LIFESTYLE JOURNALISM

Ranging from travel to wellbeing and fashion to food, *Lifestyle Journalism* explores a wide variety of subjects within a growing field.

This edited collection examines the complex dynamics of the ever-evolving media environment of lifestyle journalism, encompassing aspects of consumerism, entertainment and cosmopolitanism, as well as traditional journalistic practices. Through detailed case studies and research, the book discusses themes of consumer culture, identity, representation, the sharing economy and branding while bringing in important new aspects such as social media and new cultural intermediaries. International and cross-disciplinary, the book is divided into four parts: emerging roles; experience and identity in lifestyle media; new players and lifestyle actors; and lifestyle consumerism and brands.

Featuring case studies from a variety of countries including Turkey, the US, Chile and the UK, this is an important resource for journalism students and academics.

Lucía Vodanovic, PhD, is Senior Lecturer at London College of Communication (UAL) and Course Leader of the MA in Arts and Lifestyle Journalism at the same institution. She completed her MA and PhD in Cultural Studies at Goldsmiths College. Her research interests focus on social aesthetics, lifestyle media, the 'everyday' and amateurism in its links with self-organisation and self-reliance, among others. Her work has been featured in publications such as *Journal of Visual Art Practice; Travesía: Journal of Latin American Cultural Studies* and the edited collection *Materiality and Popular Culture: The Popular Life of Things* (Routledge, 2016).

LIFESTYLE JOURNALISM

Social Media, Consumption and Experience

Edited by Lucía Vodanovic

LONDON AND NEW YORK

First published 2020
by Routledge
2 Park Square, Milton Park, Abingdon, Oxon OX14 4RN

and by Routledge
52 Vanderbilt Avenue, New York, NY 10017

Routledge is an imprint of the Taylor & Francis Group, an informa business

British Library Cataloguing-in-Publication Data
A catalogue record for this book is available from the British Library

Library of Congress Cataloging-in-Publication Data
Names: Vodanovic, Lucia, 1974- editor.
Title: Lifestyle journalism : social media, consumption and experience / edited by Lucía Vodanovic.Description: London ; New York : Routledge, 2019. | Includes bibliographical references and index.
Identifiers: LCCN 2019008467 (print) | LCCN 2019018926 (ebook) | ISBN 9781351123389 (ebook) | ISBN 9780815357971 (hardback : alk. paper) | ISBN 9780815357995 (pbk. : alk. paper)
Subjects: LCSH: Social media and journalism. |
Journalism, Consumer. | Newspapers–Sections, columns, etc. |
Food writing.Classification: LCC PN4766 (ebook) |
LCC PN4766 .L54 2019 (print) | DDC 302.23–dc23
LC record available at https://lccn.loc.gov/2019008467

ISBN: 978-0-815-35797-1 (hbk)
ISBN: 978-0-815-35799-5 (pbk)
ISBN: 978-1-351-12338-9 (ebk)

Typeset in Bembo
by Integra Software Services Pvt. Ltd.

CONTENTS

CONTRIBUTORS

Arturo Arriagada, PhD, is Associate Professor at the School of Communications and Journalism at Adolfo Ibáñez University, Chile. He holds a PhD in Sociology and an MSc in Media and Communications from the London School of Economics (LSE). He conducts research at the intersection of media, culture and technologies. His interests include social media production, consumer culture, the economy of social media and political communication. His work has been published in the *Journal of Communication* and the *International Journal of Communication*. He is also the Director of Social Media Culture, a research lab for the reflection of the role that social media has in the media and creative industries (www.culturasocialmedia.com).

Dalia Cárdenas-Hernández graduated with honourable mentions with both a bachelor's degree in Communication Sciences from the National Autonomous University of Mexico (UNAM) and with a master's degree in Communication at Iberoamerican University, Mexico City, with a dissertation in lifestyle journalism led by Dr Sergio Rodríguez-Blanco. She also worked as a journalist and an editor for some of the most important companies in this area of Mexico. She is currently studying for a PhD in Communication at the Iberoamerican University, with research that analyses how the imaginary around the privileged class has been built in Mexico for the last 50 years.

Sabrina Faramarzi is a lifestyle journalist and trend forecaster. She holds a BA (Hons) in Trend Prediction and Forecasting from the University of East London and an MA in Arts and Lifestyle Journalism from the University of the Arts London (UAL). She has worked as a trend forecaster with numerous clients across art, fashion, beauty, retail, interiors, architecture, food, travel and hospitality. In journalism, she worked on *The Guardian*'s features desk, fixing exclusive interviews with celebrities, politicians, artists, activists, designers and innovative thinkers for their flagship interview slots. She also writes for a number of digital and print publications about lifestyle trends, Internet culture and society. She now lives in Berlin, Germany, currently exploring how trend forecasting, journalism and futurology can stay relevant in more fragmented, digital global futures.

Unni From, PhD, is Associate Professor at the School of Communication and Culture at Aarhus University, Denmark. Her research areas include cultural and lifestyle journalism; media reception studies; television critique and television drama. She is currently a participant in the research project 'From ivory tower to Twitter: rethinking the cultural critic in contemporary media culture' (funded by Independent Research Fund Denmark, 2015–2019). She has published books on media and journalism and most recently the edited book *Cultural journalism and cultural critique in a changing media landscape* (co-edited by Nete Nørgaard Kristensen, Routledge 2017).

Francesc Fusté-Forné, PhD, is a researcher at the Blanquerna-Ramon Llull University School of Communication and International Relations, Barcelona, where he earned a PhD in Communication Studies, and he is a visiting researcher at Fordham University, New York, U.S. He has also earned a PhD in Tourism, Law and Business at the University of Girona, Catalonia, where he is currently Associate Professor, and he has carried out research as a visiting scholar at Lincoln University, New Zealand. He is currently undertaking research on the role of gastronomy with regards to mass media and as a driver of social changes. Additionally, he studies culinary heritages from a geographical and tourist perspective.

Amanda Hinnant, PhD, is an Associate Professor at the School of Journalism at the University of Missouri, U.S. Her research focuses on health and science communication, journalism studies and media sociology. She has recently focused on how journalists communicate social and environmental determinants of health. Her articles have appeared in *Climatic Change; Health Communication; Health Education Research; Health Education & Behavior; Journalism & Mass Communication Quarterly; Communication Research; Science Communication; Journalism Studies* and *Feminist Media Studies*. She has worked professionally in lifestyle service magazines.

Francisco Ibáñez is a sociologist at the Pontificia Universidad Católica, Chile, and Associate Researcher in Social Media Culture. He is the co-author of the study 'Musicians, labels and fans in the digital age' (2017, with Arturo Arriagada). His interests include technology, everyday life and digital culture.

Joy Jenkins, PhD, is Assistant Professor of Digital Journalism at the University of Tennessee, Knoxville, and recently a postdoctoral research fellow in digital news at the Reuters Institute for the Study of Journalism at the University of Oxford, England. Her research uses a sociological approach to examine changing organisational identities and practices in newsrooms, with a particular focus on local media. She also studies the experiences of women journalists and the functions news organisations play in spurring public discourse about feminism and gender roles. Her work has been published in journals including *Journalism Studies; Journalism Practice; Journalism; Journal of Media Ethics* and *Feminist Media Studies*. She has worked professionally as an editor at a city magazine.

Myles Ethan Lascity, PhD, is an Assistant Professor and Director of the Fashion Media in the Meadows School of the Arts at Southern Methodist University, Dallas, Texas, U.S. He was formerly an Assistant Professor of Communication at Chestnut Hill College, Philadelphia, Pennsylvania, U.S. He holds a doctorate in Communication, Culture and Media from Drexel University, Philadelphia, and a master's in Costume Studies from New York University. He is the co-editor of *Consumer identities: agency, media and digital culture* (Intellect, 2019). His research interests include popular culture and fashion communication, and his work has been published in various journals, including *Fashion Theory, Fashion Practice* and *Film, Fashion and Consumption*.

Pere Masip is a Professor at the School of Communication and International Relations at the Blanquerna-Ramon Llull University, Barcelona, Catalonia. His main research interests are media convergence, digital journalism and the impact of technology on journalistic and communication practices. He has participated in several national and international projects. He is currently coordinating a research project funded by the Spanish Ministry of Economy and Competitiveness entitled 'Active audiences and agenda-setting in the digital public sphere'. He has published articles in journals such as *The International Journal of Press and Politics; Journalism Studies; Digital Journalism; International Communication Gazette; American Behavioural Scientist* and *Journalism Practice*.

Aaron McKinnon is a graduate student at the Erasmus Mundus joint master's degree programme in Journalism, Media and Globalisation at Aarhus University, Denmark, and Hamburg University, Germany. His research interests centre around public understanding of climate science, marine debris policy and intercultural communication. He hopes to employ his research to inform communication campaigns and audience engagement efforts in multimedia.

Sidonie Naulin, PhD, is a sociologist at Sciences Po Grenoble and Pacte University, France. She specialises in economic sociology, media studies and food studies. She received her doctorate in sociology from Paris-Sorbonne University, and she held a postdoctoral position at the Max Planck Institute for the Study of Societies (MPIfG) in Cologne, Germany. Her PhD aimed to understand the production of information regarding food and gastronomy. It led to the book

Des mots à la bouche. Le journalisme gastronomique en France (Presses Universitaires de Rennes, 2017), which received the 'Prix des Assises du Journalisme' (journalism award) in 2018. Her recent research examines the current changes in the labour market and careers in the food industry. It focuses on the role that events and the Internet play in building careers and shaping public image of individuals and professional groups.

Nete Nørgaard Kristensen, PhD, is Professor of Media Studies at the University of Copenhagen's Department of Media, Cognition and Communication, Section for Film, Media and Communication. Her research interests include cultural journalism and cultural critique; lifestyle journalism and constructive journalism; political journalism and political communication; and war and conflict reporting. She is currently principal investigator of the project 'From ivory tower to Twitter: rethinking the cultural critic in contemporary media culture' (funded by Independent Research Fund Denmark, 2015–2019). Her work has appeared in international journals such as *Journalism; Journalism Studies; Journalism Practice; Digital Journalism; Television & New Media* and *Media, War & Conflict*. Her most recent books are *Cultural journalism in the Nordic countries* (co-edited with Kristina Riegert, NORDICOM, 2017) and *Cultural journalism and cultural critique in a changing media landscape* (co-edited with Unni From, Routledge, 2017).

Bryan Pirolli, PhD, obtained his doctorate from the Sorbonne Nouvelle in Paris, after studying journalism at New York University, U.S. A committed traveller, he has worked as a freelance journalist for publications including *CNN* and *Time Out* while also researching and teaching at the Sorbonne Nouvelle and at London College of Communication, University of the Arts London (UAL). A member of the Sorbonne Nouvelle's research lab, *Irméccen*, he focuses on travel media and professional journalism as it evolves online. His first book, *Travel journalism: informing tourists in the digital age* (Routledge, 2018), deals with innovations to the profession as it develops with the Internet. Straddling both academic and professional worlds, he most recently worked as a travel editor in Asia, bringing his research and writing experiences to a new market.

Sergio Rodríguez-Blanco, PhD, is a researcher and senior lecturer at the Department of Communication at the Iberoamerican University, Mexico City, where he coordinates the Journalism area. He belongs to the National System of Researchers of Mexico (SNI) and he is a supervisor of the Commission on Latin-American Accreditation in Journalism Studies (CLAEP). His research interests focus on the discourses and aesthetics that shape our understanding of culture, consumerism and citizenship through the mediation of journalism, visual culture, photography and art and media practices. He is the author of *Alegorías capilares* (Hiperlibro, 2011), where he studies materiality, trauma and memory, and *Palimpsestos mexicanos: apropiación, montaje y archivo contra la ensoñación* (Conaculta, 2015), where he analyses the contrast between opulence and violence in contemporary photography. He studied journalism at the Complutense University of Madrid, Spain, and completed his PhD at the National Autonomous University of Mexico (UNAM), where he also received the prestigious Alfonso Caso medal for the best doctoral dissertation.

Feyda Sayan-Cengiz, PhD, is Assistant Professor of Political Science and International Relations at Manisa Celal Bayar University, Turkey. She received her PhD in Political Science from Bilkent University, Ankara, Turkey, in 2014. She was a visiting researcher at Columbia University's Anthropology department from 2009 to 2010. She has previously worked at Istanbul Bilgi University's Department of Media. She has been published in edited books and journals, such as *Women's Studies International Forum* and *New Perspectives on Turkey*. Her book, *Beyond headscarf culture in Turkey's retail sector* was published by Palgrave Macmillan in 2016. Her research interests include political sociology, politics of gender, Islamic consumerism, social movements and media studies.

Lucía Vodanovic, PhD, is Senior Lecturer at London College of Communication (UAL) and Course Leader of the MA in Arts and Lifestyle Journalism at the same institution. She completed her MA and PhD in Cultural Studies at Goldsmiths College. Her research interests focus on social aesthetics, lifestyle media, the 'everyday' and amateurism in its links with self-organisation and self-reliance, among others. Her work has been featured in publications such as *Journal of Visual Art Practice; Travesía: Journal of Latin American Cultural Studies* and the edited collection *Materiality and popular culture: the popular life of things* (Routledge, 2016).

INTRODUCTION

Lifestyle journalism: social media, consumption and experience

Lucía Vodanovic

Lifestyle journalism is a genre that constitutes a significant and growing portion of mainstream journalism yet continues to be an under-researched field. While Folker Hanusch's *Lifestyle journalism* (2013) made the case for it to be considered an important dimension of journalism, rather than a 'lesser' form of it, and a subject worth scholarly inquiry, research about the field continues to occupy a marginal space. The author's most recent work, written alone or in collaboration with others (Hanusch and Hanitzsch, 2013; Hanusch, 2017), and that of Thomas Hanitzsch and Tim Vos (2018), has been focused more directly on the role of the journalist as a professional who can adopt different functions such as marketer, service provider, friend, connector, mood manager, inspirer and guide. The emphasis, however, is not necessarily on lifestyle journalism and its diverse interpretations. This book aims to extend Hanusch's project by incorporating several aspects not included in that initial attempt to map the ground, such as the crucial importance of social media, new agenda setters (bloggers and other cultural intermediaries) and the 'experiential' dimension of lifestyle journalism. It also includes contributions that explore the potential roles of the genre as a reflective, democratic, constructive or even aesthetic form.

While lifestyle journalism continues to carve its niche in an academic setting, it is important to acknowledge how the field nods back to these traditional journalism studies that academics are now looking to challenge. Numerous works have sought to define, redefine and further redefine journalism, especially in a digital world (see Peters and Broersma, 2017). However, trying to define journalism in one clean definition is precisely why lifestyle journalism has often gone overlooked: it does not fit into the civically oriented definitions that most researchers ascribe to the profession and that recent scholarship argues needs to change (Hanitzsch and Vos, 2018). Barbie Zelizer (2013) has called for such reconsiderations, emphasising the multiplicity and variety of journalism (2009), both in terms of its roles and functions and the ways in which different forms of journalism work. Slowly, academics are responding, which is crucial now when 'multiplicity has become more pronounced as journalism has necessarily mutated' (Zelizer, 2009, p. 1). There is also renewed academic interest in scholarship that has traced the function of journalism within the private sphere beyond its democratic role (Hartley, 1996; van Zoonen, 1998), which has asserted that private and everyday life could also be the subject of democratic scrutiny (Costera Meijer, 2001) and/or that has reclaimed the 'social' in journalism in addition to its 'public' and political aspects (Gutsche and Hess, 2018). The explicit or implicit understanding of the different roles and trajectories of journalism informs various contributions in this volume.

Journalism, as an ideology—that is, as an understanding of the field in terms of how journalists give meaning to and self-legitimise their work (Deuze, 2005)—does not have static values (Ahva, 2013). It has been established, for instance, that values considered essential to the field for decades— such as public service, objectivity, autonomy, immediacy and a sense of ethics (Deuze, 2005)—have been complicated by developments such as multimedia journalism and multiculturalism (Deuze, 2005; Jenkins, 2018). If applying this same ideology to lifestyle media, however, it cannot even be presumed that such shared ideologies are exactly the same for all types of journalisms. Beyond different genres and audiences, modes of production and distribution also differ, with various influences from digital media and changing economic structures. There exists no one-size-fits-all approach. As Mark Deuze and Tamara Witschge suggest, the "amplification and acceleration of more or less new news genres, forms, products and services today point towards the fact that the occupational ideology of journalism allows for many different 'journalisms' to flourish" (2017, p. 121).

Encompassing aspects of entertainment and cosmopolitanism, as well as traditional journalistic practices, lifestyle journalists continue to work in an ever-evolving media environment. Fashion, food, travel, cinema and other cultural and consumer topics are arguably more pervasive now than ever as professional media clamours to attract readers and as current-events reporting succumbs to increased tabloidization. Some of those sectors have been more researched than others, with travel and fashion appearing particularly well catered-for through the work of Pirolli (2016, 2018) or Fürsich and Kavoori (2001), for instance, among many other authors writing about travel journalism, and Rocamora (2012), Bradford (2015) and Boyd (2015), working on fashion and blogging. There is also the comprehensive body of work of From and Kristensen (2015) on cultural journalism, which shares several challenges with lifestyle journalism, such as being marginalised by traditional scholarship and increasingly transformed by the role of "amateur experts" (Baym and Burnett, 2009). While some of the chapters in this collection are focused on various subsectors within lifestyle journalism, in all cases the scope goes beyond the niche and speaks of the wider issues at play, exploring themes such as reflectivity, branding, representation, the dynamics between local and global culture, the experience and sharing economies, social media and others.

As all of these conversations about what journalism is, who journalists are and how all of these definitions are more fluid than ever, this book takes a unique look at lifestyle journalism. While acknowledging that the discussion of boundaries is one of the key dimensions of contemporary journalism studies (Carlson and Lewis, 2015; Loosen, 2015), it also proposes that the position of lifestyle journalism is unique and useful as the site to articulate that discussion.

Lifestyle media and lifestyle journalism

Given the emphasis on identity and self-expression in the field, it would be possible to define contemporary lifestyle journalism as "the journalistic coverage of the expressive values and practices that help create and signify a specific identity within the realm of consumption and everyday life" (Hanusch and Hanitzsch, 2013, p. 947). That link between consumption and identity speaks of the need to place lifestyle journalism in the wider context of lifestyle media research, which has opened up a growing field of scholarly work dedicated to cultural intermediaries, yet obliquely touching on the role of journalism within it. It is perhaps surprising that this role has not been discussed further, given that some of the qualities or roles attributed to intermediaries—for example, the fact that they "cannot enforce desires or purchases; rather, they create the conditions for consumers to identify their tastes in goods" (Smith Maguire, 2014, p. 20)— would be useful to frame some of the contemporary practices within lifestyle journalism.

Taking a more historical approach, authors such as David Bell and Joanne Hollows (2005, 2006) and particularly Tania Lewis (2008, 2014) have traced lifestyle media back to Victorian 'etiquette' manuals and early twentieth-century forms of advice focused on aesthetics, care of the self and the family. A smaller yet substantial history of practical advice for men is also present in this lineage, Lewis argues (2008, 2014), in terms of a certain "domestic masculinity" that could be considered the precursor of DIY culture, particularly in the U.S. As part of this genealogy, lifestyle journalism, in its contemporary form, has a more prominent presence from the 1950s onwards, as it is the period associated with an explosion of lifestyle publications, moving away from service magazines (even though those still exist) and 'making do' culture to a new focus on lifestyle as a construction of personal identity. This would then be expanded in the next decade with a much more commercialised version of lifestyle journalism, "which uses advertising and editorial to position readerships as consumers and as lucid participants in the selection and maintenance of gendered lifestyles" (Conboy, 2004, p. 145). The emergence of subcultures and the growth of disposable income also contributed to the explosion of the field (Conboy, 2004).

Following Lewis (2008) and McKay (2008), Julian Matthews has furthered the understanding of this role within journalism beyond the historical emergence of 'lifestyle', by attempting to define journalism as an 'intermediary' and high-lighting how the contemporary media ecology is "peppered with journalists who dispense advice and shape tastes on cultural matters in their role of self-portrayed 'expert'" (2014, p. 148). This has created specific 'modes of address' that have indeed diversified the practice of journalists covering different topics like music, film, food and travel, among others, all of which have their own particular conventions and foster a peculiar relationship between the addresser and the addressee.

The former suggestions bring the discussion much closer to Pierre Bourdieu's (1984) sociology of cultural consumption and its emphasis on the creation of taste. Indeed, even though the concept of lifestyle is employed in different ways and in different contexts, it only gained a clear place in critical theory from the 1960s and 1970s onwards, when the shift towards post-Fordism and its emphasis on consumption had settled for good. Thereafter, the question around the erosion of "traditional social structures which forms the basis for identity" and their replacement "with an imperative to choose how we construct our identities through lifestyle practices" (Bell and Hollows, 2005, p. 3) emerged more clearly.

Several of the contributions to this volume address issues of consumption, identity and taste, and so make explicit links between lifestyle journalism and lifestyle media more broadly. However, the aim here is to also establish what makes knowledge production in lifestyle journalism different from other forms of lifestyle content. This question demands a longer and more complex answer: what form does that mediation adopt and how does this sit with other traditional journalistic roles and values, if at times it seems to be in its complete opposition? These are two of the basic questions addressed in this volume.

From consumption to identity

The subtitle of 'social media, consumption and experience' expresses some of the factors that offer both constraints and possibilities to the production and reception of journalism in the current context. 'Social media' and 'consumption' are terms that receive significant attention in contemporary critical theory. While the former has been particularly well researched in terms of how it has transformed journalistic practices, and continuous to be in a recent wave of publications (Bruns, 2018; Hill and Bradshaw, 2018; Lugmayr and Dal Zotto, 2016), the latter—with a much longer and varied history in academic research, freshly gathered in the collection *Routledge handbook on consumption* (Keller *et al.*, 2017)—is rarely addressed to talk about journalism outside the lifestyle niche. There is also an added complexity derived from the fact that social media has not only transformed journalism dramatically, it has also changed our consumer habits—how we buy and sell things, where we shop, how we interact and socialise, how we are exposed to commodities, our everyday practices of consumption—and, as a result, our lifestyles, consumer cultures and consumer identities (Keller *et al.*, 2017, p. 405). In this volume, both concepts are used to explore the potentials and the clashes with traditional journalistic values and roles in the lifestyle field, acknowledging that they might have an even more prevalent function here than in other forms of journalism, given its consumer-oriented nature and the presence of lifestyle actors outside the profession. Examples of those actors are fashion bloggers in Arriagada and Ibáñez's chapter, amateur food bloggers in Naulin's, TV travel hosts in McKinnon's, and trend forecasters in Faramarzi's.

Lastly, the use of the term 'experience' refers to what James Gilmore and Joseph Pine (1998, 2011) influentially termed as "the experience economy", a fourth economic sector preoccupied with the production of services instead of end products. Given that the notion of 'engagement' is key for both the experience economy and contemporary journalism (Broersma *et al.*, 2017), some of the essays in this collection explore the form of that engagement, as news outlets strive to offer novel forms of content production and companies outside the traditional journalistic space—for instance, Airbnb in the essay by Pirolli, or clothing companies in the one by Lascity—adopt journalism as a way of constructing a 'lifestyle' around their products that goes beyond traditional marketing to become an experiential form of consumption. Other chapters take this concept to other realms; for instance, the articulation of private/professional dynamics within the lived experience of a journalist and his/her readers—in the case of Vodanovic's contribution about dialogues in 'below the line' comments—the portrayal of an idealised and almost virtual experience of a city in Jenkins and Hinnant's chapter, or the links between consumption, identity, religious values and travel experiences in Sayan-Cengiz's.

It is noteworthy that contributions to this volume deal with issues of lifestyle journalism in a variety of countries—Turkey, Mexico, Chile, Denmark, the U.S. and several others—which constitutes an interesting addition to a research field that, up until now, had been almost exclusively matured in Scandinavian and Northern European nations. This also speaks of the significant growth of the sector in recent years, which now forms a substantial portion of the journalism being produced across the globe. Even though the contributions are very varied in their scope, they have been grouped in four parts to emphasise some of the propositions of this collection; yet those groupings do not limit the dialogue between them and the shared themes around consumer culture, identity, representation, the sharing economy, branding and others.

Part I discusses the emerging roles of lifestyle journalism—and of lifestyle journalists—at a time in which different news organisations are looking at new forms of storytelling and audience engagement. It makes the case for lifestyle journalism as a reflective practice and a producer of niche audiences and communities, at times showing continuity, at others disruption, of traditional roles. Chapter 1 serves as an introduction to several of the topics discussed in the collection, by placing lifestyle journalism as a response to broader sociocultural transformations such as commercialisation, individualisation and digitalisation, while positioning the field in relation to both 'service journalism' (Eide and

Knight, 1999) and the relatively new practice of 'constructive journalism'; as a result, it also unpacks new relations between the traditional divisions of 'hard' and 'soft' news. Chapter 2 presents an extensive discussion of sociologist Jean Baudrillard's theories of simulacra and simulation—extremely influential for media studies, yet seldom used in journalism research—to argue that city magazines, through promoting particular lifestyles and products to specific groups of readers, play active roles in creating simulated presentations of reality, distributing images that constitute a desire-driven, simulated world. The audience of these simulations are the city inhabitants rather than tourists, and so these magazines fulfil a different role to that of the more traditional travel beat. In the last chapter of this first section, Vodanovic uses notions of individualisation, authenticity and agency, among others, to explore the different roles that a lifestyle journalist adopts in her interactions with the audience in 'below the line' comments, using the beauty section of *The Guardian* as a case study to argue that the exchanges in those forums bring together a variety of discourses: professional and personal; institutional and private.

Part II looks at emerging identities and 'ways of being' in lifestyle media, with particular attention to journalism; it acknowledges the possibilities of lifestyle media in the creation of new subjectivities, in tension with the contemporary citizen identity of a 'consumer' of goods and also of experiences. In this vein, Chapter 4 addresses consumerism in Turkey through a case study of *Aysha* magazine that provides an insight into the creative ways in which religion and consumerism are reconciled in Islamic lifestyle media, and shows that the magazine not only offers suggestions about what to consume, it also advises on how to reconcile a consumerist lifestyle with a religious one. Chapter 5 looks at identity in the context of difference through the discussion of cultural mediation and 'othering' in travel journalism and travel TV shows; acknowledging that travel journalism has a significant role in defining foreign cultures to audiences at home, it argues that the late Anthony Bourdain, in his CNN travel show *Parts Unknown*, engages in a different process of cultural mediation to that of traditional travel journalism. It features the ordinariness of a given location through an interplay between political structures and the cultural practices of common citizens, sometimes criticising his profession's unintended propagation of self-serving tourists and constructing more complex representations of 'otherness' through conversations about everyday life with locals. Lastly, Chapter 6 looks at the tensions between journalistic values and consumption more directly, by researching journalists' perceptions and practices with regard to the social media accounts of various mainstream news outlets with lifestyle content in Mexico, arguing that the use of these platforms is perceived as benefiting the commercial interests of the media, establishing a mixture of information and advertising.

New actors and lifestyle players are discussed in Part III of this collection. As bloggers, amateur 'foodies' and trend forecasters co-exist, take the space of or sometimes work with journalists, this part takes a close look at the values and practices that drive their content. These actors have been challenging traditional journalism norms, but can also enrich lifestyle media experiences and influence lifestyle journalists' practice (e.g. Pirolli 2016). The role of agencies that manage fashion bloggers in Chile is explored in Chapter 7, discussing how the content produced by these bloggers is part of a network of economic and social relations linking different actors, e.g. branding agencies, audiences and platforms. These bloggers work as cultural intermediaries shaping consumers' decisions by working with other intermediaries, specifically branding agencies, in order to create 'branded content' and consumption experiences around brands and products on digital platforms. Another intermediary, the 'amateur expert' in the food blogging sphere in France, is researched in Chapter 8, an exploration that allows the author to discuss the boundaries between lifestyle journalism and other forms of lifestyle media. A different, less commonly known form of intermediation is addressed in Chapter 9, which discusses the role of the trend forecaster as a 'coolhunter' and establishes its parallels and links with some of the work that lifestyle journalists do.

Lastly, Part IV looks at consumption in relation to specific genres of lifestyle journalism (travel and food) as speaking to and being spoken by commercial agents and markets. It also acknowledges further roles for lifestyle journalism not discussed in the first section, such as journalism as a form of "brand communication" (Bull, 2013). In Chapter 10, Fusté-Forné and Masip study how gastronomy is imagined daily in the lifestyle sections of newspapers in both Spain and the U.S. to argue that food journalism could be a vehicle to define social trends and ways of life. Travel in the context of the 'sharing economy' is the focus on Chapter 11, where Pirolli looks at how Airbnb, emblematic of this sector, offers new opportunities and challenges to journalists, especially as it began to publish its own glossy magazine. The chapter discusses how Airbnb and its community of hosts and customers becomes a source for journalists working in the magazine, arguing that there is potential for such branded content that goes beyond the simple interests of the company in question. Finally, the last chapter in this collection explores and compares how the clothing brands Uniqlo and Abercrombie & Fitch have used forms of lifestyle journalism in their efforts to build consumable images, establishing the links between lifestyle journalism and lifestyle branding and looking at each brand's marketing materials to perform an interpretative deconstruction in the vein of Consumer Culture Theory.

This brief summary shows that lifestyle journalists are still journalists, and a core set of practices and ethics do exist; pinpointing them and understanding how these professional practices speak to the greater state of lifestyle media is another matter. Further complicating this sort of research is the near-constant evolution of journalism as a profession thanks to digital media and other changes. The goal of this book is not to build a border between lifestyle journalism and other types of reporting; instead, it attempts to sketch out the Venn diagrams that overlap with lifestyle journalism, to understand its many facets at the beginning of the twenty-first century. Ideally, it would be able to further Hanusch's 2013 work in order to strengthen the foundation for future journalism scholars.

References

Ahva, L. (2013) 'Public journalism and professional reflexivity', *Journalism*, 14(6), pp. 790–806. doi:1464884912455895.

Baym, N. K. and Burnett, R. (2009) 'Amateur experts: international fan labour in Swedish independent music', *International Journal of Cultural Studies*, 12(5), pp. 1–17.

Bell, D. and Hollows, J. (2005) *Ordinary lifestyles: popular media, consumption and taste*. Maidenhead and New York: Open University Press.

Bell, D. and Hollows, J. (2006) *Historicizing lifestyle: mediating taste, consumption and identity from the 1900s to the 1970s*. London: Routledge.

Bourdieu, P. (1984) *Distinction: a social critique of the judgement of taste*. Boston: Harvard University Press.

Boyd, K. (2015) 'Democratizing fashion: the effects of the evolution of fashion journalism from print to online media', *McNair Scholars Research Journal*, 8(1), pp. 17–34.

Bradford, J. (2015). *Fashion journalism*. London: Routledge.

Broersma, M. *et al.* (2017) 'Repositioning news and public connection in everyday life: a user-oriented perspective on inclusiveness, engagement, relevance and constructiveness', *Media, Culture & Society*, 39(6), pp. 902–918. doi: 10.1177/0163443716679034.

Bruns, A. (2018) *Gatewatching and news curation: journalism, social media and the public sphere*. New York: Peter Lang.

Bull, A. (2013) *Brand journalism*. Oxon: Routledge.

Carlson, M. and Lewis, S. (eds) (2015) *Boundaries of journalism: professionalism, practices and participation*. London: Routledge.

Conboy, M. (2004) *Journalism: a critical history*. London, California and New Delhi: Sage.

Costera Meijer, I. (2001) 'The public quality of popular journalism: developing a normative framework', *Journalism Studies*, (2)2, pp. 189–205. doi: 10.1080/14616700120042079.

Deuze, M. (2005) 'What is journalism? Professional identity and ideology of journalists reconsidered', *Journalism*, 6(4), pp. 442-464.

Deuze, M. and Witschge, T. (2017) 'What journalism becomes', in Peters, C. and Broersma, M. (eds), *Rethinking journalism again: societal role and public relevance in a digital age*. Oxon: Routledge, pp. 115–130.

Eide, M. and Knight, G. (1999) 'Public/private service: service journalism and the problems of everyday life', *European Journal of Communication*, 14, pp. 525–547.

From, U. and Kristensen, N. (2015) 'Cultural journalism and cultural critique in a changing media landscape', *Journalism Practice*, (9)6, pp. 760–772. doi: 10.1080/17512786.2015.1051357.

Fürsich, E. and Kavoori A. P. (2001). 'Mapping a critical framework for the study of travel journalism', *International Journal of Cultural Studies*, 4(2), pp. 149–171.

Gutsche, R. and Hess, K. (2018) 'Journalism and the social sphere: reclaiming a foundational concept for beyond politics and the public sphere', *Journalism Studies*, (19)4, pp. 483–498. doi: 10.1080/1461670X.2017.1389296.

Gilmore, J. and Pine, J. (1998) 'Welcome to the experience economy', *Harvard Business Review*, pp. 97–105.

Gilmore, J. and Pine, J. (2011) *The experience economy*. Boston: Harvard University Press.

Hanitzsch, T. and Vos, T. (2018) 'Journalism beyond democracy: a new look into journalistic roles in political and everyday life', *Journalism*, 19(2), pp. 146–164.

Hanusch, F. (ed.) (2013) *Lifestyle journalism*. London and New York: Routledge.

Hanusch, F. (2017) 'Journalistic roles and everyday life', *Journalism Studies*. doi: 10.1080/1461670X.2017.1370977.

Hanusch, F. and Hanitzsch, T. (2013) 'Mediating orientation and self-expression in the world of consumption: Australian and German lifestyle journalists' professional views', *Media, Culture & Society*, 35(8), pp. 943–959.

Hartley, J. (1996) *Popular reality: journalism, modernity, popular culture.* London: St Martin's Press.

Hill, S. and Bradshaw, P. (2018) *Mobile-first journalism: producing news for social and interactive media.* London: Routledge.

Keller, M. *et al.* (2017) *Routledge handbook on consumption.* Abingdon and New York: Routledge.

Jenkins, J. (2018) 'Elevated influences', *Journalism Studies.* doi: 10.1080/1461670X.2018.1486729.

Lewis, T. (2008) *Smart living: lifestyle media and popular expertise.* New York: Peter Lang.

Lewis, T. (2014) 'Lifestyle media', in Smith Maguire, J. and Matthews, J. (eds) *The cultural intermediaries reader.* London: Sage, pp. 134–144.

Lugmayr, A. and Dal Zotto, C. (eds) (2016) *Media convergence handbook – volume 1: journalism, broadcasting and social media aspects of convergence.* Berlin: Springer.

Loosen, W. (2015) 'The notion of the "blurring boundaries": journalism as a (de-differentiated phenomenon', *Digital Journalism*, 3(1), pp. 68–84. doi: 10.1080/21670811.2014.928000.

Matthews, J. (2014) 'Journalism', in Smith Maguire, J. and Matthews, J. (eds) *The cultural intermediaries reader.* London: Sage, pp. 145–155.

McKay, S. (2008) 'Advice columns as cultural intermediaries', *Australian Journal of Communication*, 35(2), pp. 93–103.

Peters, C. and Broersma, M. (2017) *Rethinking journalism again: societal role and public relevance in a digital age.* London: Routledge,

Pirolli, B. (2016) 'Travel journalists and professional identity', *Journalism Practice*, 11(6), pp. 740–759. doi: 10.1080/17512786.2016.1193821.

Pirolli, B. (2018) *Travel journalism: informing tourists in the digital age.* London: Routledge.

Rocamora, A. (2012) 'Hypertextuality and remediation in the fashion media: the case of fashion blogs', *Journalism Practice* 6(1), pp. 92–106.

Smith Maguire, J. (2014) 'Bourdieu on cultural intermediaries', in Smith Maguire, J. and Matthews, J. (eds) *The cultural intermediaries reader.* London: Sage, pp. 15–24.

van Zoonen, L. (1998) 'A professional, unreliable, heroic marionette (M/F): structure, agency and subjectivity in contemporary journalisms', *European Journal of Cultural Studies*, 1(1), pp. 123–143. doi: 1 0.1177/136754949800100108.

Zelizer, B. (2009) *The changing faces of journalism.* London: Routledge.

Zelizer, B. (2013) 'On the shelf life of democracy in journalism scholarship', *Journalism*, 14(4), pp. 459–473.

PART I

Emerging roles of lifestyle journalism

1

UNPACKING LIFESTYLE JOURNALISM VIA SERVICE JOURNALISM AND CONSTRUCTIVE JOURNALISM

Unni From and Nete Nørgaard Kristensen

Lifestyle journalism has often been defined as a specific journalistic beat of a softer nature. Lifestyle media content covers consumer-related topics such as travel, fashion, beauty, health, fitness, food, gardening, parenting, celebrity and personal technology (e.g. Bell and Hollows, 2005, p. 9). Moreover, it has been connected to "the journalistic coverage of the expressive values and practices that help create and signify a specific identity within the realm of consumption and everyday life" (Hanusch and Hanitzsch, 2013, p. 947). In this chapter, we focus on lifestyle journalism as a specific approach in journalism (see From and Kristensen, 2018), influenced by three strong sociocultural developments: commercialisation, individualisation and digitalisation. In combination with media institutional changes, these transformations have influenced journalistic sub-fields across the traditional distinction between hard and soft news. Approaches associated with lifestyle journalism, such as guidance, service, 'feel good' and empowerment news, have more recently been adopted within more traditional hard news reporting.

To analyse these new relations between soft news and hard news, we first unpack lifestyle journalism in a media institutional context to demonstrate how lifestyle journalism is one of various responses to the broader sociocultural transformations of commercialisation, individualisation and digitalisation. The main focus is on lifestyle journalism in the news media and in the press in particular, but with connections to lifestyle media in a broader sense across media types. We aim to show that lifestyle journalism is not only characterised by addressing the audience as consumers but also involves more complex conceptualisations of the audience in line with notions of the audience presented by service journalism, an umbrella term for softer types of journalism introduced in the 1980s and 1990s. Service journalism is characterised by a strong emphasis on guiding and empowering the audience to deal with problem solving in modern life. Thus, second, we show how service journalism may serve as a useful pathway to the broad field of lifestyle journalism in terms of conceptualising the hybrid nature of audiences as part citizens, part consumers and part clients (Eide and Knight, 1999; Eide, 2017). However, we also argue that the intentions of service and lifestyle journalism to guide audiences and focus on positive problem solving have more recently migrated to other journalistic fields. To exemplify this argument, we, third, examine how approaches typically associated with lifestyle journalism are adopted in some parts of hard news reporting. Taking our point of departure in a relatively new journalistic practice, constructive journalism, we analyse how such stories in some cases incorporate stylistic formats from service journalism and lifestyle journalism and argue that the fields are in similar ways rooted in processes of commercialisation, individualisation and digitalisation.

Research context

Lifestyle journalism has long been a well-established sub-field within Western news institutions. Even though lifestyle journalism is often associated with entertainment and leisure, it is now present across print and digital newspaper sections—from the main news section, to the business section and in supplements addressing topics of everyday life, life politics or sub-political subjects (From, 2010, 2018). Lifestyle topics have also had a strong presence on television, including public service media, especially since the 1990s (e.g. Brunsdon, 2003; O'Sullivan, 2005). Lifestyle content is popular with audiences and producers (Bell and Hollows, 2005) and a profitable area of journalism (e.g. Hanusch, 2017).

Lifestyle journalism and the growth of lifestyle media content have often been viewed in scholarly debates as an example of the tabloidization of journalism or the weakening of journalism as an important democratic institution (see Brunsdon, 2003; Kristensen and From, 2012). Franklin argues that "the task of journalism has become merely to deliver and serve up what the customer wants; rather like a deep-pan pizza" (1997, p. 5). Journalism outside the realm of the political domain is a neglected research area, resulting in "comparatively little knowledge about its structures, processes of production, content and effects it may have on audiences" (Hanusch, 2012, p. 3). Compared to studies of the development of journalism more generally, comprehensive historical analyses of the development of lifestyle journalism are more sporadic or even non-existent (From, 2018). However, lifestyle journalism may be regarded as a reflection of the development of modern democracies based on liberal and capitalist ideologies (Hartley, 1996, 1999; see also From, 2018) and the changed relations between media institutions, market, society and consumers. As such, lifestyle journalism may be seen as an integrated part of the development of modern journalism, because it reflects the social reality and provides sense-making practices of modernity (Hartley, 1999). Therefore, the historical development of lifestyle journalism as a specific beat and as a specific mode of addressing audiences is an important point of departure for scholarly enquiries into the field.

Commercialisation as a driving force in lifestyle journalism

Commercialisation is a prominent perspective that has often been associated with lifestyle media content in general and lifestyle journalism more specifically (e.g. From, 2018). The importance of lifestyle media content is tied to consumerism, consumption and the rise of industrial societies in the late eighteenth and early nineteenth centuries, and later the shift from modernity to postmodernity or late capitalism (Bell and Hollows, 2005, pp. 2–3). The industrial revolution opened up new markets and made more consumer goods available to the developing middle class, i.e., made "the relative democratisation of consumption" possible (Lewis, 2008, p. 28). Advertisers saw newspapers as useful platforms for marketing consumer goods, and media institutions saw advertising as a source to finance the production and distribution of editorial content, advertising became an inevitable part of the news industry (Barnhurst and Nerone, 2001; From, 2018).

The literature on lifestyle journalism demonstrates that commercialism takes different shapes as a driving force in the development of the beat during the nineteenth and twentieth centuries (e.g. From, 2018). Two examples can be highlighted: even though newspapers began to cover more popular culture forms in the eighteenth century, the coverage was characterised by an instrumental approach to audiences. Lewis (2008) argues that lifestyle content in the early phases was more formalistic and practically oriented. The coverage of food, for example, focused on how to get the most out of ingredients (Jones and Taylor, 2013). By the 1980s and 1990s, the interplay of commercialisation and individualisation, as we demonstrate below, meant that lifestyle journalism became a matter of taste and cultural identity more than solely a matter of consumption. Brunsdon (2003, p. 10) shows that in the mid-twentieth century, British hobby programmes on television were mainly didactic, providing instructions on 'how to', while the lifestyle programmes of the 1990s and onwards combined 'instruction and spectacle' as the make-over element became a centre of attention.

Commercialisation has thus constituted an important element of lifestyle journalism all along and has generally triggered an interest in the private sphere and provided more engaging ways of addressing the audience, as is also the case with constructive journalism (see below). The genres and modes of address in lifestyle journalism are often inspired by the language used in advertising. The more recent emergence of advertorials and branded content, which are particularly pronounced in lifestyle journalism (e.g. Eckman and Lindlof, 2003; Zhou, 2012), exemplify this. Hanusch also emphasises the private sphere and entertainment as important features when defining lifestyle journalism as "a distinct journalistic field that primarily addresses its audiences as consumers, providing them with factual information and advice, often in entertaining ways, about goods and services they can use in their daily lives" (2012, p. 2). Accordingly, research has often pointed to commercial influences as a critical element of the journalistic profession and of lifestyle journalism in particular. Using travel journalism as an example, Fürsich argues that many have criticised the "poor state of travel journalism and its dependency on free trips and giveaways" (2012, p. 15). At the same time, lifestyle journalism's "connection to the current unique historic socio-political situation" (Fürsich, 2012, p. 15) makes it relevant as a source of inspiration in the development of journalism practice more generally, as the case of constructive journalism also demonstrates.

In summary, commercialisation is more generally a key characteristic of late modernity and has, by extension, been a driving force in the development of the media industry and journalism during the twentieth century. The development of lifestyle journalism exemplifies media institutions' acknowledgement of commercialism, consumerism and consumption as important to their audiences and to their business models. As we demonstrate in the following sections, devoted to service journalism and constructive journalism, changed market conditions in conjunction with social and technological change compelled journalism to re-invent itself in the 1980s and at the beginning of the twenty-first century, reiterating and renewing lifestyle journalism.

Individualisation and changed audience conceptions

Other theoretical perspectives often applied to explain the development of lifestyle journalism are individualisation and late modern processes of de-traditionalisation or disembedding (Beck, 1992; see Hanusch and Hanitzsch, 2013, p. 945). Individualisation marks a fundamental social change beyond but related to commercialisation and the development of a capitalist society, which has attached great importance to lifestyle media components especially from the 1980s and onwards, because lifestyle content provides the individual with the opportunities to choose values and identity detached from class and family ties. Such processes of individualisation are reflected in lifestyle content and modes of addressing the audiences.

In terms of content, lifestyle journalism and marketing material on lifestyle issues have placed greater emphasis on aesthetic representations and consumer goods as markers of taste cultures, pointing to the close ties between lifestyle products and cultural tastes and identities. Lewis (2008, p. 35), for example, argues that the symbolic and cultural dimensions of consumption became dominant features of lifestyle media from the 1980s and onwards. Popular culture and lifestyle issues were and continue to be covered in their own right, acknowledged as an important part of identity formation and "self-styling" (Lewis, 2008, p. 35) or "self-authorship" (Raisborough, 2011, p. 21). Hanusch and Hanitzsch (2013, p. 945) also point to the formative elements of lifestyle, as they adopt Chaneys' conceptualisation of lifestyles as "patterns of action that differentiate people" and argue that contemporary lifestyle has formative, reflexive and articulative dimensions.

Processes of commercialisation and individualisation have also influenced the modes of addressing the audience. As argued above, commercialisation led to an increased journalistic and commercial attention to the personal and the private sphere. In parts of the scholarly debates, this has been viewed as a sign of consumerism replacing citizenship (e.g. Eide and Knight, 1999, p. 536). However, in the last decades of the twentieth century, lifestyle journalism also developed along with more complex understandings of the audience, applying a service-oriented way of guiding the public in the complex late-modern (consumer) society (Eide and Knight, 1999; Hjarvard, 1995). Eide and Knight have introduced the notion of service journalism, which is a term that encompasses how media institutions increasingly combined modes of address in particular types of journalism directed towards audiences with a hybrid identity. They argue that service journalism reflects a more advanced individualism that "embraces aspects of the citizen (rights) and the consumer (self-interest) mediated through the subjectivity of the client whose relation to self and to others, especially those who inform and advise, is shaped by the ethics of responsibility" (Eide and Knight, 1999, p. 542). The identity of 'citizen' adheres to traditional ideas about journalism, democracy and audiences; the identity of 'consumers' links to audiences as consumers of both lifestyle goods and media content; and the identity of 'client' is linked to professional media taking on the role of advising audiences to solve and act on everyday life problems.

The 2018-story series 'Seven ways to' in *The Guardian* exemplifies this, as it takes its point of departure in (public) lifestyle and health issues but advises individuals on how to cope with them, e.g. 'Seven ways to deal with post-traumatic stress disorder' (Robinson, 23 July 2018), 'Seven ways to improve your balance' (Carter, 16 July 2018), or 'Seven ways to minimise the risk of having a stroke' (Robinson, 11 June 2018). This conceptualisation links service journalism to broader political and economic issues and structures of public relevance and not merely the social and personal problems of individuals. From a media institutional perspective, individualisation, combined with commercialisation, thus manifests itself by an increasing audience orientation and segmentation. The increase in lifestyle sections and lifestyle programming exemplifies how news media used lifestyle and cultural coverage to build distinct media brands and segment audiences in the increasingly competitive media market of the 1980s and 1990s (Bell and Hollows, 2005; Kristensen and From, 2012, 2015).

All in all, service journalism points to a hybrid social role for journalists, serving both the consumer and the citizen as a continuum rather than as distinct or separate categories (From, 2018; From and Kristensen, 2018). It also suggests that processes of individualism have led to a promotionally driven kind of lifestyle journalism and a service-oriented kind of lifestyle journalism. However, as will be outlined below, commercialisation and individualisation also constitute important contexts for newer and broader developments in journalism in the digital media landscape, as exemplified by constructive journalism.

Lifestyle journalism in a digitalised media landscape

In the contemporary digital media environment, institutionalised media compete with numerous news and lifestyle content providers, producing and sharing such content on digital media platforms. Ordinary people express their views and opinions about lifestyle and consumption on vlogs and social media; semi-professional communicators, such as social media influencers or micro-bloggers (e.g. Maares and Hanusch, 2018), provide both original and branded content about lifestyle and consumer goods; and advertisers or marketing and PR professionals from the consumer industry promote lifestyles and goods on websites and social media. They all publish content on lifestyle issues by mimicking, adopting and transforming traditional journalistic genres into various stylistic media formats (e.g. Fulton, 2015; Kristensen and Christensen, 2017; Maares and Hanusch, 2018). The opportunities provided by digital media technologies for many different voices to produce and comment on lifestyle issues have occasioned yet another boom in media texts about lifestyle content. Besides the obvious argument that the Internet provides unlimited space for distributing lifestyle content, research has also pointed to a stylistic correspondence between communication patterns of soft journalism, particularly lifestyle journalism and social media logics. These include the often more subjective and opinion-based modes of communication of softer types of journalism and the more personalised communication patterns associated especially with social media (Kristensen and From, 2018). One example is fashion blogging, which has circumvented traditional taste hierarchies in the fashion industry and in fashion journalism. Fashion blogging is not about communicating fashion, based on expertise and novelty, but about the bloggers' performance of identity by means of a personalised or individualised everyday life approach to fashion (Kristensen and Christensen, 2017).

Today's digital media landscape has re-contextualised processes of commercialisation and individualisation, and a recurring issue in academia and in the public debate is how the digital media landscape is changing journalism more generally. A key concern is how the authority and legitimacy of journalism, as illustrated by the example of fashion communication, is challenged by digital media technologies, necessitating a rethinking of journalism. As we return to below, constructive journalism is one such an attempt, as it is dedicated to providing more trustworthy and unique stories by approaching audiences in new ways; or, in fact, in ways similar to those of service and lifestyle journalism. Accordingly, the above outlines of commercialisation, individualisation and digitalisation cannot, of course, be isolated as historical and societal contexts for the development of lifestyle journalism alone. Rather, they are broader processes embedded in and representing constituting factors of late modernity. This implies that news and political reporting have also been influenced by these perspectives. More personalised and subjective stylistic trends are emerging across different types of journalism, as interpretation (Cushion, 2015; Salgado, Strömbäck and Aalberg, 2017), emotion (Wahl-Jorgensen, 2016) and intimacy

(Steensen, 2016) are strategies that potentially give news media and journalists the opportunity to regain authority and a place in the digital information circuit; that is, they are approaches with a long tradition within soft journalism, including lifestyle journalism and journalism on arts and culture (e.g. Chong, 2017; Kristensen and From, 2015). While these trends may not be driven solely by digitalisation, digital media technologies—especially the emergence of social media—have occasioned as well as facilitated them. Scholars have argued that the boundaries between hard and soft news, the public and the private, the professional and the personal, the objective and the subjective, have become increasingly blurred in the digital media landscape (Kristensen and From, 2015, 2018; Sjøvaag, 2015; Steensen, 2016). One important aspect of this re-thinking of journalism concerns conceptions of the audience. Newer trends in hard news reporting, such as constructive journalism, seem to adopt modes of addressing audiences similar to those of service journalism and lifestyle journalism more specifically.

Constructive journalism and a changed mode of addressing audiences

The notion of constructive journalism emerged in a newsroom setting in the late 2000s, where it was developed to improve political news reporting (Gyldensted, 2015; Haagerup, 2017; From and Kristensen, 2018). A research agenda is now slowly developing (e.g. Ahva and Hautakangas, 2018; Hermans and Drok, 2018; Mast, Coesemans and Temmerman, 2018), though scholars also suggest that constructive journalism is not a completely new invention (From and Kristensen, 2018). It shares practices and values with action journalism or public journalism (e.g. Bro, 2018) and solutions journalism (McIntyre, 2017). The practice-based concept occurred at a time when the increased circulation of information and disinformation via digital media technologies, including fake news, necessitated a re-thinking of traditional news and journalism. In that sense, it can be seen as yet another attempt to remedy audiences' distrust in journalism in recent years. The solution to this crisis, suggested by constructive journalism, is for journalism to provide answers and guide people in a complex modern society. Our argument is that the journalistic tools applied in constructive journalism and its modes of addressing audiences are, in some respects, in line with not only action journalism, public journalism and solutions journalism but also with modes of addressing audiences in service journalism, and lifestyle journalism more specifically, and the hybrid audience identity encapsulated by these types of journalism (see also From and Kristensen, 2018).

Definitions of constructive journalism are still evolving, and the practice-based, bottom-up nature of the concept means that its explanations are often based either on normative dogmas or very concrete examples of articles or reporting. According to one definition, constructive journalism could be viewed as a new professional value—or news criteria—providing "new ideas, new solutions, new practices and new knowledge to existing problems in culture and society" (Haagerup, 2017, p. 57). This signals a clear break with traditional journalism based in objectivity and distance, because the constructive journalist plays a more active or engaged role. Moreover, this definition contradicts types of journalism driven by conflict and sensation as main news criteria, as finding common ground and pinpointing solutions is a priority. Thus, constructive journalism resembles the aims of service journalism and lifestyle journalism in terms of empowering the individual and, by extension, society in late modernity (From and Kristensen, 2018; From, 2018).

One of the pioneer practitioners in the field, Danish journalist and news editor Ulrik Haagerup, has provided six key ideas about constructive journalism. These ideas exemplify constructive journalism as a reaction to the broader challenges related to the digital media landscape, while at the same time suggesting a changed conception of the social role of journalism; one solution to these challenges is for journalism to address audiences in new ways. The six ideas state that constructive journalism 1) has to be unique by making alternative frames for understanding public events available to the audience; 2) has to be based on proximity by relating to people's lives, emotionally or geographically; 3) is caring as journalism should not mainly pinpoint problems and leave audiences in fear and distress but provide solutions and guidance; 4) has to be reflective by adding comprehension, knowledge and overview to current events; 5) has to be trustworthy (as any other type of journalism); and 6) must help audiences to prioritise and make relevant choices (Haagerup, 2017, p. 54). These ideas suggest a redefinition of the role of journalism, sharing several traits with service journalism and, more specifically, lifestyle journalism (From and Kristensen, 2018). A common ambition is to provide original content based not in breaking news logics and timeliness but in a reflective approach to broader human-interest issues and phenomena of our time. Rather than merely pointing to human conditions and problems, constructive journalism, as well as parts of lifestyle and service journalism, aim to facilitate and provide audiences with ways to cope with these issues.

The daily radio programme *Public Service*, produced by the Danish Public Broadcasting Company, DR, launched in January 2018 and aired on the radio channel P1, may serve as an example of content-labelled constructive journalism but also with service and lifestyle journalism connotations. This programme tries to dig one step deeper into current issues and stories by pointing to potential solutions to some of the problems raised and hereby guiding audiences in their everyday practices (https://www.dr.dk/radio/p1/public-service/public-service-98/). A more specific example of a constructive news theme on this radio show concerns how to solve the recurring problem of lack of housing for students in many (Danish) university cities (P1, 08.08.2018). Taking its point of departure in concrete cases, e.g. a student not able to find a place to live, the programme is organised as a dialogue between the host, an expert panel and audiences responding to this specific problem, and solutions are provided in collaboration between the experts, the panel and the ordinary listeners. This organisation of the programme resembles sub-genres of lifestyle journalism with 'advice' as a dominating feature, as suggested by Fürsich (2012, p. 14), where the interaction between audiences, experts and journalists, as well as the facilitation of solutions, are key features. The personal needs of the audience are at the centre, as the stories strive to guide the audience to handle specific situations in everyday life, but in this manner they also try to provide solutions to broader social problems. Thus, the example shows how constructive journalism shares lifestyle and service journalism's ambitions of not only addressing audiences as individuals but also as citizens.

Another example of constructive journalism is *The Guardian*'s special section 'The upside', launched in February 2018 and editorially framed as journalism that "seeks out the people, innovations and movements offering possible solutions to some of the world's thorniest problems" (https://www.theguardian.com/info/2018/feb/12/ about-the-upside-a-guardian-series). The online version is organised in different sub-sections: a general news section and five thematic sections named Enterprise, Environment, Communities, Health and Technology. These sub-themes overlap with topics often found in lifestyle supplements, among them also *The Guardian*'s own lifestyle section on 'Health & Fitness'. Even though 'The upside' stories focus more on issues from the social and political sphere, compared to articles in the lifestyle section, they share the ambition of providing solutions to significant individual and, by extension, societal problems. The lifestyle sub-section 'Health & Fitness', for example, brings the story 'The lost art of concentration: being distracted in the digital world', written by freelance broadcast and print journalist Harriet Griffey (2018), who has published a book on the topic and, in this article, advises readers on how to deal with distraction when constantly surrounded by digital media. The article exemplifies the strong commercial ties often found in lifestyle journalism, as it almost connotes branded content and includes consumer information on the price of the book. At the same time, the article provides input to solving a problem faced by many individuals in the digital age. Mental health is also the focus of attention in stories under the sub-section 'Health' of 'The upside'. In the article 'Our mental health is fracturing. Here's what I'd wish I had done …', the section editor Marc Rice-Oxley (2018), for example, diagnoses mental illness as a widespread cultural and social phenomenon of our time, and based on personal experience, he advises on how to remedy this mental state. At the end of the article, a link guides the reader to amazon.co.uk, where a Kindle version of Marc Rice-Oxley's memoir can be purchased. As such, the two articles share their thematic and guiding approach in terms of how individuals can cope with challenges in contemporary society. Furthermore, they share the inevitable commercial tie between journalism and cultural agents and thus exemplify cases characterised by blurring boundaries between lifestyle journalism and constructive journalism.

As indicated by these examples, constructive journalism perceives journalists as well as audiences in broader terms compared to traditional conceptions of journalism, proposing that journalists should be even more engaged in empowering audiences and in taking responsibility for their wellbeing. This notion of constructive journalism resonates with Gyldensted's (2015) and McIntyre's (2015, 2017) audience-oriented work, based on positive psychology, which has demonstrated that constructive news may, in fact, have an engaging and empowering effect on audiences. However, the pioneers of constructive journalism have also emphasised that this type of journalism should have social relevance. This implies perspectives that seemingly go beyond traditional definitions of lifestyle journalism, i.e., perspectives that transcend the traditional (critical) conceptualisation of lifestyle journalism as solely connected to consumerism and as symbolising the decline of journalism's democratic and social role. As argued in this article, however, if lifestyle journalism is seen as one aspect of the broader approach encapsulated by service journalism, it carries the potential of breaking down the dichotomy of the public and the private, the consumer and the citizen, as oppositional terms in ways similar to those of constructive journalism. The journalistic approaches both capture central processes of commercialisation, individualisation and digitalisation, and share some of the same ambitions and potential to empower the individual in a contemporary setting (Eide and Knight, 1999; Fürsich, 2012).

Conclusion

In this chapter, we have demonstrated that commercialism and individualism are key theoretical perspectives to explain the emergence and transformation of lifestyle journalism in Western news media, especially during the twentieth century. Or put differently, lifestyle journalism seems to have been a media institutional and journalistic response to and reflection of pivotal historical processes of late modern society. Likewise, the emergence of constructive journalism in the early twenty-first century may be viewed as a response to the challenges that media institutions and professional journalism are facing in the digital age, to some extent echoing these broader late-modern sociocultural transformations. In that sense, these types of journalism, and especially their particular mode of addressing audiences, represent various phases of journalism, influenced by particular media historical, institutional and technological circumstances as well as particular sociocultural conditions. They share a common denominator in that they have all entailed increasingly blurred boundaries between soft news and hard news and adopted increasingly complex modes of addressing audiences. Analytically, lifestyle journalism and constructive journalism share a conceptualisation of audiences as part consumers, part citizens and part clients; a hybrid identity originally associated with the umbrella term service journalism (see Eide and Knight, 1999; From and Kristensen, 2018). As such, they share a civic as well as a political potential. This double potential is often overlooked in scholarly debates, especially about lifestyle journalism, because the field is often, and understandably so, explained by its close ties to the market and to commercial interests. However, scholars in critical theory have argued that the genres used and mode of address applied in lifestyle journalism may empower audiences. Fürsich (2012, p. 23) for example, shows that different lifestyle sub-genres, such as travel journalism and music reviews on world music, may activate but also impede the negotiation of ongoing cultural change. Taste cultures, negotiated in lifestyle journalism, resonate with wider socio-political issues such as class, social mobility and identity (Fürsich, 2012, p. 13). This suggests that certain forms of lifestyle journalism may mobilise social change in ways similar to the more recent constructive approaches in political news journalism. Similarly, the pioneer practitioners and scholars of constructive journalism argue that by adding a more solution-oriented, caring and trustful dimension to hard news, reporting of international as well as everyday social and political problems may engage audiences in new ways (e.g. McIntyre, 2017). Thus, service journalism, lifestyle journalism and constructive journalism all include a continuum of civic and political identities, i.e., view such identities as complementary rather than opposites.

References

Ahva, L. and Hautakangas, M. (2018) 'Why do we suddenly talk so much about constructiveness?', *Journalism Practice*, 12(6), pp. 657–661. doi: 10.1080/17512786. 2018.1470474.

Barnhurst, K. G. and Nerone, J. (2001) *The form of news: a history*. Hove: Guildford Press.

Beck, U. (1992) *Risk society: towards a new modernity*. London: Sage.

Bell, D. and Hollows, J. (2005) 'Making sense of ordinary lifestyles', in Bell, D. and Hollows, J. (eds) *Ordinary lifestyles*. Berkshire: Open University Press, pp. 1–18.

Bro, P. (2018) 'Constructive journalism: Proponents, precedents, and principles', *Journalism*, pp. 1–16. doi: 10.1177/1464884918770523.

Brunsdon, C. (2003) 'Lifestyling Britain: the 8–9 slot on British television', *International Journal of Cultural Studies*, 6(1), pp. 5–23. doi: 10.1177/1367877903006001001.

Carter, K. (2018) 'Seven ways to improve your balance', *The Guardian*, 16 July. Available at: https://www.theguardian.com/lifeandstyle/2018/jul/16/seven-ways-to-improve-your-balance (Accessed: 27 December 2018).

Chong, P. (2017) 'Valuing subjectivity in journalism: bias, emotions and self-interest as tools in arts reporting', *Journalism*, pp. 1–17. doi: 10.1177/1464884917722453.

Cushion, S. (2015) *News and politics: the rise of live and interpretive reporting*. London: Routledge.

Eckman, A. and Lindlof, T. (2003) 'Negotiating the gray lines: an ethnographic case study of organizational conflict between advertorials and news', *Journalism Studies*, 4(1), pp. 65–77. doi: 10.1080/14616700306507.

Eide, M. (2017) 'The culture of service journalism', in Kristensen, N. N. and Riegert, K. (eds) *Cultural journalism in the Nordic countries*. Göteborg: Nordicom, pp. 195–204.

Eide, M. and Knight, G. (1999) 'Public/private: service journalism and the problems of everyday life', *European Journal of Communication*, 14(4), pp. 525–547. doi: 10.1177/0267323199014004004.

Franklin, B. (1997) *Newszak and news media*. Oxford: Oxford University Press.

From, U. (2010) 'The reading of cultural and lifestyle journalism', *Northern Lights: Film and Media Studies Yearbook*, 8(1), pp. 157–175. doi: 10.1386/nl.8.157_1.

From, U. (2018) 'Lifestyle journalism', in *Oxford encyclopedia of journalism studies*. Oxford: Oxford University Press. doi: 10.1093/acrefore/9780190228613.013.835.

From, U. and Kristensen, N. N. (2018) 'Rethinking constructive journalism by means of service journalism', *Journalism Practice*, 12(6), pp. 714–729. doi: 10.1080/17512786.2018.1470475.

Fulton, J. (2015) 'Are you a journalist? New media entrepreneurs and journalists in the digital space', *Javnost*, 22(4), pp. 362–374. doi: 10.1080/13183222.2015.1091624.

Fürsich, E. (2012) 'Lifestyle journalism as popular journalism', *Journalism Practice*, 6(1), pp. 12–25. doi: 10.1080/17512786.2011.622894.

Griffey, H. (2018) 'The lost art of concentration: being distracted in a digital world', *The Guardian*, 14 October. Available at: https://www.theguardian.com/lifeandstyle/2018/oct/14/the-lost-art-of-concentration-being-distracted-in-a-digital-world (Accessed: 27 December 2018).

Gyldensted, C. (2015) *From mirrors to movers: five elements of positive psychology in constructive journalism*. Lexington, KY: GGroup Publishing.

Haagerup, U. (2017) *Constructive news*. Aarhus: Aarhus University Press.

Hanusch, F. (2012) 'Broadening the focus: the case for lifestyle journalism as a field of scholarly inquiry', *Journalism Practice*, 6(1), pp. 2–11. doi: 10.1080/17512786.2011.622895.

Hanusch, F. (2017) 'Journalistic roles and everyday life: an empirical account of lifestyle journalists' professional views', *Journalism Studies*. doi: 10.1080/1461670X.2017.1370977.

Hanusch, F. and Hanitzsch, T. (2013) 'Mediating orientation and self-expression in the world of consumption: Australian and German lifestyle journalists' professional views', *Media, Culture & Society*, 35(8), pp. 943–959. doi: 10.1177/0163443713501931.

Hartley, J. (1996) *Popular reality: journalism, modernity, popular culture*. New York: Arnold.

Hartley, J. (1999) 'What is journalism? The view from under a stubbie cap', *Media International Australia*, 90(1), pp. 15–33. doi: 10.1177/1329878X9909000105.

Hermans, L. and Drok, N. (2018) 'Placing constructive journalism in context', *Journalism Practice*, 12(6), pp. 679–694. doi: 12048/10.1080/17512786.2018.1470900.

Hermes, J. (1998) 'Cultural citizenship and popular fiction', in Brants, K., Hermes, J. and Van Zoonen, L. (eds) *The media in question: popular cultures and public interests*. London: Sage, pp. 156–167.

Hjarvard, S. (1995) *Nyhedsmediernes rolle i det politiske demokrati ('The news media's role in political democracy')*. København: Statsministeriet.

Jones, S. and Taylor, B. (2013) 'Food journalism', in Turner, B. and Orange, R. (eds) *Specialist journalism*. London: Routledge, pp. 96–107.

Kristensen, N. N. and Christensen, C. L. (2017) 'The mediatization of fashion: the case of fashion blogs', in Driessens O. et al. (eds) *Dynamics of mediatization. Transforming communications – studies in cross-media research*. Cham: Palgrave Macmillan, pp. 225–245.

Kristensen, N. N. and From, U. (2012) 'Lifestyle journalism: blurring boundaries', *Journalism Practice*, 6(1), pp. 26–41. doi: 10.1080/17512786.2011.622898.

Kristensen, N. N. and From, U. (2015) 'Cultural journalism and cultural critique in a changing media landscape', *Journalism Practice*, 9(6), pp. 760–772. doi: 10.1080/17512786.2015.1051357.

Kristensen, N. N. and From, U. (2018) 'Cultural journalists on social media', *Mediekultur*, 34(65), pp. 76–97. doi: https://orcid.org/0000-0002-8782-7179.

Lewis, T. (2008) *Smart living*. New York: Peter Lang.

Maares, P. and Hanusch, F. (2018) 'Exploring the boundaries of journalism: Instagram micro-bloggers in the twilight zone of lifestyle journalism', *Journalism*. doi: 10.1177/1464884918801144.

Mast, J., Coesemans, R. and Temmerman M. (2018) 'Constructive journalism: concepts, practices, and discourses', *Journalism*. doi: 10.1177/1464884918770885.

McIntyre, K. (2015) *Constructive journalism: the effects of positive emotions and solution information in news stories*. PhD thesis. University of North Carolina at Chapel Hill. Available at: https://cdr.lib.unc.edu/indexablecontent/uuid:83b99a42-951c-4205-a129-44c9bf7ad8f3 (Accessed: 27 December 2018).

McIntyre, K. (2017) 'Solutions journalism. The effects of including solution information in news stories about social problems', *Journalism Practice*. doi: 10.1080/17512786.2017.1409647.

O'Sullivan, T. (2005) 'From television lifestyle to lifestyle television', in Bell, D. and Hollows, J. (eds) *Ordinary lifestyles*. Berkshire: Open University Press, pp. 21–34.

Raisborough, J. (2011) *Lifestyle media and the formation of the self*. Hampshire: Palgrave Mcmillan.

Rice-Oxley, M. (2018) 'Our mental health is fracturing. Here's what I wish I'd done', *The Guardian*, 22 July. Available at: https://www.theguardian.com/society/2018/jul/22/advice-improve-mental-health-anxiety-wellbeing-depression (Accessed: 27 December 2018).

Robinson, A. (2018) 'Seven ways to deal with post-traumatic stress disorder', *The Guardian*, 23 July. Available at: https://www.theguardian.com/lifeandstyle/2018/jul/23/seven-ways-to-deal-with-post-traumatic-stress-disorder-ptsd (Accessed: 27 December 2018).

Robinson, A. (2018) 'Seven ways to minimise the risk of having a stroke', *The Guardian*, 11 June. Available at: https://www.theguardian.com/lifeandstyle/2018/jun/11/seven-ways-to-minimise-the-risk-of-having-a-stroke (Accessed: 27 December 2018).

Salgado, S., Strömbäck, J. and Aalberg, T. (2017) 'Interpretive journalism', in de Vreese C., Esser, F. and Hopmann, D. N. (eds) *Comparative political journalism*. London: Routledge, pp. 50–70.

Steensen, S. (2016) 'The intimization of journalism', in *The SAGE handbook of digital journalism*. London: Sage, pp. 113–127.

Sjøvaag, H. (2015) 'Hard news/soft news: the hierarchy of genres and the boundaries of the profession', in Carlson, M. and Lewis, S. C. (eds) *Boundaries of journalism: professionalism, practices and participation*. New York: Routledge, pp. 101–117.

Wahl-Jorgensen, K. (2016) 'Emotion and journalism', in *The SAGE handbook of digital journalism*. London: Sage, pp. 128–144.

Zhou, S. (2012). '"Advertorials": a genre-based analysis of an emerging hybridized genre', *Discourse & Communication*, 6(3), pp. 323–346. doi.org/10.1177/1750481312446265.

2

IDEALISED AUTHENTICITY

Analysing Jean Baudrillard's Theory of Simulation and its applicability to food coverage in city magazines

Joy Jenkins and Amanda Hinnant

Magazines play a compelling role in the construction of mediated reality, from covers adorned with meticulously styled celebrities to spreads of lavishly decorated homes to articles filled with tips for eating, working and living better. Unlike newspapers, magazines typically target clearly defined groups of readers in both their conception and execution based on particular lifestyles and interests (Le Masurier, 2014) as well as characteristics such as age, gender and race. Magazines, and their advertisers, also cultivate two-way customer relationships (Turow, 2005), categorising audiences and appealing to them through the promotion of specific topics, activities and products. Thus, magazines have been criticised for participating in an overall culture of consumption that contributes to stimulating people's needs and providing instructions on how to meet them. As Duffy (2013) pointed out, women's magazines tend to be filled with contradictions, emphasising discourses of the 'real' and 'authentic' within individualised notions of empowerment and capitalistic-consumerist structures. Through promoting particular lifestyles and products, magazines do not force readers to comply with these suggestions, but they have been instrumental in the emergence of modern consumer culture and often endorse ways of life that are difficult to achieve (Kitch, 2015).

In these ways, magazines play active roles in creating a simulated presentation of reality, distributing images that constitute a desire-driven, simulated world. French sociologist Jean Baudrillard argued that reality has become so overwhelmed by signs that the only way we can perceive our surroundings is as simulations. That is, "signs have now taken priority over the things signified. In fact, things have just about disappeared altogether" (Baudrillard, 2010, p. 1554). Baudrillard suggested that signs are represented by simulacra, which imply representation but also include aspects of the "counterfeit, sham, or fake" (Baudrillard 2010, p. 1554). Simulacra have referents, but ultimately, they signify the absence, rather than the presence, of the objects they represent. As a result, we can no longer recognise our actual needs but only our hyperreal, media-driven needs, which lack referents in reality and are driven by consumption.

In arguing that reality has given way to hyperreality, Baudrillard presents an extreme view. His early works suggested that consumerism changed the way we see objects, shifting our focus from their utilitarian function to their symbolic function. For example, we no longer purchase items for our homes because they fulfil a particular purpose but because they help us achieve an ideal as presented in media images. They represent symbols of class or status, thereby allowing us to become part of a particular category of consumers. Mass media depict lifestyles that audiences may attempt to emulate through fashion, travel, fine dining, or luxury homes. In doing so, audiences yield to simulation, willingly taking part in an image-driven categorisation of needs.

This chapter focuses on city magazines—publications that focus their editorial content on a particular city or group of cities through a blend of service journalism and feature writing (O'Grady, 2004)—a genre whose portrayals may affect how readers perceive and behave in the places they live. Developed to promote cities in the post-World War II population boom (Hynds, 1995a), city magazines served as "'urban survival manuals' for the relatively affluent—guides to the best shopping, the best dining, the best entertainment that a city had to offer" (Riley and Selnow, 1989, p. 3). City magazines also often sought to serve as alternative news sources in their cities (Hynds, 1995b). Indeed, Burd (1969) suggested that the rise of city magazines signalled an "alert urban press" that aims to "maintain a metropolitan image of the city, but crusade for as well as boost civic morale, and which appeal to a rather small, quality-minded elite who are influential in urban decision-making and move across political boundaries in the metropolis" (p. 319).

Although similar in style and content to travel magazines that cover a city, region, or multiple countries through guides and essays, city magazines largely cater to citizens, rather than travellers, providing insights for how to better understand and experience their cities as well as in-depth packages on local issues and distinctive storytelling styles and visual approaches (Sivek, 2014). City magazines reflect different ownership approaches, including individual and chain ownership, and although each market is different, city magazines receive revenues largely from print advertising, as well as subscriptions and newsstand sales. Although facing revenue declines in the aftermath of the 2008 recession, city magazines have carved out niches in their communities, including remaining authorities in content areas where newspapers have scaled back coverage, such as dining, shopping and long-form journalism (Rehagen, 2017). However, to cater to a particular readership—their readers tend to be in their 40s and 50s and are college educated with a median household income of $162,000 (Rehagen, 2017)—city magazines have also emphasised idealised versions of cities, relying on class-based assumptions about what is good and desirable (Jenkins, 2016a).

These hyperreal representations, therefore, offer intriguing case studies for applying Baudrillard's theories.

Background and early works

Baudrillard was deeply influenced by Frankfurt School theorists Max Horkheimer and Theodor Adorno's critiques of the culture industries and by Barthes' semiotic criticism (Leitch, 2010). In the late 1960s, Baudrillard affiliated with the Situationists, a group combining Marxist analysis with criticism of consumer society and bourgeois values (Leitch, 2010). This Marxist influence was evident in two of Baudrillard's early works, *The system of objects* and *The consumer society*. In *The system of objects* (1968), Baudrillard considered objects in terms of their ideological roles in an integrated consumer capitalist system (Pawlett, 2007), suggesting that they serve as a means of achieving a higher social status (Lane, 2000). As Hegarty (2004) suggested, individuals choose from among different objects and products, but they do so within media-created categories, thus subjecting themselves to a "corporate imposition of identities" (p.16). Similarly, in *The consumer society* (1998), Baudrillard argued that our everyday life is defined by "the reception and manipulation of goods and messages" (p. 25). Individuals are not forced to consume objects; consumption creates an "abstract happiness" (p. 29) that resolves tensions. The consumer society, thus, presents objects as magical, miraculous, or even "a blessing of nature" (Baudrillard, 1998, p. 32).

In the essay 'The ideological genesis of needs', Baudrillard characterised objects as myths consisting of nothing but "different types of relations and significations that converge, contradict themselves, and twist around" (1969, p. 255). Objects also have symbolic exchange values, serving as hierarchical signs and constituting social control through norms and values. Mass media play key roles in this process by disseminating mythology and consumable signs (Baudrillard, 1998). It is assumed that individuals cannot be "citizens of the consumer society" (Baudrillard, 1998, p. 100) if they do not keep up with the trends media recognise. Therefore, rather than addressing the complexities of reality, the media present a world that is "visualizable, endlessly segmentable, and readable in images" (Baudrillard, 1998, p. 123), and audiences are expected to respond only within a select range of ideologies.

Baudrillard and simulation

Later, simulation began to define Baudrillard's critiques of contemporary culture. In *Symbolic exchange and death* (1976), Baudrillard proposed that simulation has become the dominant way we experience the world. For Baudrillard, all of reality is mediated and humans' conception of what is real falls between a process of "symbolic exchange" of meanings and simulation and is all the product of simulacra (Hegarty, 2004). In *The precession of simulacra* (2010), Baudrillard charted how simulation took hold and became "the map (that) … precedes the territory" (2010, p. 1557). Although "representation tries to absorb simulation by interpreting it as false representation, simulation envelops the whole edifice of representation as itself a simulacrum" (Baudrillard, 2010, p. 1560). This process occurs in four phases: in the first, there is a reflection of basic reality; in the second, the reflection masks and perverts basic reality; in the third, the representation marks an absence of basic reality; and in the fourth, the reference ceases to exist and is instead a simulation. When this transition occurs, the real has disappeared, opening the door through which "nostalgia assumes its full meaning" (Baudrillard, 2010, p. 1561). This is followed by a panic of material production to recapture the real, including objects and places.

Magazines as modes of simulation

Although Baudrillard's media criticism focused largely on the influence of television on society, magazines evoke many of the concepts he espoused as playing vital roles in simulation, including their emphasis on presenting appealing images of locations, people and objects; entanglement with consumerist society; and ability and desire to signal particular classes and lifestyles, thereby demonstrating the utility of his theories for journalism research. Magazines are arbiters of taste, promoting products, experiences, places and even people so that readers who embrace these suggestions may experience 'the good life'. Holmes (2007) described magazines' significant focus on readers, whom they spend much time researching in order to meet their "needs, desires, hopes, fears and aspirations" (p. 514). Magazines, then, take on the role of media Baudrillard suggested in *The system of objects* (1968), using images to promote objects that satisfy a particular type of consumer or lifestyle. Magazines suggest that consumers may choose from among a range of options, when, in reality, they choose from a determinate, media-defined set of objects.

Magazines are not only products of particular social realities but also shape reality by defining ideology and culture (Abrahamson, 2007). In discussing the democratisation of culture in *The consumer society* (1998), Baudrillard discussed publications such as *La Bible, Les Muses, Alpha, Le Million* and art and music publications. He said the audience for these publications embraced the middle class—such as white-collar workers and low and middle managers—and "long fed the demand for culture of the 'potentially upwardly mobile'" (Baudrillard, 1998, p. 107). Readers gravitated to magazines as a "mark of membership" (Baudrillard, 1998, p. 107) in an imagined community with the same interests and desires, a characteristic of magazines that remains. Class is also a key component. With *Nouvel Observateur*, Baudrillard said, "to read that magazine is to affiliate oneself to the readers of that magazine; it is to use a 'cultural' activity as a class emblem" (1998, p. 108). Although readers may have said they turned to these publications because they desired the knowledge in the content, their goal was largely encapsulated in the cultural exchange value of the publications and the status they conferred.

Magazines that focus on 'serving' the reader stimulate anxieties and then attempt to quell them. Eide and Knight (1999) argue that through the lens of service journalism, modernity makes everyday living problematic, creating a need for resolution and simplification in the form of knowledge, advice, expertise and information. Service journalism makes problems seem actual, no matter how manufactured, by complicating everyday life:

> The engineered 'realism' of the topical magazines threatened to deepen the passivity of the reader in several senses. In the main, it tended to encourage the idea that 'real' life was beyond the pale of the reader's existence […] The effect, therefore, was to create the feeling that *others* experienced the real—the sense that the reader, too, was an outsider looking in. […] the reader was first awed by its complexity and then counseled by 'experts' ostensibly closer to the action.
>
> *(Wilson, 1983, p. 61)*

Using authoritative language and providing expert advice, magazines tell readers how to identify problems in their lives and offer suggestions for how to address them, all while reinforcing shared consumer behaviours, leisure interests and attitudes (Machin and Van Leeuwen, 2005). Magazines, then, strive to cultivate a shared identity among readers rooted in a circular pattern of constructing and meeting media-constructed needs.

City magazines and the hyperreal

Although Baudrillard's concepts could be applied to almost all types of magazines, we focus on a genre that is generally under-studied in mass communication research: city magazines. Although geographically focused lifestyle magazines exist around the world, we particularly focus on their development in the U.S. The first U.S. city magazine, Hawaii's *Paradise of the Pacific*, emerged in the late nineteenth century and focused on serving as an "ambassador-at-large", emphasising positive characteristics of the Hawaiian islands to attract tourists (Riley and Selnow, 1991). The publication that set the precedent for the contemporary city magazine genre was *San Diego* (Tebbel, 1969), and the genre proliferated in the post-World War II population shifts of the 1960s and 1970s (Hayes, 1981; Hynds, 1995a).

These magazines aimed to provide readers with information about dining, travel and entertainment in their cities, while occasionally addressing community needs (Hynds, 1995a). City magazines also tended to attract "a sophisticated, class-conscious audience that buys new cars, stereo equipment and fine clothes and is highly attractive to advertisers" (Shaw cited in Hynds, 1995b, p. 176), a focus that continues today. Because city magazines cater to upwardly mobile residents with time and income to spare, they tend to focus on branding cities as a means of reaching middle- and upper-class "consumers" (Greenberg, 2000). In case studies of three notable city magazines, *Atlanta, New York* and *Los Angeles,*

Greenberg (2000) found that these publications increasingly replaced coverage of controversial topics and in-depth reporting with an emphasis on advertising and entertainment. As a result, challenges to communities, such as economic and racial inequalities, were overshadowed by lifestyle coverage.

Therefore, city magazines might not present actual depictions of cities but—in Baudrillard's term—simulations of cities. These media representations, offered through images, text and an authoritative tone, may convince readers that through particular experiences, perspectives, or purchases, they can participate in the realities of city life while often neglecting to publish direct calls to action that improve cities (Jenkins, 2016a).

In 'Hyperreal America' (1993), Baudrillard argued that America lacks the historical grounding of other nations and, therefore, exists in a perpetual present, or a "perpetual simulation" (p. 245). For Baudrillard, American cities are not defined by traditional ideas of urbanism but by images. In particular, he juxtaposed referential cities, such as London, Paris and Rome, which "have a territory, a memory, and a history", and fictional ones, such as Disney World and Las Vegas. Las Vegas, he said, is "a pure contiguity of advertising signs" (Baudrillard, 1993, p. 246).

City magazines often encourage their targeted readers, who are typically educated and affluent, to more fully experience their cities through consumption. By informing readers where to eat, what clothes to buy, how to decorate their homes and what events to attend, city magazines simulate a sense of community, which can never be gained through individual consumption. In doing so, though, they cater to those who can afford such luxuries, potentially contributing to alienation rather than camaraderie.

These magazines also reduce cities—and their problems—into digestible media packages. By emphasising photographs of the most appealing sites and people and ignoring images that may present a less-appealing view, city magazines can present a "false representation" (Baudrillard, 2010, p. 1560) of reality. City magazines represent the 'real' life that the reader should be leading, which is unattainable because of its artificiality. The magazines must deter readers from the realisation that there is no achievable way to live a 'real' city life to perpetuate their own monthly existence, maintaining a myth that is just out of reach.

Food coverage and 'authentic' culture

One part of city magazines that epitomises cultural differentiation while simulating the quest for the 'real' or authentic is food coverage. To closely examine how city magazines characterise foods to promote Baudrillard's simulation of a particular lifestyle, we purposively sampled award-winning U.S. city magazines. The magazines reviewed have consistently won awards from the City and Regional Magazine Association, a nonprofit organisation offering professional development and training for member magazines, and the texts analysed ranged from 2008–2011. Award-winners were selected because other publications often seek to emulate another publication's success. More specifically, we used intensity sampling of restaurant review guides, which often run multiple times in the same magazine over several issues and years, to locate information-rich cases. Critical discourse analysis (Van Dijk, 2001) allowed us to understand how authenticity was approached, demonstrated and fetishised through the food coverage. We approached the concept of 'authenticity' through the ways the magazines rhetorically constructed their area's most desirable foods, restaurants and dining districts, and in doing so attempted to connect these choices to the distinctive history, culture or feel of a city, all while adhering to conventions of city magazines.

The gastroporn elements of city magazines take up significant editorial realestate, including frequent appearances on the covers of these magazines via 'Best Restaurants', 'Cheap Eats', 'Best Breakfasts' and similar features. Despite these magazines' presence in 66 cities and regions across the U.S. (City and Regional Magazine Association, 2017), they have become increasingly standardised, adopting many of the same editorial topics and approaches (Jenkins, 2016a). These techniques can result in publications less focused on uniquely addressing their geographic bases than perpetuating the norms of a specific media genre. For example, as Greenberg (2000) found, images on every January cover of *New York* magazine and *Atlanta* magazine between 1990 and 1995 featured "glossy close-ups of platters of gourmet delicacies prepared in one of the 'top 10 area restaurants'" (p. 252). There are several practical reasons for city magazines to cover area restaurants, most prominently advertising and audience interest. City magazines use their service editorial to suggest that they are giving lists of choices for consumers, but they are doing so from within an institutional need to promote a certain idealised dining environment.

French bistros, Spanish tapas, Japanese sushi and Italian food receive critical attention in city magazines, possibly because they are part of a checklist of what is most in demand for gourmet eaters. One city-magazine food critic wrote: "For a city to be known as a dining destination, it's essential that strong, classic French fare be part of the mix" ('Stellar', *5280*★).[1] The writer emphasises that any American city should, whether actual French influence is present or absent via immigrants or history, have the representation of French influence via an 'Old World' dining establishment. Although 'Old World' is not explicated in the magazines, it is typically used to imply Europe and a quality of charm from the past. French cuisine for any given American city signifies a standard of restaurant food quality. Saying that French cuisine is required for legitimacy echoes Baudrillard's contention that American cities are disconnected from culture and history in ways that European cities are not. The 'nostalgia' for Parisian food intensifies the simulated quality of reality.

These descriptions, of course, are not limited to France. For example, one city magazine states, "there is something essential about Italy itself in the lightly scored surface of the *garganelli*" ('Drago Centro', *Los Angeles*). In this quote, not only is the culture distilled into a food, but it is further compartmentalised into the imagined preparation of the food. Playfulness with 'Old World' references also occurs, with a West Coast magazine describing a dish that would "make a St. Louis hausfrau proud" ('Eva', *Los Angeles*). There is both reverence and irreverence for the 'Old World' just as there is for authenticity. The continual signifying of the 'Old World' exhibits a "fetish of the lost object" (Baudrillard, 1983, p.142) in that the city magazines cultivate a nostalgia for something that has always been absent in American cities.

Obsession with whether something is authentic or aware of being inauthentic—and thus acceptable—is pervasive. One city magazine applauds: "We would call Providence elegant, but the restaurant is better than that: It is real" ('The 75 best restaurants in L.A.', *Los Angeles*). A chef is described as "embracing the honesty of the Italian table" ('Stratta', *Las Vegas Life*). Sometimes the authenticity is mocked with 'artisanal' used in quotation marks. Foods are playfully accused of hiding "their sophistication under a convincing layer of tradition" ('Greenwood's on Green Street', *Atlanta*). Alternatively, the 'real' can be heralded or knowingly discarded: "Many of the old soul-food restaurants have become caricatures, but this is the real deal" ('Busy Bee Cafe', *Atlanta*). Age, in this case, does not even grant authenticity. In fact, authenticity can sometimes be ironically dispensed with in city magazines. One sentence describing a restaurant reads: "It's never been about authenticity here; it's been about craft" ('Border Grill', *Los Angeles*). Just as 'foodies' have a nostalgia for the lost object in the home-cooked meal as representation of evaporated culture and values, city magazines maintain nostalgia for the cultural history that American cities are too new to have.

The origin of the actual food served in restaurants is a mystery in city magazine text, unless restaurants offer the sources of their food distributors. Also noteworthy is how a distributor's localness adds to the appeal of a food, such as arugula, grass-fed beef, or eggs. Localness simulates a seasonal tie to the land that is mostly nonexistent in urban settings. "Robust earthiness" is celebrated, and food is described as "woodsy" or evocative of "the forest floor". A seared king salmon is unironically described to carry "the purity of the waters in which it swam" ('Savory', *Los Angeles*). That said, most magazine food coverage, and especially covers featuring food photography, is interchangeable in that it is not distinctive of any particular city. A feature on 'Best Burgers' could as easily appear in Memphis as in Dallas or Portland. Stories are, in fact, de-origined by their repetitive and widespread nature.

The desire for non-mass-produced food is emphasised in an institution that is mass-producing food. Along with the adulation of items that are sourced locally, house-made and not mass-produced are items that are from "sustainable" farms that have been "sourced with a conscience" ('Forage', *Los Angeles*), as one magazine put it, by the restaurants. This evokes a desire to have a real person behind the food and to have it appear that it is one person cooking for another person. Rarely is the producer of the food shown, which might prevent the reader from inserting an imagined idea of who produced the food or even connecting with the producer.

In addition to representing the 'Old World', city magazines reveal restaurants to be drawing from global influences: "meatball *tagine* evokes the souks of Marrakech" ('Cleo', *Las Vegas Life*), "stewed chrysanthemums" ('Urasawa', *Los Angeles*), "the ramekin of sun-dried daikon sounds an ancestral note" ('Kiriko Sushi', *Los Angeles*). Turkey, Mexico and Japan are posed as sources for non-'Old World' inspiration. This approach relates to how city magazines, like the American cities they represent, do not reference connections to particular cultures but rather seek to promote a generalised "international dining scene".

Hand-in-hand with the idea that having French fare is 'essential' is verbiage from other city magazines about 'needs'. For example, "Best breakfasts: 75 restaurants you must check out" (*Chicago*) or the carrot-dangling routine of "you've had this, but not this", or plain directives telling readers what to eat all revolve around the concept of needing the food. Baudrillard (1969) argues that 'need' is not a natural phenomenon as it is assumed to be in a class bourgeois economy. He writes,

> consumption does not arise from an objective need of the consumer, a final intention of the subject toward the object; rather there is social production, in a system of exchange, of a material of differences, a code of significations and invidious [...] values.
>
> *(Baudrillard, 1969, p. 68)*

The exhaustive nature of food coverage, with every food category deemed acceptable to upper-middle-class readers, in part reveals the mechanised creation of food needs. Does anyone need to know about 75 best breakfast spots? The system, in this case city magazines, describes dining experiences to seek out, cultivates desires where they didn't exist, creates gaps to be filled and manufactures food needs to be met so that the magazines can survive.

Most importantly, the articles about food are never about people who actually need food in a city, those who do not have funding or access to quality food. In city magazines, money is rarely mentioned. There are generalised dollar-sign symbols, but seldom does the reader find out the actual cost of food, which is the main barrier for people who need food security. The food coverage serves as a form of social classification, or a means for the reader to differentiate him or herself from other classes. The idea of food as a natural need also reveals a fetishising of the lost object. In the U.S. and in many parts of the world, too much food is more deadly than too little food with regard to disease prevalence (Institute for Health Metrics and Evaluation, 2017). People with food insecurity suffer more from diabetes and obesity as demonstrated by the "obesity-hunger paradox" (Drewnowski and Specter, 2004) because cheaper foods are generally less nutritious and higher in calories (Darmon and Drewnowski, 2015; James *et al.*, 1997). The idea of not being able to get food is a "lost object" for people who are middle class or above. Because the real need for food is gone, we see a panic of production of editorial food coverage in order to recapture it. City magazines suggest an environment where upper-class 'foodies' thrive, while others seek what the magazines construe as 'less authentic' options.

Conclusion

Through their topic selection, photographic approaches and tone, magazines often create a bright picture of cities that are clean, easy to navigate and rife with opportunities for consumption by affluent residents. City magazines are ostensibly speaking to millions of citizens, but, in many cases, the main form of engagement they offer people is through their buying power (Greenberg, 2000; Jenkins, 2016a). This preserves American cities' disconnect from culture, history and memory, all while fostering a connection to the "hyperreal" city within the magazines' pages. 'Authentic' experiences, which allow residents or visitors to take part in the distinctive culture of a place, can be consumed (literally) through food and culture is a pastiche of borrowed referents to evoke nostalgia for 'Old World' or 'street' experiences.

Despite their applicability to these aspects of city magazines, Baudrillard's frameworks also present limitations. In particular, Baudrillard presents a strong, potentially technologically deterministic view of the media and their power in society, leaving little room for response from audiences. Indeed, multiple critics have raised concerns about Baudrillard's removal of the "real world" of reality (Leitch, 2010, p. 2). Specifically, his concepts of simulation and the hyperreal have been viewed as "politically apathetic" (Leitch, 2010, p. 2) in that they swallow narratives, truth claims and the real world without permitting critical response (Smith, 2001). As Merrin (2005) suggested, once Baudrillard's theory has been realised, we have no ability to deny it. Even Baudrillard suggested that his aim was not for his theory to be true or empirically testable. Rather, it should present a symbolic challenge offered with the hope that the real will eventually reemerge (Merrin, 2005).

Scholarship should consider how media depictions deviate from reality and the effects of these simulations on readers. In this, we veer from Baudrillard's suggestion that hyperreality is present and cannot be contested. Although the depictions of cities offered in city magazines may not represent reality but a glossy, consumer-oriented, easily digestible image of cities created to appeal to readers and advertisers—a "hyperreality"—audiences may not necessarily accept these depictions at face value. Rather, they may engage with magazines for their escapist qualities, seeking recommendations for restaurants and shopping destinations while also recognising that cities face challenges that may go unaddressed in these publications. Perhaps readers of city magazines are aware that they are essentially paying not to read about the challenges facing cities in the form of poverty, corruption, environmental damage and other challenges that population-dense spaces face. City magazines, as their editors have argued, may also serve a public-service function, informing and educating readers about both well-known and little-known aspects of their cities and how to engage with them (Jenkins, 2016b). These magazines offer the freedom to imagine a 'lifestyle' and be instructed on how to live in it, even if it has nothing to do with occupying an urban space.

Note

1 The articles cited in the findings of the discourse analysis come from resturant reviews that run consistently—over multiple issues and years, in some cases—in the back pages of city magazines. These articles often do not include authors. Because the focus of our anlaysis is city magazines' overall discursive construction of authenticity through food coverage, the particular authors and years of publication are less vital. Therefore, we cited only the name of the restaurant or the title of the feature in which the article appeared and the magazine title.

References

Abrahamson, D. (2007) 'Magazine exceptionalism', *Journalism Studies*, 8(4), pp. 667–670.
Baudrillard, J. (1968). *Le Système des objets* ('The system of objects'). Paris: Gallimard.
Baudrillard J. (1969) 'The ideological genesis of needs', in Schor, J. B and Holt, D. B. (eds) *The consumer society*. New York: The New Press, pp. 57–80.
Baudrillard, J. (1976). *L'échange symbolique et la mort* ('Symbolic exchange and death'). Paris: Gallimard.
Baudrillard, J. (1981) *Simulacra and simulation*. Ann Harbor: University of Michigan Press.
Baudrillard, J. (1983). *Simulations*. Los Angeles: Semiotext[e].
Baudrillard, J. (1993) 'Hyperreal America', *Economy and Society*, 22(2), pp. 243–252.
Baudrillard, J. (1998) *The consumer society: myths and structures*, Vol. 53. London: Sage.
Baudrillard, J. (2010) 'The precession of simulacra', in Leitch, V. B. (ed.) *The Norton anthology of theory and criticism* (2nd ed.). New York: WW Norton and Co, pp. 1553–1556.
Burd, G. (1969) 'The mass media in urban society', in Schmandt, H. J. and Bloomberg, Jr. W. (eds) *The quality of life*. Beverly Hills, CA: Sage, pp. 293–322.
City and Regional Magazine Association (2017) Member Directory. Available at: http://www.citymag.org (Accessed: 1 October 2017).
Darmon, N. and Drewnowski, A. (2015) 'Contribution of food prices and diet cost to socioeconomic disparities in diet quality and health: a systematic review and analysis', *Nutrition Reviews*, 73(10), pp. 643–660.
Drewnowski, A. and Specter, S. E. (2004) 'Poverty and obesity: the role of energy density and energy costs', *American Journal of Clinical Nutrition*, 79(1), pp. 6–16.
Duffy, B. (2013) 'Manufacturing authenticity: the rhetoric of "real" in women's magazines', *The Communication Review*, 16(3),pp.132–154.
Eide, M. and Knight, G. (1999) 'Public/private service: service journalism and the problems of everyday life', *European Journal of Communication*, 14(4), pp. 525–547.
Greenberg, M. (2000) 'Branding cities: a social history of the urban lifestyle magazine', *Urban Affairs Review*, 36(2), pp. 228–263.
Hayes, J. P. (1981) 'City/regional magazines: a survey/census', *Journalism & Mass Communication Quarterly*, 58(2), pp. 294–296.
Hegarty, P. (2004), *Jean Baudrillard: live theory*. London: Continuum International Publishing Group.
Holmes, T. (2007) 'Mapping the magazine', *Journalism Studies*, 8(4), pp. 510–521.
Hynds, E. C. (1995a) 'City magazines have diverse roles', *Mass Comm Review*, 22(1–2): pp. 90–100.
Hynds, E. C. (1995b) 'Research review: city and regional magazines', in Abrahamson, D. (ed.) *The American magazine: research perspectives and prospects*. Ames, IA: Iowa State University Press, pp. 172–185.

Institute for Health Metrics and Evaluation (2017) 'GBD compare sata visualisation'. Available at: http://vizhub.healthdata.org/gbd-compare (Accessed: 17 August 2018).

James, W. P. T. *et al.* (1997) 'Socioeconomic determinants of health: the contribution of nutrition to inequalities in health', *Bmj*, 314(7093), p. 1545.

Jenkins, J. (2016a) 'The good life: the construction of imagined communities in city magazines', *Journalism Studies*, 17(3), pp. 319–336.

Jenkins, J. (2016b) 'Public roles and private negotiations: considering city magazines' public service and market functions', *Journalism*, 26(5), pp. 619–635.

Kitch, C. (2015) 'Theory and methods of analysis: models for understanding magazines', in Abrahamson, D. and Prior-Miller, M. R. (eds) *The Routledge handbook of magazine research*. New York: Routledge, pp. 9–21.

Lane, R. J. (2000) *Jean Baudrillard*. New York: Routledge.

Le Masurier, M. (2014) 'What is a magazine?', *TEXT*, 25, pp. 1–16.

Leitch, V. B. (2010) 'Jean Baudrillard', in Leitch, V. B. (ed.) *The Norton anthology of theory and criticism* (2nd ed.). New York: WW Norton and Co, pp 1–36.

Machin, D. and Van Leeuwen, T. (2005) 'Language style and lifestyle: the case of a global magazine', *Media, Culture & Society*, 27(4), pp. 577–600.

Merrin, W. (2005) *Baudrillard and the media: a critical introduction*. Cambridge: Polity.

O'Grady, M. (2004) 'The 2003 relaunch of *Vancouver* magazine'. Unpublished doctoral Dissertation. Simon Fraser University.

Pawlett, W. (2007) *Jean Baudrillard: against banality*. London: Routledge.

Rehagen, T. (2017) 'City magazines, dependent on print, face uncertain future amid wave of deals', *Columbia Journalism Review*, 18 April. Available at: https://www.cjr.org/busines s_of_news/city-magazines-journalism-longform-emmis.php (Accessed: 17 August 2018).

Riley, S. G., and Selnow, G. W. (1989). *Index to city and regional magazines of the United States*. Westport, CT: Greenwood Publishing Group.

Riley, S. G. and Selnow, G. W. (1991) *Regional interest magazines of the United States*. Westport, CT: Greenwood Press Inc.

Shaw, D. (1976) 'List grows: magazines of the cities, a success story', *Los Angeles Times*, April 5.

Sivek, S. C. (2014) 'City magazine editors and the evolving urban information Environment', *Community Journalism*, 3, pp. 1–22.

Smith, M. W. (2001) *Reading simulacra*. Albany: State University of New York Press.

Tebbel, J. W. (1969) *The American magazine: a compact history*. New York, NY: Hawthorn Books.

Turow, J. (2005) 'Audience construction and culture production: marketing surveillance in the digital age', *The ANNALS of the American Academy of Political and Social Science*, 597(1), pp. 103–121.

Van Dijk, T. A. (2001) 'Critical discourse analysis', in Schiffrin D., Tannen, D. and Hamilton, H. E. (eds) *The handbook of discourse analysis*. Malden, MA: Blackwell Publishing, pp. 352–371.

Wilson, C. P. (1983) 'The rhetoric of consumption: mass market magazines and the demise of the gentle reader, 1880–1920, in Fox, R. W. and Lears, T. J. J. (eds) *The culture of consumption: critical essays in American history*, 1880–1980. New York: Pantheon.

3

JOURNALISM 'WITHOUT NEWS'

The beauty journalist private/professional self in *The Guardian*'s 'below the line' comments

Lucía Vodanovic

'Below the line' comments constitute one of the many forms of participatory journalism that has transformed the relationship between journalists and audiences, sometimes challenging the top-down model of news organisations (Graham, 2013). Like other digital platforms, they provide opportunities for users to comment on, criticise, praise, clarify or interrogate news content, while also allowing readers to like or dislike other users' posts and engage in direct conversations with them; the former has been characterised as "user-content interactivity" and is primarily aimed at providing feedback to the content creator, while the latter has been described as "user-user interactivity" and takes the form of a dialogue or conversation between commenters (Ksiazek *et al.*, 2016).

These interactions have the potential to strengthen one of the roles that journalism can adopt as a result of the rise of citizen and user content, in terms of facilitating people's public connection within groups based on the significance of sharing news, fostering communities, creating common terms of reference and aiding social integration (Swart *et al.*, 2018, p. 2). Yet as Todd Graham has identified, they are also unique and different to other forms of user-generated content:

> ['Below the line' comments] not only unite and join together journalistic content with content produced by the audience, they also allow the articles to move on, evolve and develop in a (sometime) deliberative manner, producing a new type of journalism product for readers.
>
> *(2013, p. 119)*

Beyond issues of popularity and rankings, recent research about 'below the line' comments has started to articulate the changes that they have brought for both the journalist and the audience, and also their relationship. Coddington *et al.* (2016), for instance, have developed the notion of "reciprocity" to conceptualise this new journalist/audience dialectic, describing how journalists are encouraged to seek comments from the public even when they feel ambivalent about it, and that readers expect that to happen. The authors identify different forms of reciprocity: while sharing, liking and commenting are forms of direct reciprocity on the side of the audience, a straightforward answer to a question would be the equivalent on the side of the journalist. Conversely, a form of indirect reciprocity could be just the witnessing and sharing of a piece of news, a practice that both journalists and audiences engage with. Over time, a form of "sustained reciprocity" could be developed, which "resituates journalists in the network. It casts them in a community manager role" (Coddington *et al.* 2016, p. 167). Another example is the work of Ksiazek *et al.* (2016), who focus more exclusively on the audience to argue how its participation constitutes a significant step-up in terms of engagement and reflective capacity:

> While it is one thing to simply read or watch a news story, making the decision to publicly contribute your reaction or opinion in response to the story indicates an individual that is more invested, aware, and attentive—in other words, more engaged—with the content.
>
> *(Ksiazek* et al. *2016, p. 505)*

Unlike the former contributions, this chapter looks at the audience/journalist interaction in the context of roles, values and definitions of the lifestyle journalist, and how that identity emerges in the exchanges with the reader. It proposes that 'below the line' comments are a useful site to articulate that identity, as this field is very often staffed by freelancers or "atypical media workers" (Deuze, 2008)—the majority of whom are female—not physically present in the newsroom, which generates particular dynamics between the professional and the private persona of the journalist. The primary research analyses this interactivity in *The Guardian*'s weekly beauty column, which is published every Saturday both in the print and the online versions of the British newspaper.

This beauty section, one of several under the heading of 'lifestyle journalism' alongside fashion, food, family and others, is part of *The Guardian*'s 'news you can use' or service journalism offer, as it helps to make sense of consumer issues and speaks to the audience's mixed identity of "part consumer, part citizen and part client", the mode of address usually present in service journalism (Eide and Knight, 1999, p. 527). The words and main picture of the beauty column are identical in both the digital and the print versions, with the sole difference being that the online platform contains affiliated links to the products mentioned by the beauty writer, added by subeditors after the journalist has filed her copy. Given that the direct interaction between journalist and audience is only possible on the online site, the research analyses the comments field of the column at guardian.co.uk, which represents the online version of both *The Guardian* and *The Observer* and is open and available to everyone to read, registered or not. In terms of traffic, *The Guardian* is one of the leading online newspapers in the UK; it regularly comes very high in the rankings of English language newspaper sites and, crucially, provides one of the most extensive uses of comments in British written journalism (Graham, 2013, p. 117).

While the lifestyle pages of the site have always included beauty features, this column was launched in 2011 and has become almost synonymous with the beauty journalist who writes it, Sali Hughes. She is also literally the face of it, as a picture of Hughes holding or wearing the products or trends alluded to in the article accompanies each weekly column. Despite the regularity and longevity of her column, she works for the organisation on a freelance basis, and on some occasions writes longer features, celebrity interviews and other lifestyle content, broader than the beauty niche. In addition to her role as resident beauty columnist for *Guardian Weekend* magazine, she writes features and comment pieces for a range of publications such as *Grazia* and *Red*, contributes to various radio programmes and is the creator and presenter of the YouTube series 'In the Bathroom', based on very long interviews with industry insiders and creators about life, work and beauty, conducted in the bathroom of the interviewee's house, very often seated on the toilet or inside the bathtub. She is also author of two books, *Pretty Honest* (2014) and *Pretty Iconic* (2016), with a third publication scheduled for 2019, and the co-founder of Beauty Banks, a charity that provides free toiletries and sanitary pads to people in need, operating similarly to food banks.

Method

The early iterations of Hughes' online column included video content in the form of practical step-by-step tutorials—a series of 'how-to's such as how to apply liquid eyeliner, or the secrets for achieving voluminous hair, and 'best-of's, such as the best high street moisturisers or serums—but now it only includes written material. The research analysed a total of 1,065 posts from Saturday 13 July 2013 to Saturday 14 July 2018 by the journalist in response to readers' comments, as it is rare for Hughes to post something that is not prompted by or a direct response to a reader question, observation or criticism. The latter only occurred in ten of the posts analysed; in all those cases, the journalist either posted a follow-up to her column, because, as she explains, she did not have enough space to include everything she wanted to or because there was a product update after she had filed her copy, or explained a change of format for her section.

While it would also be interesting to explore "user-to-user interactivity" in this forum, particularly because the idea of a community of readers and beauty lovers features heavily in the comments—and indeed this notion of a "community" has been used to define service journalism (Usher, 2012)—on this occasion the research questions are better answered by focusing on the conversations in which the journalist is directly involved. For that reason, the analysis looks at each individual post by Hughes and the conversation in which it emerged, either as a response to a singular reader comment or to a series of posts by different members, in order to understand the context of her contribution; this allows me to establish how the role that the journalist adopts in the comments section arises in the context of that conversation.

A qualitative content analysis has been employed to answer the questions that guided the research: What role does the journalist adopt in her interactions with the audience?; what journalistic values does she attribute to the content produced?; how does she negotiate her private and her professional persona in these interactions? As the analysis discusses, these questions are closely linked; very detailed conversations about the role and the production of journalism, for instance, often emerge in the context of an interaction that refers to domestic issues taking place in the life of the journalist. For this reason, the analysis also speaks of wider trends and issues within lifestyle journalism and journalism more broadly, such as notions of individuation—the shift from the news organisation to the individual journalist—and the variety of roles that journalism provides, including those in the private sphere. This context is discussed in the following two sections of this chapter, before providing the research findings and analysis.

Journalism of the self

As different authors have started to pay attention to the functions of journalism beyond the political in order to include those related to everyday life (Hanusch, 2017; Hanitzsch and Vos, 2018), the management of the self (Eide and Knight, 1999) and the construction of identity (Hanusch and Hanitzsch, 2013), the role of the journalist, as a professional, has also been expanded in order to embrace its potential position as a connector, mood manager, inspiratory and guide (Hanitzsch and Vos, 2018); someone who is "able to dispense advice and shape tastes on cultural matters" (Matthews, 2014, p. 148).

This contemporary research has given renewed attention to a lineage of thinking about the role of journalism in the private sphere in addition to its political and public one, or even a rethinking of those boundaries altogether; Hanitzsch and Vos (2008), for instance, have asserted that journalism operates in the "everyday life", a terrain that has consequences for political life but cannot be reducible to the political either. This lineage is expressed by John Hartley in this quote from his seminal *Popular reality: journalism, modernity, popular culture*, a text originally published in 1996 that continues to inform the discussion of what we might refer to as journalism of the self or journalism of the domestic and private spheres:

> Another unusual feature of this book compared with most treatments of the topic is that it does not confine journalism to news, if by that is understood the daily reporting of the political public sphere as traditionally defined. It is just as interested in what has become known as 'style',

'consumer' and 'lifestyle' journalism, especially that which addresses a feminized readership. Clearly 'hard' news is an important component of journalism, perhaps its professional cutting-edge, but it is not a self-explanatory, self-evident object of study. Journalism has always included coverage of the public as well as the private sphere, and it is in fact a fundamental thesis of this book that these 'two' spheres have never been as separated as is sometimes supposed; on the contrary, new political movements have tended to develop in the private sphere, while public politics have progressively been privatized over the past century or so.

(Hartley, 1996, p. 6)

This trajectory that challenges the private/public division in journalism and reclaims the potential political aspects of everyday choices is also exemplified by the work of feminist media scholar Lisbet van Zoonen (1998), who suggests that the high status of traditional news journalism has been based on the assumption that it delivers what is required for a healthy democracy, yet that the profession has also always provided people with what is required to "make sense of" reality, both in the public world and the private sphere (1998, p. 125). This more reflective stance could then take journalism beyond the traditional boundaries of hard or soft news, to the 'new' as a space of reflexivity or an encounter with a fresh view, narrative or practice. Some authors have even spoken about disentangling journalism from 'the news' (Le Masurier, 2015, p. 139), if it is assumed that only hard-hitting, financial and international affairs news qualify as such. Other authors have emphasised that the private sphere could be a site for news culture in its own right and indeed could contribute to democracy and social reflection: "By showing the creative and inventive nature of everyday life, journalism might contribute to a more balanced representation of the civic importance of life's private and public spheres" (Costera Meijer, 2001, p. 195).

These offerings challenge the assumed contrast between the political life of the public sphere and the intimacy of the private one, which includes issues of domesticity, consumption and identity. They also invite research into the practices and roles of journalists, making a distinction between those practices and the assumed normative and institutional functions of journalism (Hanitzsch and Vos, 2018). Given this shift, Julian Matthews has argued that research into these new roles of the journalist in the private sphere requires a consideration of the professional's activities "as the object of analysis rather than the subject of external influences" (2014, p. 146), suggesting that traditional journalism research has privileged the discussion of external factors such as financial constraints, ownership and regulations, instead of the actual activities and practices that take place in those settings, and how journalists navigate those imposed structures. This relates the discussion of roles to ideas of agency and individualisation, the other important framework for the discussion that is addressed in this chapter.

The individual journalist

In 'The politics of journalistic creativity: expressiveness, authenticity and de-authorization', Tim Markham argues that, in the context of media convergence, contemporary discourses of journalism and the creative industries tend to associate creativity with a specific conception of agency, which in the case of lifestyle journalism takes the form of "self-determination" (2012, p. 189). According to the author, this stands in contrast to the romantic notion of journalism as a craft, trade or tribe, as this form of agency "is demonstrably individualistic, tied up with the authentic voices or trusted authority of particular journalists" (Markham, 2012, p. 189). The choice of the word "authentic" is relevant: while credibility has been considered one of the essential traits of a good, trustable journalist, authenticity points to something different, to do with genuineness and integrity, with the conception of a truthful self and a valorisation of personal experience. Markham cites many expressions or examples of this individual agency, from the increased use of head shots online and in print, to the activity of journalists in comment forums and Twitter feeds. Perhaps less directly, the noticeable presence of the personal authorial voice in news writing—usually referred to as "subjective and confessional journalism" (Coward, 2013), a genre that has both passionate fans and acute detractors—is also a consequence of this; quite literally, "you cannot and should not write yourself out of your work" (Markham, 2012, p. 188). These discourses, he argues, can be problematic, as the freedom to "be yourself" does not guarantee a freedom to act without the constraints of traditional journalistic structures.

Other authors such as Mark Deuze (2008) have also looked at issues of professional identity in the context of convergence—understood not simply as a technological process but also as the increasing merging of work, life and play, and the blur between media production and consumption that has allowed the audience to become a source within news reports, opinions and analysis—. Deuze argues that journalists, particularly freelancers, are "increasingly forced to give meaning to their work and thus construct their own professional identity in the context of rapidly changing and often overlapping work contexts" (2008, p. 111). This process takes the form of a constant negotiation between the dynamics of the journalist as a person and as a professional working within an organisation, sometimes adopting different identities as journalists move across different platforms, news organisations and roles.

With a different emphasis, Ulrika Olausson (2017) has described this shift towards the "individualisation" of journalism in terms of self-promotion and branding:

> There is a noticeable trend among the most active journalists to exploit social media to create personal brands and promote themselves as individual professionals rather than (or possibly in parallel with) their role as employees of a particular news organisation.
>
> *(2017, pp. 1–2)*

This echoes the work of others such as Logan Molyneux and Avery Holton (2015, 2017), who argue that journalists spend more time building a personal rather than an organisational brand; and Ulrika Hedman and Monika Djerf-Pierre (2013), who write about journalists' self-promotion through social media, very much using their own personalities as their currency. "Being 'personal' is crucial in building a personal brand by means of social media" (Hedman and Djerf-Pierre, 2013, p. 372). Olausson (2017) summarises these processes of self-production, commodification and promotion within journalism with the notion of a "celebrified" journalist.

Despite its different nuances, all this literature suggests an increasing shift from the news organisation that journalists represent to the journalist as an individual, stressing also how the dialogue with the audience—through social media, 'below the line' comments and other forums—is one important cause and determinant of this change: "That organisation-centred definition is being challenged as journalists adapt to new technologies and new involvement of the audience in the newsgathering process" (Molyneux and Holton, 2015, p. 227).

The space of beauty journalism in the UK is peppered with examples of branding and entrepreneurialism, from the pioneer Jane Cunningham—known as the British Beauty Blogger, one of the first journalists to launch a commercial blog to build her portfolio career—who has become more known through her blogging presence than through her travel journalism signed by her real name, to Alex Steinherr, the beauty editor of *Glamour* magazine, who has launched a range of skincare products with Primark, a mass-market clothing and lifestyle store known for its very low prices. In addition to affiliated links, there are a number of sponsored posts to be found on the British beauty blogger sites, such as on Nadine Baggott's—another popular British beauty journalist—YouTube channel; both have collaborated with a number of recognisable British and international brands such as Marks & Spencer, Clinique, Blink Blow Bar and several others.

The work of Sali Hughes also constitutes an example of the portfolio career of contemporary lifestyle journalists, known as individuals beyond the news organisation in which they are based. Managed by the talent agency Arlington, she hosts corporate events for a number of brands and retailers, such as Selfridges, Boden, Triumph, John Lewis, Olay, Liberty and many others; by late 2018, her Instagram account shows over 115K followers and her online presence in this platform is a mixture of posts about her private life (her wedding, her evening meals cooked at home, her dog, Sylvie), posts about her professional activities (book tour announcements, links to events that she is hosting), and her charity work through Beauty Banks. But her case is also different, as she has a regular column in a national newspaper, in which, as the analysis below discusses, she strongly defends her total independence from the beauty industry and from advertisers and takes various different roles in her interactions with the readers.

Analysis and discussion

After a first cycle of analysis, a set of categories was established and then the posts where coded against those themes. The full list of categories is as follows: 'product recommendations', 'beauty advice', 'life', 'production of journalism', 'industry', 'criticism' and 'work outside *The Guardian*'. For the second cycle, the posts that contain small interactions and/or very little information—comments like 'thanks', 'see above', 'see my previous reply' or corrections to spelling mistakes in previous posts—were left out as they don't say enough about the qualities of her journalistic role, even though they are telling of the quantity of her audience interactions. When a post contains material that could be included in different categories, the theme most clearly expressed—nearly always prompted by the original comment of the reader—was chosen, unless there was almost a total overlap, in which case the post was coded against more than one category and a note was made about which themes were overlapping. After that, the role that the journalist adopts in that conversation was established to seek patterns of professional identity in relation to those topics.

The majority of the posts were coded against the themes of 'product recommendations' and 'beauty advice'—604 and 236 respectively—something that reinforces the journalist in her role of 'beauty expert' and this section within *The Guardian* as 'news you can use' content. Advice in these categories includes very comprehensive recommendations of specific skincare and makeup products, with detailed, almost prescriptive information about brands and formulations. It also includes equally comprehensive advice on application techniques, how to layer products, makeup tips, etcetera, sometimes verging on the medical: even though Hughes often recommends readers to visit their GP, a number of the interactions engage with topics such as adult acne, melasma, hyperpigmentation and psoriasis, and the journalist often offers instructions based on her own experience as a sufferer of melasma and her close friends' issues with adult acne, for instance. Unlike other roles that would be discussed below, in this function of 'beauty expert', Hughes is very much cast as a trusted and authoritative figure, suggesting a top-down approach present in these interactions instead of feedback between the audience and the professional.

The third category with the highest number of posts is 'life', with 75 interactions, ranging from bereavement to fashion and breastfeeding; this also includes short, fun and snappy interactions, as if the journalist was sharing a joke with her readers. Here, the journalist adopts a 'horizontal' role that could be described as 'friend' or companion. These interactions below the line of the column 'Beauty: how makeup can help in the hardest times' (Hughes, 2015), written after, as it is revealed in the text, the journalist's close friend had passed away, are examples of much more intimate and personal forms of dialogue, prompted by the readers' response to the piece:

[Reader1] 14 Nov 2015 8:48

What a beautiful and heartbreaking read. When I tragically lost my cousin a couple of years ago I spent ages choosing my lipstick for his funeral. To me it was a hugely important part of controlling what I could during such a deeply traumatic day.

Beautiful piece Sally. One I will always remember. I am so sorry for your loss.

(in Hughes, 2013)

salihughes [Reader1] 15 Nov 2015 0:04

I write in my book about my identical feelings on the day of my father's funeral.

It's a need some of us have to regain some control. I think it's healthy. Sx

(in Hughes, 2013)

[Reader2] 14 Nov 2015 7:56

My closest friend died on Monday. In the last fortnight of her life, when I had to be out of the Country for a few days, I arranged delivery of a gift-wrapped Dior Addict lipstick. When it arrived, we were able to share our delight, by text, of the rich but subtle colour and the slick magnetic closure of that lovely crystalline tube. When all else seems to be swept away, these little moments of seemingly frivolous normalcy helped us to navigate the wilderness. Sorry for your loss, Sali.

(in Hughes, 2013)

salihughes [Reader2] 15 Nov 2015 0:09

This is lovely. I sent Carey products all the time, because she loved them and there was so little else I could do from three hundred miles away. In her last two months, we put lots of them on, and chatted as we went. I'll never forget those hours and days. They changed my life, truly. An enormous privilege. I am so sorry for your loss. It's horrible. I can only imagine how awful you feel, especially so soon after the event. Please know I am thinking of you, and do make sure you take time to look after yourself. Sx

(in Hughes, 2013)

In both cases, the experience of loss on the reader's side is matched on the side of the journalist—sending products to a dying friend; choosing a lipstick shade for a funeral—describing the rituals of beauty and the importance it has for some people in moments of intimacy and vulnerability, while fostering a community of beauty lovers. The mode of address here is significantly different from the consumer speak of the previous 'beauty expert' role and much less hierarchical. A similar tone and the 'matching' of experiences can be found in several exchanges about women being criticised or considered frivolous because of their love of makeup or skincare, which also reinforces the notion of a community of beauty lovers.

A third role of an 'independent journalist' is taken most explicitly in the posts responding to accusations of branded content and addressing 'criticism' in general, or discussing issues to do with the 'production of journalism', the 'industry' and her 'work outside *The Guardian*'. Indeed, those are the categories that often present overlaps between themes, particularly between 'criticism' and the 'production of journalism'. Any criticism about the perceived commercial nature of the column is addressed with very detailed explanations of the production of journalism—the fact that headings are written by the subeditor, for instance, or why her image is always on the column even though she mentions that she is not comfortable with it, or what she does with all the products she gets sent—and comments about *The Guardian*'s editorial integrity. Overall, there is a mix of comments that suggest implicit disagreements between her professional self and the news organisation, and others that defend *The Guardian* as a valuable provider of journalism. The following quote is an example of the latter and constitutes the single post of the journalist in 2018:

> To reiterate, I make not a penny from affiliate beauty product links in The Guardian. Never have, never will. Moreover, I have never once been asked by The Guardian to favour any brand for any reason, affiliated or otherwise. They've never attempted it, and I would leave if they did.
>
> *(Hughes, 2018)*

This role of independent and 'professional journalist' is reinforced in comments about the beauty industry, showing a similar mix of disagreements with its practices—calling out the limited offer of shades for non-Caucasian skin tones by some brands, for instance—and positive comments about it.

Within this theme, posts addressing concerns about animal welfare and animal testing in the beauty industry are, arguably, the most clear example of feedback between readers and the journalist; the analysis of the history of the interactions shows that this was a concern that readers started to express in those conversations early on, culminating with a rich exchange between them in the column 'Beauty: the end of animal testing' (Hughes, 2013), which coincided with the deadline for all companies to implement the EU ban on animal testing. This particular column also generated a number of exchanges about the production of journalism, in particular the fact that the headline could be regarded as misleading given that animal testing was only banned in the EU then and that companies that sell in China, for instance—including European ones—must go through a compulsory process of animal testing to access the Asian market, even though the regulations about this are also changing now. While the tone used to address criticism is primarily informative—variations of the claim "I don't agree with the title but it is written by the subeditor"—the conversation also suggests a horizontal community in which the journalist educates the reader and vice versa, which implies that listening to readers' concerns is also an important feature of the professional journalist.

The last role that the journalist adopts in this history of exchanges could be described as 'individual', which is also more present in the last few categories/themes. Even though she sometimes alludes to events in her private life when acting as 'expert' and as 'friend', her identity outside work is most clearly displayed when answering critical comments, including those arguing that she is not interested in or taking enough time to answer readers' questions. Posts that directly explain that she can't answer questions on the day the column is published because it is her son's eighth birthday, or because her children are at home during half term, while also clarifying that she gets paid for the column but not for those interactions with the readers, speak of her complex identity of regular columnist, freelancer, professional journalist and mother, and of the challenges and possibilities that 'below the line' comments can provide.

Conclusion

This analysis of 'below the line' comments suggests that various discourses—some personal, some professional—are brought together in the conversations between the journalist and her audience, very often merging the individual and the institutional. Different roles and modes of address were identified—'expert', 'friend', 'professional journalist' and 'individual'—in response to these comments. The shift from the organisation to the individual is perhaps not as sharp as the term 'individualisation' would imply; Hughes' work, particularly the interaction with audiences but also how she describes the production process of her column, suggests an agency and subjectivity embedded in the institutional, rather than an anti-institutional or beyond institutional, approach. This brings together the personal and the social and sits very much in the terrain of consumption, identity, self-expression and sometimes politics, as the conversations about race and animal testing in the context of the beauty industry suggest, which emphasises the potential civic importance of our private lifestyle choices.

The space devoted to comments and fairly detailed explanations about the production of journalism speaks of a strong defence of traditional professional values—independence, integrity, trust—in a niche sector that perhaps is perceived in the popular imaginary as working closely with brands. This is in line with what Olausson (2017) has written about the industry's recent transformations: as the boundaries between professional journalists and other information brokers have become increasingly blurred, journalists now work hard to distinguish themselves from other providers while being both flexible and multi-skilled. Interestingly, industry here does not just refer to the journalistic one, as there are substantial conversations about beauty brands, the production of cosmetics, ethics and the normalisation of certain forms of appearance and aesthetics over others. This suggests that the professional journalist is navigating the dynamics and tensions of both the news organisation for which she works and the industry that provides her sources, material and, literally, stock.

References

Bruns, A. (2012) 'Journalists and Twitter: how Australian news organisations adapt to a new medium', *Media International Australia Incorporating Culture and Policy*, 144, pp. 97–107.

Coddington, M. *et al.* (2016) 'From participation to reciprocity in the journalist-audience relationship', in Broersma, M. and Peters, C. (eds) *Rethinking journalism again: societal role and public relevance in a digital age*. London: Routledge, pp. 161–174.

Costera Meijer, I. (2001) 'The public quality of popular journalism: developing a normative framework', *Journalism Studies*, 2(2), pp. 189–205, doi: 10.1080/14616700120042079.

Coward, R. (2013) *Speaking personally: the rise of subjective and confessional journalism*. Houndmills: Palgrave Macmillan.

Deuze, M. (2008) 'The professional identity of journalists in the context of convergence culture', *Observatorio (OBS*) Journal*, 7, pp. 103–117.

Eide, M. and Knight, G. (1999) 'Public/private service: service journalism and the problems of everyday life', *European Journal of Communication*, 14(4), pp. 525–547.

Graham, T. (2013) 'Talking back, but is anyone listening? Journalism and comment fields', in Broersma, M. and Peters, C. (eds) *Rethinking journalism: trust and participation in a transformed news landscape*. London and New York: Routledge, pp. 116–127.

Hanitzsch, T. and Vos, T. (2018) 'Journalism beyond democracy: a new look into journalistic roles in political and everyday life', *Journalism*, 19(2), pp. 146–164.

Hanusch, F. (2017) 'Journalistic roles and everyday life', *Journalism Studies*. doi: 10.1080/1461670X.2017.1370977.

Hanusch, F. and Hanitzsch, T. (2013) 'Mediating orientation and self-expression in the world of consumption: Australian and German lifestyle journalists' professional views', *Media, Culture & Society*, 35(8), pp. 943–959.

Hartley, J. (1996) *Popular reality: journalism, modernity, popular culture*. London: St Martin's Press.

Hedman, U., and Djerf-Pierre, M. (2013) 'The social journalist: embracing the social media life or creating a new digital divide', *Digital Journalism*, 1(2), pp. 368–385. doi: 10.1080/21670811.2013.776804.

Hughes, S. (2013) 'Beauty: the end of animal testing', *The Guardian*, 28 December. Available at: https://www.theguardian.com/fashion/2013/dec/28/beauty-end-animal-testing-china (Accessed: 11 December 2018).

Hughes, S. (2014) *Pretty honest: the straight-talking beauty companion*. London: Fourth State.

Hughes, S. (2015) 'Beauty: how makeup can help in the hardest times' (comments section), *The Guardian*, 14 November. Available at: https://www.theguardian.com/fashion/2015/nov/14/beauty-how-makeup-can-help-at-hardest-times-in-life (Accessed: 11 December 2018).

Hughes, S. (2016) *Pretty iconic: a personal look at the beauty products that changed the world*. London: Fourth State.

Hughes, S. (2018) 'The best workout makeup' (comments section), *The Guardian*, 14 July. Available at: https://www.theguardian.com/fashion/2018/jul/14/the-best-workout-makeup (Accessed: 11 December 2018).

Ksiazek, T. *et al.* (2016) 'User engagement with on-line news: conceptualizing interactivity and exploring the relationship between online news videos and user comments', *New Media & Society*, 18(3), pp. 502–520. doi: 10.1177/1461444814545073.

Le Masurier, M. (2015) 'What is slow journalism?', *Journalism Practice*, 9(2), pp. 138–152. doi: 10.1080/17512786.2014.916471.

Matthews, J. (2014) 'Journalism', in Smith Maguire, J. and Matthews, J. (eds) *The cultural intermediaries reader*. London: Sage, pp. 145–155.

Markham, T. (2012) 'The politics of journalistic creativity: expressiveness, authenticity and de-authorization', *Journalism Practice*, 6(2), pp. 187–200. doi: 10.1080/17512786. 2011. 616651.

Molyneux, L. and Holton, A. (2015) 'Branding (health) journalism: perceptions, practices, and emerging norms', *Digital Journalism*, 3(2), pp. 225–242.

Molyneux, L. and Holton, A. (2017) 'Identity lost? The personal impact on brand journalism', *Journalism*, 18(2), pp. 195–210.

Olausson, Ulrika (2017) 'The celebrified journalist', *Journalism Studies*. doi: 10.1080/1461670X.2017.1349548.

Swart, J. *et al.* (2018) 'Shedding light on the dark social: the connective role of news and journalism in social media communities', *New Media & Society*. doi: 10.1177/1461444818772063.

Usher, N. (2012) 'Service journalism as community experience', *Journalism Practice*, 6(1), pp. 107–121. doi: 10.1080/17512786.2011.628782.

van Zoonen, L. (1998) 'A professional, unreliable, heroic marionette (M/F): structure, agency and subjectivity in contemporary journalisms', *European Journal of Cultural Studies*, 1(1), pp. 123–143. doi:10.1177/136754949800100108.o

PART II

Experience, consumption and identity

4

RECONCILING RELIGION AND CONSUMERISM

Islamic lifestyle media in Turkey

Feyda Sayan-Cengiz

The landscape of journalism in Turkey has witnessed an increasing focus on life-styles, consumption and popular culture since the 1980s, and a surging trend to address media audiences as consumers. The transformation of journalism unfolded after the *coup d'état* in 1980, which resulted in a process of depoliticisation of society, economic liberalisation and rising consumerism. In the decades that followed, Islam's influence was increasingly seen in Turkey at the political, economic, social and cultural levels. The Islamic bourgeoisie, which has flourished in the process of economic liberalisation and the multifaceted rise of Islamic influence, gained more visibility in the public sphere, particularly following the 1990s. This process engendered new markets and consumption patterns that both reflected and shaped new Islamic lifestyles and identities. Islamic identity, which used to be perceived as a sign of 'backwardness', failure to modernise, or being from a lower class in comparison to secular identity, started to assert its existence in urban spaces particularly through the appearance of the middle class, educated women wearing stylish items of Islamic fashion (Sandıkçı and Ger, 2007, 2010) and wealthy Islamic families enjoying gender-segregated holidays and leisure-time activities. Consumption was an ineluctable part of how the new middle-class Islamic identity defined itself vis-à-vis secular identity and displayed itself in the public sphere.

Islamic media—including TV, radio channels and newspapers—were among the new markets that flourished, along with Islamic leisure tourism and modest fashion. As a part of the global "new genre" of Islamic lifestyle media (Lewis, 2010), Islamic fashion and lifestyle magazines followed suit. These magazines guide their readers through the world of fashion, style and consumer products much like the Western-based popular glossy fashion magazines such as *Vogue*, as well as helping them convey a middle-class Islamic identity through consumption. They also circulate images and narratives of global Islamic consumerism.

The first of such magazines in Turkey, *Âlâ*, was published from 2011 to 2016. The magazine, which was called the "Vogue of the Veiled" by *The New York Times* (Bilefsky, 2012), was so popular that it was soon followed by a number of similar magazines that aimed to take a slice of the advertisement pie in the burgeoning Islamic fashion market. As of today, when Islamic fashion media shifts to the digital realm, *Aysha*, which began publishing in 2013, is the only in-print Islamic fashion and lifestyle magazine on the market in contemporary Turkey. Besides giving advice on fashion, beauty, health and fitness, *Aysha* also provides guidance on leisure consumption, including luxury leisure and Islamic tourism consumption, such as Hajj tourism. The magazine also includes several pages of religious and spiritual advice.

This study focuses on *Aysha* and explores how Islamic lifestyle media constructs the relation between religiosity, spirituality and leisure consumption through the advice it provides regarding what to consume in leisure time, religious tourism and how to experience religious rituals. The content of *Aysha* sheds light on the creative ways in which religion and consumerism are reconciled in Islamic lifestyle media, as well as the tensions and contradictions that reflect broader discussions regarding piety and materiality. How is the reconciliation between religion and consumerism formulated? How does the magazine relate leisure consumption to religious and spiritual experiences? What is the role of Islamic lifestyle media and journalism in the articulation of the Islamic identity through consumption?

Method

To answer these questions, the study relies on in-depth qualitative analysis of ten issues of *Aysha* magazine. I coded a total of 26 articles published in *Aysha*. Of those 26 articles, 12 provide advice on leisure consumption and religious tourism particularly during religious holidays, such as Ramadan, and 14 articles offer religious and spiritual advice. The timeframe for the selection of magazine issues is from July 2017 to May 2018. By covering one whole year, I aimed to eliminate biases of seasonal variation, such as Ramadan and Hajj periods. The issues of *Aysha* were obtained by contacting the magazine's office in İstanbul.

The surge of middle-class Islamic consumption patterns—particularly the consumption of Islamic fashion and the transformation of Islamic identities in interplay with rising consumerism—has been well documented and extensively discussed with regard to both Muslim majority (Sandıkçı and Ger, 2005, 2007, 2010; Gökarıksel and Secor, 2009, 2012, 2016; Tepe, 2011; Jones, 2010), and non-Muslim majority contexts (Tarlo, 2007; Lewis, 2015). Previous research on Islamic fashion and lifestyle magazines has focused on the perceived contradictions between established expectations of what religious Muslims represent and how Islamic fashion and lifestyle magazines represent them (Sehlikoğlu, 2016), how they reconcile Islamic understanding of female modesty and piety with fashion and materiality (Lewis, 2010; Jones, 2010), as well as the social change they both represent and constitute (Dinç, 2014).

The contribution of this study is twofold: first, by employing the perspective provided by scholarship on lifestyle journalism, the study attains a new understanding of the ways in which religion and consumerism are reconciled through media. Research on lifestyle journalism points out its increasing role in a context where consumption has become essential to constructing and expressing identities (Hanusch and Hanitzsch, 2013). This line of research sheds light on the significance of Islamic lifestyle media in circulating narratives of religious identity articulated through consumption. Second, the study focuses on the mediation of the Islamic consumption of leisure, an issue that remains underresearched despite its potential to provide insight about the changing relations between consumerism, religiosity and Islamic lifestyles in Turkey.

The study is organised as follows: I start by outlining the literature on lifestyle journalism in its relation to consumerism; then, I trace the historical context of the concomitant development of lifestyle journalism, consumerism and Islamic lifestyle media in Turkey. The paper then concludes with a discussion of the findings.

Lifestyle journalism: circulating meanings for consumer goods

The prominent defining aspects of lifestyle journalism include addressing the audience first and foremost as consumers, focusing on the private domain and guiding the audience in navigating everyday life (Hanusch 2012, p.2; Hanusch, Hanitzsch and Laurer, 2017, p.142). Elfriede Fürsich (2012, pp. 13–16) argues that lifestyle journalism is distinguished from other types of journalism through its functions of reviewing consumer goods; giving direct, individual level advice to the readers, as well as its close connection to commercial influences and rising consumerism. This study takes lifestyle journalism in line with these definitions that highlight its close relation with increasing consumerism.

One major stream in the literature on lifestyle journalism consists of studies that investigate its public and political relevance. On the one hand, it is argued that the trend of 'softening' of news corresponds directly to declining quality (Patterson, 2003; Plasser, 2005; Karlsson, 2016). In contrast to such arguments, research conducted on different types of lifestyle media, such as travel journalism (McGaurr, 2010) and food journalism (Duffy and Yang, 2012), suggests that lifestyle journalism not only has public relevance but also the potential of playing a political role (Hanusch, 2012, p. 8). Fürsich challenges the binary understanding of serious media catering to "informed citizenry" vs "popular media which frivolously focus on individual pleasure and consumption" (2012, p. 17). Instead, she suggests that lifestyle media is capable of contributing to the democratisation of the public sphere by enhancing social cohesion (2012, pp. 18–19).

Another stream in the literature discusses the surging role of lifestyle journalism within the social and cultural context of late capitalism, where consumerism takes over as a "type of social arrangement that results from recycling mundane, permanent and so to speak 'regime neutral' human wants, desires and longings into the principal propelling and operating force of society" (Bauman, 2007, p. 28). Kristensen and From (2012) investigate the expansion of lifestyle journalism with regard to this context, referring to Jansson's (2002) framework of culturalisation and mediatisation of consumption. As consumption becomes a way of expressing identity, even the consumption of functional commodities becomes culturalised (2002, p. 12). In the process of creating meanings, images and lifestyles for products (Fürsich, 2012, p. 13), the significance of lifestyle media's function to "circulate discursive knowledge" (Jansson, 2002, p. 14) increases. Along these lines, Hanusch and Hanitzsch (2013) emphasise lifestyle journalism's increasing role in helping shape and express identities through consumption. Indeed, this role does not solely unfold within national boundaries. As Jansson (2002) argues, the internationalisation of the media system leads to new transnational communities of belonging that are forged through the "sharing of lifestyles and certain cultural tastes" (p. 15).

There is substantial debate about whether Islam stands in an adversary relation to the diversification of lifestyles and identities promised by consumerism (Turner, 1994), or whether contemporary Islamic identities and subjectivities are also reconstructed and redefined by global consumerism (Ismail, 2004). The globally flourishing Islamic lifestyle media is a fertile field, which enables us to observe how lifestyle media circulates images and narratives that shape new Muslim subjectivities, formulating a "commercial version of Muslim lifestyle culture" (Lewis, 2010, p. 59) and guiding Muslim consumers in a global discourse of Islamic identity articulated through consumerism. As Lewis (2010) and Jones (2010) emphasise, Islamic lifestyle magazines face unique challenges in their roles as "cultural intermediaries" (Fürsich, 2012, p. 13) as they try to reconcile the notion of Islamic identity with a discourse of consumerism that emphasises continuously shifting "individual choices" and the desire to remake the self.

Such challenges present themselves in particular ways in the case of Turkey's Islamic lifestyle magazines. These challenges reflect the social and historical context of Turkey's last three decades, within which Islamic identity and lifestyle have gained more visibility and popularity in the public sphere, along with the simultaneous rise of consumerism and major transformations in media landscape.

Consumption, identity politics and changing journalism in Turkey

Lifestyle journalism in Turkey has flourished in the process of rising consumerism and the retreat of political discussion from the public sphere in the aftermath of the *coup d'état* in September 1980. After the *coup*, Turkey witnessed a suppression of the leftist movement, a strict oppression of freedom of expression, and a concomitant depoliticisation of the public (Bek, 2004, p. 374), alongside a larger process of economic liberalisation and the promotion of consumerism. The 1980s and 1990s were also decades of major transformations in Turkey's media landscape. Media ownership was increasingly concentrated in the hands of big business with investments in a range of other sectors such as banking and construction. Meanwhile, there was a substantial expansion in terms of media outlets, especially after the private sector entered the TV and radio broadcasting market in the 1990s, breaking the state's monopoly on media (Kaya and Çakmur, 2010).

Within this context, media content was increasingly dominated by commercial concerns, which arguably led to the hegemony of popular entertainment shows, an ever-increasing focus on popular culture and journalism that highlights 'personal stories', i.e. the private domain (Ergül, 2000; Bek, 2004; Kaya and Çakmur 2010, p. 528; Öncü, 2012). Bek's research demonstrates that in the early 2000s, Turkey's private TV news showed a strong tendency to personalise politics, as well as focus either on the tragedies of the very poor or the glamorous lives of the very rich, without touching upon any discussions on social inequality (Bek, 2004, p. 381). Yet, it has also been argued that private TV channels in Turkey provided an accessible and popular alternative to the official, homogenising language of state and institutional politics (Öncü, 2000). On the other hand, from the 1980s onwards, newspapers and magazines increasingly catered to the young, urban, professional, well-to-do readers, addressing them as consumers, especially through columnists who extensively wrote about their own consumption of luxury and entertainment (Bali, 2002, pp. 233–244). In the context of the privatisation and commercialisation of TV and radio broadcasting, Islam also became an issue of popular public discussion, unlike the standardised official representations that were dominant in broadcasts in the 1990s from state television channel TRT. Öncü (1995) argues that commercial television presented Islam in simplified, interpretive packages ready to be consumed by the audience.

The 1990s also witnessed a flourishing of Islamic media, including TV and radio channels, newspapers and magazines that catered to the Islamic population. These Islamic media outlets emerged amidst the rising political, social and cultural influence of Islam in Turkey, a process that resulted in the Justice and Development Party (JDP) coming to power in 2002. This influence was supported by the accumulation of wealth among small- and medium-scale capitalists of conservative Anatolian cities in the context of economic liberalisation and integration into networks of global business (Buğra, 2002; Gülalp, 2003; Demir, Acar and Toprak, 2004).

On this point, it is essential to emphasise the relationship between consumption, consumer markets and identity politics in Turkey with regard to the much-discussed social and cultural polarisation between Islamic and secular identities. During the course of the 1990s, the Islamic bourgeoisie gained visibility in the public sphere, particularly through new lifestyles and patterns of consumption that gave rise to new sectors ranging from Islamic fashion to gender-segregated holidays. The "Islamic consumptionscapes" (Sandıkçı and Ger, 2002) were established on a discourse that strongly emphasised the distinction between Islamic and secular consumption patterns. Moreover, these new patterns were presented as ways to assert an Islamic identity. In response, urban shopping malls and national brands that defined themselves as secular followed suit and manifested their loyalty to secularism through advertisements in national media, tapping into politically relevant symbols such as pictures of Mustafa Kemal Atatürk, the founder of the Turkish Republic. As Navaro-Yashin aptly states, the "habits of consumption became central markers of internal cultural difference in Turkey" (2002, p. 85). In other words, consumption became a crucial element of identity politics, not just marking but also contributing to the construction of a politics of Islamic identity (Sayan-Cengiz, 2016, pp. 25–54). In particular, consumption of Islamic veiling fashion by urban, educated and increasingly wealthier women became the prominent markers of Islamic identity articulated through consumerism.

Findings

Islamic fashion and lifestyle magazines catering particularly to wealthy women consuming Islamic veiling fashion were products of this context. In line with the transformation of journalism in Turkey in the post 1980 era, the emerging Islamic lifestyle media also adopted journalistic practices that distinguish lifestyle journalism, such as addressing an audience assumed to be urban, middle-class consumers and giving direct, individual-level advice to this audience and keeping close contact with commercial influences (Fürsich, 2012).

Aysha magazine is an example of this genre. *Aysha* is a monthly women's magazine that declares its focus as 'life and style' on its cover. The magazine is owned by Pınar Küçükşabanoğlu, a businesswoman who also manages a company that organises events, ranging from concerts to political party gatherings; the latter includes those of the incumbent JDP, with which the magazine has close ties (Meşe, 2015). Küçükşabanoğlu declares the aims of the magazine as responding to the needs of conservative women who need guidance in their consumption choices:

> This magazine is a mission for me. I was raised in a conservative environment and constantly heard women looking for advice on what to wear, how to shop. There was a gap for both younger and elder conservative women. I published *Aysha* as a real women's magazine. It includes news on culture and art as well.
>
> *(Çetinkaya, 2014)*

In other words, the owner highlights that the magazine aims to give direct consumption advice to the target audience and help them navigate the world of consumption, without breaking the codes of an Islamic conservative environment. The practice of journalism in the magazine reflects this objective, as it includes sections on fashion, as well as news reports on the latest advances on women's health, nutrition, beauty and fitness. However, these sections are almost exclusively designed to include commercial recommendations about what to consume. In that sense, the line between editorial and advertorial content is very thin and the boundaries between informing the audience and promoting certain goods and services, including certain specific brands, are blurred.

The covers and fashion shoots of *Aysha* more often than not include models with headscarves. Even though its content is very similar to other fashion and lifestyle magazines addressing women, *Aysha* distinguishes itself from secular magazines through its sections offering advice on religion and spirituality and through its support of traditional gender roles that reflect the conservative life-style that it endorses (Meşe, 2015, p. 153).

Each issue of *Aysha* contains one short editorial piece and several pages on fashion and style that introduce modest clothes and footwear by various brands, ranging from relatively affordable to highly luxurious. Besides several pages on fashion, style, health, motherhood, beauty, nutrition, psychology, the magazine also includes interviews with celebrities, most of whom identify themselves as religious Muslims. In each issue, one can find two to five pages of religious and spiritual advice, and occasional pages including advice on how to spend leisure time, especially holidays. I focus on the sections of religious and spiritual advice and the pages on the consumption of leisure.

Pious consumerism

Previous research investigating the ways in which neoliberal capitalism and con-sumerism interact with Islamic culture has uncovered various ways in which they intermingle and shape each other (Adaş, 2006; Atia, 2012; Rudnyckyj, 2009). *Aysha* is a case in point: the magazine introduces to its readers luxurious restaurants, hotels and spas within a narrative that highlights the spiritual benefits of consumption in terms of augmenting the religious experience. This narrative is particularly accentuated in the issues published during or before Ramadan, the holy month of fasting, and before Hajj, the annual pilgrimage to Mecca in Saudi Arabia.

During Ramadan, several pages of *Aysha* introduce and suggest *iftar* (the meal for breaking fast) services offered by expensive restaurants and hotels in Istanbul, suggesting that its readers should experience the satisfaction that will be derived from celebrating spiritual moments in "elegant" places. In an article entitled 'You can make this Ramadan unforgettable', the magazine declares: "The iftar table undoubtedly provides the most special moments that make Ramadan more meaningful. Those moments with family and friends can become even more meaningful and elegant in these special venues that we picked for you" (*Aysha*, 2018, p. 48).[1] What follows is an introduction of 15 different venues that offer *iftar* meals, including five-star hotels with views of the Bosphorus, as well as luxury restaurants that do not serve alcohol. It is emphasised that the *iftar* ser-vices include open buffets prepared by award-winning chefs and served at "pres-tigious" venues. Each introduction is accompanied by enticing photos of abundant food, glamorous table decorations and a view of the Bosphorus strait in the background.

In this example, it is remarkable how conspicuous consumption is not only justified but even promoted in spiritual and religious terms, as a way to add "more meaning" to a religious practice. This discourse is reminiscent of Mona Atia's concept of "pious neoliberalism" (2012, p. 808), by which she refers to promoting entrepreneurship and business skills as components of Islam and piety—except that, in this case, *Aysha* is promoting conspicuous consumption as a part of the experience of Ramadan, marking "pious consumerism".

The paragraphs introducing the venues do not include any critical reviews of these restaurants but instead read like press releases by PR companies, which marks very thin, if not non-existent, lines between *Aysha*'s advertorial and editorial content. It is possible to observe similarly fine lines in the content related to the Hajj pilgrimage and the related advertorial/editorial pages introducing hotels and tours to Mecca to observe Hajj or Umrah (religious visit to Mecca that can be made at any time of the year, unlike Hajj, for which there is a fixed time period).

Luxurious Hajj and Umrah services are introduced in two different issues of *Aysha*. The January 2018 issue includes two pages promoting an international hotel chain and its five-star hotels in Mecca and Medinah, Saudi Arabia, both holy cities for Muslims. It is underlined that the hotels provide comfort, elegance and modern decoration to those who visit these two cities for religious reasons. It is emphasised that the hotel in Mecca offers an ideal location as it is very close to the Holy Kaaba (a building at the centre of Islam's most important mosque, Al-Masjid Al-Ḥarām), as well as to a shopping mall hosting more than 450 stores. These two venues—Holy Kaaba and the shopping mall—are enlisted as "must-sees" in the same breath, along with Jabal al-Nur, where Prophet Muhammed is believed to have received his first divine revelation. Along similar lines, the religious advice section of the July/August 2017 issue is allocated to the promotion of a Turkish tourism company that is known for its highly-priced Hajj and Umrah tours. Using the expression "Hajj with 7-star comfort", the text underlines that the company offers its customers a luxurious tent with air conditioning and open buffet meals even during the prayers on Mount Arafat, where millions of Muslims climb and pray together, observing the most important rite during the Hajj period with seamless, white, uniform garments that are aimed to mark equality among Muslims.

In their study focusing on "alternative tourism" and gender-segregated Islamic holiday venues, Sehlikoğlu and Karakaş find that the religious customers of such venues formulate their leisure consumption practices "as a means of bridging spirituality and holiday in order to create memorable experiences" (2014, p. 9). They also underline that alternative tourism taps into the emergence of new Islamic subjectivities "evolving in search of global aspirations triggered by desires and new lifestyles", recognising and responding to these demands and desires (Sehlikoğlu and Karakaş, 2014, p. 3). *Aysha*'s content combines the religious practices of fasting during Ramadan and pilgrimage to Mecca—two of the five pillars of Islam—with the consumption of luxury, which marks a new level of consumerism inherent to the evolution of new Islamic subjectivities. This content also uncovers the ways in which Islamic lifestyle journalism contributes to shaping, justifying and expressing the interpenetration of religious practices and consumerism by providing a narrative that opens up the possibility to utter the desires for luxury, comfort and prestige in the same breath with Hajj and Ramadan, which are believed to aim for the control of *nafs* (material and bodily desires), humility and the feeling of equality among Muslims.

Tension between promoting consumerism and advising against it

Interestingly enough, the narrative that celebrates consumption as a way of intensifying religious experience is challenged by more orthodox Islamic views that also appear in *Aysha* magazine. This tension, which complicates the articulation of religiosity and Islamic identity through consumerism, surfaces occasionally in the pages of religious and spiritual advice.

The religious advice pages are occasionally written by Nursen Turgut, a theologian, and Hikmet Anıl Öztekin, an Islamic-oriented writer, YouTuber and motivational speaker. These pages seem to almost stand separately from the rest of the magazine in both content and design, with longer texts and very few, if any, visual material. For example, in the September 2017 issue, a month after the magazine promoted the luxury Hajj tour with the open buffet meals on Mount Arafat, Nursen Turgut wrote the following:

> Hajj is a comprehensive form of religious practice and includes various symbols and levels. It is a long-term practice, it does not consist of a journey or a set of performances. Hajj is a journey to one's own soul; it unsettles your outlook on life, your relation to the space that surrounds you, and your lifestyle.... The reason of your visit to Arafat is to change the purpose of your life and become one of Allah's beloved servants.... Arafa means 'to know'. Your Hajj meets its purpose only if you come to know yourself on Mount Arafat.
>
> *(Turgut, 2017, p. 28)*

In another issue of *Aysha*, the same writer argues that "our *nafs* and body act collectively and weigh us down" (Turgut, 2018, p. 42) and suggests that we should escape the ties that bind us to the profane. Along similar lines, Hikmet Anıl Öztekin (in Öke, 2017) refers to Mevlana (Jalaluddin Rumi) to explain the benefits of controlling the *nafs* and eating, sleeping and talking less. Another author who contributed to the 'Spirituality' section in the July/August 2017 issue further accentuates the dichotomous understanding of material desires versus spirituality:

> Consumer society tries to compensate for its unhappiness by spending money. But the graceless extravagance is no cure to our personal

melancholies.… If humans had consisted solely of materiality, then you would reach your 'Nirvana' as you rejoiced in material joys. But it does not work that way, does it?… The truth of humankind lies in the spirit.

(Öke, 2017, p. 38)

These suggestions to distance oneself from material and bodily desires stand in sharp contrast to the entire content of the magazine, which is crammed with pages of fashion photos featuring professional models in expensive clothes, posing in glamorous urban settings; beauty and makeup tips; and information about anti-aging products. More importantly, the imagination of an essential and irreconcilable conflict between material desires and piety in these texts is in fundamental opposition to the predominant narrative of the magazine, which constructs a rather harmonious relation between the two. This tension complicates the narrative of reconciliation between consumerism and Islamic subjectivities, demonstrating points of contradiction. These contradictions have their roots in broader public discussions within Islamic circles in terms of coping with the transformations of lifestyles that has surfaced as a result of the process of accumulation of wealth among Islamic bourgeoisie, who constitute the readers/consumers primarily targeted by *Aysha* magazine.

Conclusion

Lifestyle journalism, as it is practised in Turkey's Islamic lifestyle media, acts as a "cultural intermediary" (Fürsich, 2012, p. 13) in articulating Islamic identity within a discourse of consumerism. In Turkey, Islamic identity has found a way of articulating and asserting itself vis-à-vis secular identity, through Islamic consumption patterns. Today, the Islamic consumption patterns have diversified to address the needs and desires of people from different socioeconomic backgrounds. It is possible to argue that modern, urban, upper-class habits of consumption, such as consumption of luxury leisure during religious rituals such as Hajj pilgrimage, underline status distinction from lower-class Islamic population, rather than a distinction from secular lifestyles. Islamic lifestyle media has taken shape within this context of burgeoning bourgeoisie, and reflects the transformation of consumption patterns. However, what is more important is the way it constructs new narratives to frame those new consumption patterns as acceptable and desirable parts of Islamic lifestyle.

Aysha magazine addresses its readers as consumers who need guidance in their consumption practices and gives them direct individual advice, not only about how and what to consume, but also about how to reconcile a consumerist lifestyle with a religious lifestyle. The findings of this research demonstrate that the magazine gives new meanings to Islamic practices such as Hajj and Ramadan *iftar*s as moments of celebrating life through the consumption of luxury and the experience of corporeal comfort and pleasure. These Islamic precepts are reformulated as opportunities for spiritual cleansing, which is in line with the discursive ground of self-help literature that marks "sacralization of the self and psychologization of religion" (Kenney, 2015, p. 675).

On the other hand, *Aysha* magazine also pays lip service to more orthodox interpretations of Islam by publishing religious advice sections that particularly condemn consumerism. The glaring contradiction between promoting consumption of luxury to the point of abandoning lines between editorial and advertorial content, and publishing strongly worded advice against consumerism, stands as the elephant in the room. What this contradiction points out is the most important challenge facing Islamic lifestyle media: how to stay connected to the market that seeks to address to wealthy Islamic consumers, distinguishing them from lower-class religious Muslims, while avoiding making statements that critically engage with the interpretations of Islam that prioritise humility, control of the *nafs* vis-à-vis corporeal and mundane pleasures and equality among Muslims.

Nevertheless, in providing narratives that justify luxury consumption in relation to and during religious rituals, even suggesting luxury consumption as a way to strengthen the religious experience, Islamic lifestyle media give new meanings to the practice of religiosity. They also shows us the high potential of lifestyle media and journalism in terms of constructing, normalising and circulating narratives that articulate identities, including religious identities, through material desires and consumption. In a world defined by consumerism, if material desires are the "principal operating force of society", as Bauman (2007, p. 28) would put it, then lifestyle journalism provides a medium through which this force operates, by constructing narratives to express consumerist subjectivities, material desires and by fostering new ones.

Note

1 *Aysha* magazine is published in Turkish. All quotations from the magazine have been translated by the author.

References

Adaş, E. B. (2006) 'The making of entrepreneurial Islam and the Islamic spirit of capitalism', *Journal for Cultural Research*, 10(2), pp. 113–137.

Atia, M. (2012) '"A way to paradise": pious neoliberalism, Islam, and faith based development', *Annals of the Association of American Geographers*, 102(4), pp. 808–827.

Aysha (2018) 'Bu Ramazan ayını unutulmaz kılabilirsiniz' (You can make this Ramadan unforgettable), May 2018, p. 48.

Bali, R. (2002) *Tarz-i hayattan lifestyle'a: yeni seçkinler, yeni mekanlar, yeni yaşamlar (From tarz-I hayat to lifestyle: new elites, new spaces, new lives)*. İstanbul: İletişim.

Bauman, Z. (2007) *Consuming life*. Cambridge: Polity Press.

Bek, M. G. (2004) 'Research note: tabloidization of news media: an analysis of television news in Turkey', *European Journal of Communication*, 19(3), pp. 371–380.

Bilefsky, D. (2012) 'A fashion magazine unshy about baring a bit of piety', *The New York Times*, 29 March. Available at: https://www.nytimes.com/2012/03/29/world/europe/a-turkish-fashion-magazine-ala-is-unshy-about-showing-some-piety.html (Accessed: 14 December 2018).

Buğra, A. (2002) 'Labour, capital and religion: harmony and conflict among the constituency of political Islam in Turkey', *Middle Eastern Studies*, 38(2), pp. 187–204.

Çetinkaya, B. (2014) 'Pınar Küçükşabanoğlu: Bütün çabamız kadınlar için' (Our effort is for women), *Türkiye Gazetesi*, 27 July. Available at: http://www.turkiyegazetesi.com.tr/yazarlar/burcu-cetinkaya/581596.aspx (Accessed: 14 December 2018).

Demir, Ö., Acar, M. and Toprak, M. (2004) 'Anatolian tigers or Islamic capital: prospects and challenges', *Middle Eastern Studies*, 40(6),pp.166–188.

Dinç, C. (2014) 'Veiling and (fashion-) magazines – 'Alâ Dergisi' magazine as a case for a new consumer image of a new devout middle class in Turkey', *Uluslararası Sosyal Araştırmalar Dergisi*, 34(7), pp. 650–665.

Duffy, A. and Yang, Y. A. (2012) 'Bread and circuses: food meets politics in the Singapore media', *Journalism Practice*, 6(1), pp. 59–74.

Ergül, H. (2000) *Televizyonda haberin magazinleşmesi (The tabloidization of news on TV)*. Istanbul: İletişim.

Fürsich, E. (2012) 'Lifestyle journalism as popular journalism: strategies for evaluating its public role', *Journalism Practice*, 6(1), pp. 12–25.

Gökarıksel, B. and Secor, A. (2009) 'New transnational geographies of Islamism, consumerism and subjectivity: the veiling fashion industry in Turkey', *Area*, 41(1), pp. 6–18.

Gökarıksel, B. and Secor, A (2012) 'Even I was tempted: the moral ambivalence and ethical practice of veiling fashion in Turkey', *Annals of the Association of American Geographers*, 102(4), pp. 847–862.

Gökarıksel, B. and Secor, A. (2016) 'What makes a commodity Islamic? The case of veiling-fashion in Turkey', in Jafari, A. and Sandıkçı, Ö. (eds) *Islam, marketing and consumption: critical perspectives on the intersections*. New York: Routledge, pp. 123–139.

Gülalp, H. (2003) *Kimlikler siyaseti: Türkiye'de siyasal İslamın temelleri (Politics of identity: the foundations of political Islam in Turkey)*. Istanbul: Metis.

Hanusch, F. (2012) 'Broadening the focus: the case for lifestyle journalism as a field of scholarly inquiry', *Journalism Practice*, 6(1), pp. 2–11.

Hanusch, F. and Hanitzsch, T. (2013), 'Mediating orientation and self-expression in the world of consumption: Australian and German lifestyle journalists' professional views', *Media, Culture & Society*, 35(8), pp. 943–959.

Hanusch, F., Hanitzsch, T. and Lauerer, C. (2017) '"How much love are you going to give this brand?" Lifestyle journalists on commercial influences in their work', *Journalism*, 18(2), pp. 141–158.

Ismail, S. (2004) 'Islam, Islamism and identity politics', *Government and Opposition*, 39(4), pp. 614–631.

Jansson, A. (2002) 'The mediatization of consumption: towards an analytical framework of image culture', *Journal of Consumer Culture*, 2(1), pp. 5–31.

Jones, C. (2010) 'Materialising piety: gendered anxieties about faithful consumption in contemporary urban Indonesia', *American Ethnologist*, 37(4), pp. 617–637.

Karlsson, M. B. (2016) 'Goodbye politics, hello lifestyle: changing news topics in tabloid, quality and local newspaper websites in the UK and Sweden from 2002 to 2012', *Observatoria Journal*, 10(4), pp. 150–165.

Kaya, R. and Çakmur, B. (2010) 'Politics and mass media in Turkey', *Turkish Studies*, 11(4), pp. 521–537.

Kenney, J. T. (2015) 'Selling success, nurturing the self: self-help literature, capitalist values, and the sacralization of subjective life in Egypt', *International Journal of Middle Eastern Studies*, 47(4), pp. 663–680.

Kristensen, N. N. and From, U. (2012), 'Lifestyle journalism: blurring boundaries', *Journalism Practice*, 6(1), pp. 26–41.

Lewis, R. (2010) 'Marketing Muslim lifestyle: a new media genre', *Journal of Middle East Women's Studies*, 6(3), pp. 58–90.

Lewis, R. (2015) *Muslim fashion: contemporary style cultures*. Durham and London: Duke University Press.

McGaurr, L. (2010) 'Travel journalism and environmental conflict: a cosmopolitan perspective', *Journalism Studies*, 11(1), pp. 50–67.

Meşe, İ. (2015) 'İslami bir moda dergisi örneğinde moda ve tesettür: ne türden bir birliktelik? (Fashion and tesettür in the case of an Islamic fashion magazine: what kind of an association?)', *Fe Dergi*, 7(1), pp. 146–158.

Navaro-Yashin, Y. (2002) *Faces of the state: secularism and public life in Turkey*. Princeton: Princeton University Press.

Öke, M. K. (2017) 'Arınmak mutluluk mu?', *Aysha*, July–August 2017, p. 38.

Öncü, A. (1995) 'Packaging Islam: cultural politics on the landscape of Turkish commercial television', *Public Culture*, 8, pp. 51–71.

Öncü, A. (2000) 'The banal and the subversive: politics of language on Turkish television', *European Journal of Cultural Studies*, 3(2), pp. 296–318.

Öncü, A. (2012) 'Television and media', in Heper, M. and Sayarı, S. (eds) *The Routledge handbook of modern Turkey*. London: Routledge, pp. 125–137.

Patterson, T. E. (2003) 'The search for a standard: market and media', *Political Communication*, 20(2), pp. 139–144.

Plasser, F. (2005) 'From hard to soft news standards? How political journalists in different media systems evaluate the shifting quality of news', *Press/Politics*, 10(2), pp. 47–68.

Rudnyckyj, D. (2009) 'Spiritual economies: Islam and neoliberalism in contemporary Indonesia', *Cultural Anthropology*, 24(1), pp. 104–141.

Sandıkçı, Ö. and Ger, G. (2002) 'In-between modernities and postmodernities: theorising Turkish consumptionscape', *Advances in Consumer Research*, 29(1), pp. 465–470.

Sandıkçı, Ö. and Ger, G. (2005) 'Aesthetics, ethics and politics of the Turkish headscarf', in Kuechler, S. and Miller, D. (eds) *Clothing as material culture*. Oxford: Berg, pp. 61–82.

Sandıkçı, Ö. and Ger, G. (2007) 'Constructing and representing the Islamic consumer in Turkey', *Fashion Theory*, 11(2, 3), pp. 189–210.

Sandıkçı, Ö. and Ger, G. (2010) 'Veiling in style: how does a stigmatized practice become fashionable?', *Journal of Consumer Research*, 37(1), pp. 15–36.

Sayan-Cengiz, F. (2016) *Beyond headscarf culture in Turkey's retail sector*. New York: Palgrave Macmillan.

Sehlikoğlu, S. (2016) 'The daring mahrem: changing dynamics of public sexuality in Turkey', in Özyeğin, G. (ed.) *Gender and sexuality in Muslim cultures*. New York: Routledge, pp. 235–253.

Sehlikoğlu, S. and Karakaş, F. (2014) 'We can have the cake and eat it too: leisure and spirituality at "veiled" hotels in Turkey', *Leisure Studies*, 35(2), pp. 157–169.

Tarlo, E. (2007) 'Islamic cosmopolitanism: the sartorial biographies of three Muslim women in London', *Fashion Theory*, 11(2,3), pp. 143–172.

Tepe, S. (2011) 'Serving God through the market: the emergence of Muslim consumptionscapes and Islamic resistance', in Sandıkçı, Ö. and Rice G. (eds) *Handbook of Islamic marketing*. Cheltenham: Edward Elgar, pp. 363–392.

Turgut, N. (2017) 'Kendi ruhuna yolculuk: Hac ibadeti', *Aysha*, September 2017, p. 28.

Turgut, N. (2018) 'Bu Miraç, insanlığımızı yeniden hatırlayalım', *Aysha*, April 2018, p. 42.

Turner, B. (1994) *Orientalism, Postmodernism and Globalism*. New York: Routledge.

5

TRAVEL JOURNALISTS AS CULTURAL MEDIATORS

A qualitative discourse analysis on the 'othering' of Anthony Bourdain's *Parts Unknown*

Aaron McKinnon

Despite its ever-changing style and format, travel journalism continues to play a significant role in defining foreign cultures to domestic audiences (Hanusch, 2010, p. 75; Buzinde *et al.*, 2014, p. 222). Episodes from a travel show can serve as both entertaining and informational articles that shape the public's view on places across the globe (Hanusch, 2010, pp. 71–73). Television coverage of foreign perspectives can show audiences a mirror to "the generalized elsewhere" from which they can better reflect upon their own locality (Meyrowitz, 1989, p. 327). The concept of "the generalized elsewhere" refers to audience conceptualisations of non-local places and cultures; information from media sources can contextualise the world outside and consequentially further delineate one's own familiar locale (Meyrowitz, 1989, p. 331). This form of ideological self-reflection allows people to better understand what Hall calls their own "covert culture", culturally oriented behavioural routines and beliefs that individuals often perceive as universal, and thus better interpret communication from people of dissimilar cultures (1976, p. 153). Media and articles by travel journalists serve as an accessible and characteristically engaging platform for readers and viewers to gain intercultural insights. What remains of interest for scholars is the analysis of varied sources of the travel beat to better understand developments to these dynamic cultural artefacts.

In efforts to create comprehensive methods of research for the travel beat, Folker Hanusch has standardised vocational dimensions, mapped international work cultures and co-published a textbook on the travel genre (2010; 2011; 2014). In his article titled 'Dimensions of travel journalism', the author identifies four interrelated fields of interest through which we can study travel journalism (Hanusch, 2010); they are the cultural mediation, market orientation, motivational aspects and ethical standards of travel journalism. In this chapter, I couple Hanusch's 'dimensions' with cultural journalism literature to focus this study on the intercultural aspects of existing travel literature. The ever-changing range and quantity of shows increases the complexity of the genre's tropes and generalisations, thus creating new demands in the study of the nuances of travel journalism. In response to this challenge, I conduct a textual analysis on intercultural communication within travel journalism media to better understand the role of travel journalists as cross-cultural mediators. Specifically, this study focuses on the constructions of cultural meaning-making in cable television travel shows, by analysing a show host's approach to representations of multiculturalism in discourse with locals, and how he or she drafts otherness in relation to local populations. To best identify developments to the intercultural meaning-making by travel journalists, I have chosen to examine the anti-hero of this beat: the late Anthony Bourdain, host of CNN's *Parts Unknown*.

Bourdain's journalistic perspective

Journalism scholars who have analysed the work of Bourdain do so within the framework of functional journalism (Greene, 2017; Buzinde *et al.*, 2014). Bourdain was not trained as a journalist, but his role as a travel show host became increasingly journalistic as his focus transitioned from foreign food onto the stories of locals with whom he dines. This role became explicit with his move to CNN in 2013, where he began his most recent series titled *Parts Unknown*. The title's double entendre nods to Bourdain's interests in both travel and food. With three cable television series and numerous publications about travel, Bourdain's level of success and influence in travel journalism remains unrivalled across mainstream media. The presenter used his background as a successful chef, writer and traveller to cover gastronomic and cultural topics around the world since his first episode of *No Reservations* in 2002.

On 8 June 2018, Anthony Bourdain took his life while abroad for an episode of *Parts Unknown*. Bourdain's passing received remembrance in the hours and days following from all major American news media outlets and fans from around the world. His legacy lives on in the many books, media and televised interactions he had with people over his lifetime.

The 'othering' of travel journalism

In the field of journalism, reporters who cover travel assume the role of interpreter-to-societies and presenter-of-otherness (Santos, 2004, p. 394; Santos, 2006, p. 639). Hanusch hails travel journalists' cultural-interpreter role as "cultural mediation" (2010, p. 78). This term represents a work-specific responsibility of journalists who bring back news of distant cultures that affords them the position to interpret ideas of the 'other'. Journalists seeking to sell an image of something new have primarily chosen to focus on the strange and different. This approach, while potentially attractive, can misguide the way audiences interpret notions of social power among represented cultures (Kassaye *et al.*,

2016, p. 776; Gerbner *et al.*, 2002, p. 44). Reporters who choose to distance their own identity from the host culture, overtly or covertly, engage in a negative form of 'othering' (Santos, 2006, pp. 639–644). For the past century, traditional media in the U.S. have produced and sold an idea of otherness when representing foreign cultures that covertly reflects their colonialist roots (Rodríguez, 1998, p. 287). Of course, variations between media systems exist (Kristensen and From, 2015, p. 773), but several studies have identified a dominant bias in Western travel journalism towards the marginalisation of, and emphasis on differences against, foreign cultures (Fürsich, 2002, pp. 223–224; Kassaye *et al.*, 2016, p. 776). This bias translates into reporting that endorses Western ideals and economic dominance with disregard for the welfare of foreign subjects (Schiller, 1976, pp. 9–16).

This 'othering' process can negatively impact the perceived and actual social cohesion of audience members to cultures around them (Kassaye *et al.*, 2016, pp. 775–782). Hanusch explains that travel journalists tend to create content focused on selling an entertaining experience "because their relationship with the travel industry can depend on audience conversion into travellers" (Hanusch, 2010, p.73). Furthermore, journalists who promote travel to dissimilar cultures risk furthering the advancement of Western ideals driven by the subsequent increase in tourists to foreign lands (Schiller, 1976, p. 7). However, hosts aren't necessarily unaware of their representation's ramifications, yet this sense of responsibility remains unstudied in most relevant literature (Hanusch, 2010, p. 76). For example, Rick Steves, bestselling travel writer and show host of the American non-profit television channel PBS, has challenged the idea of an amoral reporter with his own book and lecture series on how to *Travel as a political act* (2009).

The commodification of audience interest in travel by reporters has also begun to change for financial reasons. Newsrooms have adapted to rises in costs of foreign correspondence with the implementation of innovative and affordable forms of telecommunication (Hamilton and Jenner, 2004), as well as relocated portions of international news coverage to the travel section (Hanusch, 2014, p. 63). Regarding cable television, U.S. networks have begun to refocus their content on nonfictional stories that target audiences interested in documentary-style content and those who cannot afford to travel (Fürsich, 2002, p. 205). These recent changes to the scope of travel journalism articles have led this subgenre of lifestyle journalism to assume more traditional journalistic functions (Hanusch, 2014, p. 63).

Theoretical framework for identifying intercultural meaning-making

In coordination with Bourdain's ethnographic and culturally focused episodes, this study applies the theoretical framework of Cultural Studies to the object of research. It adopts a definition of 'culture' framed by ethnography because of this field's similar topoi to travel journalism (Grgurinović, 2012, pp. 52–54). In this vein, the authors of *Intercultural communication in contexts*, Judith Martin and Thomas

Nakayama, cautiously define the term 'culture' as "patterns of perception that influence communication" (2012, p. 88). Martin and Nakayama derive their concept of culture from sociologist Geert Hofstede, who finds that culture produces "a collective programming of the mind that distinguishes the members of one group or category of people from others" (2001, p. 9). This concept of culture defines groups in relation to their learned perceptions rather than demographics, borders or behaviours alone. While the delineation of cultural dimensions can polarise disparate peoples, scholars such as Edward T. Hall (1976) argue that these dimensions point to unique ideologies that, when aggregated, can better solve complex problems through meaningful intercultural collaboration.

Hall, an anthropologist and auto ethnographer, states that in order to understand a different culture to one's own, individuals must commit to a self-reflective process that can only "be lived rather than read or reasoned" (1976, p. 58). Just as we learn about our own culture by living in it, we can observe another's by experiencing theirs. Hall calls for disparate peoples to undergo cultural introspection by "alienating (oneself) from self and heritage" in order to avoid ethnocentric interpretations in communication exchanges (1976, p. 32). Hall's research on meaningful intercultural communication serves as a reference for my analysis on the locality of Bourdain's dialogue with his show's subjects.

The process of intercultural communication involves people from different cultures who contextualise and interpret verbal and nonverbal communication to create shared meanings from disparate ideological frameworks (Bennett, 1998; Lustig and Koester, 2006). This chapter highlights conflicting cultural dimensions between Bourdain and his show's subjects to contextualise the shared meaning-making process that occurs in intercultural discourse.

Analysing cultural mediation in travel shows

Research questions

This chapter asks the following interrelated questions about Bourdain's show *Parts Unknown*:

RQ1: What journalistic practices does Bourdain employ in order to investigate cultural tropics of an episode?
RQ2: How does Bourdain represent the ordinary?
RQ3: How does Bourdain construct representations of the other?

Method

The research uses textual analysis of *Parts Unknown* to understand how the television persona of Anthony Bourdain orients himself as a social and cultural decoder. Textual analysis allows researchers to "uncover the underlying ideological and cultural assumptions of the text" by employing literature of a specific genre to select and analyse text as "evidence for the overall argument" (Fürsich, 2009, p. 240). Of course, some degree of my personal inferences manifests in the analysis (Richardson, 1990, p. 12). Therefore, I endorse a cautious level of certainty in my inferences as suggested by Bonnie J. Dow, who accepts that textual analysis can produce "the possibility of meaning rather than its certainty" (1996, p. 224). I also engage in conversation analysis, an extension of textual analysis that deals specifically with the structure of communication exchange. In reference to this chapter's three questions, conversation analysis guides my interpretations of Bourdain's interaction with locals (Q1), representations of the ordinary (Q2) and constructions of the other (Q3).

Two examples from Bourdain's show *Parts Unknown* were selected for examination: 'Myanmar' and 'Los Angeles'. The 'Myanmar' episode was chosen to include an Asian population and location, an area that has been heavily exoticised by Western media through an association of its unique cuisine (August, 2016, pp. 193–194). This was the first episode of the series and even won an Emmy for Outstanding Cinematography. It also set the tone for the series to follow. Additionally, the 'Los Angeles' episode of season seven was chosen in order to vary the regions and population characteristics among my samples. The episode focuses predominantly on the Hispanic and Latino populations living in L.A. The two episodes aired four years apart and span from the first to the ninth season. A domestic and foreign location were chosen to account for the influence of perceived distance in prospective traveller familiarity and interest (Nicolau and Mas, 2006, p. 992), and significance of cultural proximity in audience perceptions and preferences of diverse media sources (Ksiazek and Webster, 2008, p. 584).

While my approach has the potential to reveal unrepresented dimensions about the travel genre, several limitations remain. For example, the small sample size of two episodes leaves room for additional analysis and makes identifying overarching themes difficult to determine. The aim is rather to offer a foundational understanding of *Parts Unknown*'s approach to intercultural discourse in travel journalism. Finally, it is important to say this analysis was completed two months prior to Bourdain's passing, and therefore I, as a researcher, was not emotionally influenced by his death.

Discussion

'Myanmar': away from exoticism

In *Parts Unknown* episode one of season one, host Anthony Bourdain explains in voiceover that "after 50 years of nightmare, something unexpected is happening here, and it's pretty incredible" (2013). Flashback scenes of wartime news coverage spliced frantically among shots of the host, who sits peacefully on a night train, juxtapose the past and the present representations by journalists of Myanmar. Bourdain narrates a four-minute segment, 10 per cent of the show's length, on the century-long era of military and political turmoil to which Myanmar citizens have only recently seen an end. The show quickly asserts its preference for the documentary style over the traditional travelogue approach geared towards the promotion of tourism (Hanusch, 2010, p. 72). Bourdain asserts: "My crew and I are among the first to record what has been unseen for decades by most of the world" (*Parts Unknown*, 2013). Instead of focusing on the novelty of his access, Bourdain uses the precarious situation to frame the significance of national journalistic freedoms only recently permitted. He explains:

> In 2007, a Japanese journalist was shot point-blank and killed filming a street demonstration. Be seen talking to anybody with a camera and there would likely be a knock on your door in the middle of the night. Yet so far confronted with our cameras, a few smiles, and mostly indifference at worst, shocking considering how recently the government has started to relax its grip.
>
> *(Parts Unknown, 2013)*

In this initial description of the political environment, Bourdain opts not to depend on stereotypes to characterise daily life, a common approach to discussing cultural differences in travel journalism (Bennett, 1998, p. 3), but instead expresses empathy with the struggles and hopes of locals. His comments and images challenge traditional notions of travel journalism's market orientation with a preference for information that serves the public interest over exotic and purely entertaining content. Bourdain's sentiments reflects Hanusch's description of show hosts "who travel with a critical mind and use journalistic methods at their destination" (2010, p. 77, in reference to Lischke, 2006).

Bourdain's dialogue and discussions throughout the episode centre on the ways in which citizens interpret an end to government censorship, as they question if "this loosening of government grip (will) last" (*Parts Unknown*, 2013). It could be argued that Bourdain has set out to examine a culture in transition from a large to a small "power distance" preference (Hofstede, 1984, p. 84). This concept by Hofstede describes the notion of "large versus small power distance" as "how a society handles inequalities among people when they occur" (1984, p. 83); the author explains how, for instance, cultures low on the "power distance" scale seek to overcome distinctions in social status through a balance of power (1984, p. 83). Myanmar had recently undergone egalitarian democratic reforms, which gave lower-class citizens freedoms that began to shift the country from a high to a low power distance social structure. Bourdain finds evidence of a power distance transition in public spaces where people from all levels of the social strata congregate. He narrates how "morning in Yangon has always been about tea", as a way of asserting the culinary ritual's transcendence over time, war and social inequality (*Parts Unknown*, 2013). Bourdain meets with a journalist and government watchdog named Thiha Saw for tea. Saw opens a conversation with a remark about his previous clandestine meetings at teahouses. Bourdain then contextualises the political significance of a teahouse in Yangon: "For 50 years of paranoia and repression, teahouses were also the main forum for guarded and not-so guarded discussions of the daily news" (*Parts Unknown*, 2013). In this case, teahouses serve as a fickle haven from the political elite for those with low social status to discuss personal thoughts on radical political ideas. As the research of Kyla Wazana Tompkins explains, "there is a historical relationship between food, meals and philosophical discourse" (2005, p. 245). Similarly, the format of *Parts Unknown* employs the dining table as an arena to explore contentious issues with locals assuaged by familiar tastes, sounds and customs.

The market orientation of *Parts Unknown* remains focused on a type of informed tourism where travellers consider the role and ramifications of foreign presence on the daily life of locals. Bourdain remarks on the imminent increase of tourism in the region: "It's going to mean mobility, it's going to mean prosperity for some. It will mean a lot of bad things, too. It will mean prostitution. It will mean hustling" (*Parts Unknown*, 2013). His introspection mirrors Elfriede Fürsich's idea of the newfangled "preferred traveller" of global television programs, the character of "a comparably new form of tourism growing out of the Western alternative and environmental movements that acknowledges the problems of mass tourism but actively tries to avoid them to find authentic experiences" (2002, p. 210). Fürsich relates this "preferred traveller" concept to Peter Corrigan's term "untourism", which is about "caring for people, maintaining unspoiled environments, authenticity and value-for-money" (1997, p. 145). Bourdain does not explicitly advocate "untourism", but exemplifies travel that embraces local norms abroad rather than a search for comfort or exotic thrills that economically reshape the cultural fabric of foreign lands. The host's meta-discourse casts a "critical light" on the travel industry, which suggests a motivation orientation that leans towards informative over entertainment-based content (Hanusch, 2010, p. 78).

'Los Angeles': constructions of the ordinary through local perspectives

In season nine of *Parts Unknown*, Bourdain travels to Los Angeles, a location featured several times in past series, to take a closer look at the identity and culture of the underrepresented Latino and Chicano population in L.A. The episode begins with Bourdain driving a muscle car and the same synth-pop music and 1980s aesthetic re-popularised by the movie *Drive* (2011). Bourdain tasks the audience in voiceover, "but what if we look at L.A. from the point of view from the largely unphotographed, the 47 per cent of Angelinos … doing much, if not most of the hard work of getting things done in this town" (*Parts Unknown*, 2017). The stylised cinematography and music continue over shots of Latino men and women cleaning houses and cooking in the back of kitchens, as if to suggest that both scenes are equally significant to what the hosts hails as "the landscape of our collective dreams", referring to the global cinematic influence of L.A. (*Parts Unknown*, 2017). He then asks the audience to imagine changes to the alluring cultural fabric of L.A. if the political far-right were to carry out its manifested policy goals to effectively deport all illegal immigrants. Bourdain explains:

One in 10 Angelinos are undocumented … contemplate, if you will, what would happen if anywhere near 10 per cent of the workforce were no longer here, particularly because they're rather overrepresented in those fields that most of us are not in a hurry to enter.

(Parts Unknown, 2017)

Instead of giving an answer, Bourdain meets with locals throughout the city to understand the perspective of an insider. Bourdain dines in a locally owned Mexican restaurant with professor of Chicano studies Raul Hinojosa-Ojeda to discuss food as an artefact that traces the history of Latino culture. Hinojosa-Ojeda explains that the seeds in his dish can be traced back generations and were brought to L.A. by migrant workers to the area. As an auto ethnographer immersed in international food culture, Bourdain's discourses and historical inferences about a meal can further contextualise different people and add to an audience's understanding of the 'other'. As argued by Tompkins, the act of eating could be positioned as a cultural trope (2005, p. 224), where "studying food in literature is one mode of studying material history" (2005, p. 245). The restaurant scene cuts to historical images of twentieth-century Mexican villages combined with a contemporary video of migrant workers in produce fields, which suggests a tangible connection between generations. Bourdain progresses the conversation with Hinojosa-Ojeda to discuss the potential loss of migrants who make up a significant portion of the workforce in nearly every step of the food industry's production, distribution and waste collection processes. Bourdain and Hinojosa-Ojeda postulate how a loss of migrants would mean the demise of an industry and the economy of California. However, Bourdain's subsequent conversations throughout the episode serve to construct a more dynamic identity of migrants beyond the economic roles of Latinos and Chicanos in L.A.

The political aspects of *Parts Unknown*'s intercultural discourse take place in common and unassuming locations. Bourdain sits down with Nick and Nate Diaz, two successful mixed martial arts fighters, for a plate of local cuisine. Bourdain proudly comments on the significance of a recent win by Nate Diaz over his opponent Connor McGregor, who had spouted racial slurs at the brothers prior to the fight. Earlier in the episode, Bourdain mentions that Latinos in L.A. remain largely unrepresented in the media and "don't show up so much in stupid sitcoms or superhero movies" (*Parts Unknown*, 2017). For Bourdain, the inclusion of two prominent Latino figures on the show provided an opportunity for increased positive media representation of minorities. As journalism professors Nete Nørgaard Kristensen and Unni From explain, "cultural journalism also addresses political issues through the artistic and cultural expressions it debates and contextualises" (2015, p. 762). Bourdain uses his episode to portray Nick and Nate as two Latino heroes who fight contenders with the same fervour as they combat bigotry.

Along with food and politics, ethnicity also plays a significant role in Bourdain's construction of the 'other'. To better understand ethnicity as a factor of national identity, Bourdain asks the question: "How Mexican could you be, should you be, if you were born in California with a Mexican name and of Mexican heritage?" (*Parts Unknown*, 2017). In a conversation at a *taquería*, the magazine editor Gustavo Arellano illustrates how racism becomes internalised among the Latino community with the concept, a derogatory phrase, of 'pocho'. Arellano explains, "If you say 'pocho' you basically say you're a rotting Mexican, you're completely fake, you've lost all your culture; therefore, you should be hated" (*Parts Unknown*, 2017). As Kassaye *et al.* argue, "while media discourse imposes boundaries from the 'outside', these boundaries can either be reproduced or reconstructed from the 'inside'" (2016, p. 791). Bourdain high-lights this internal 'othering' process that Latinos and Chicanos face from their countries of descent by exposing the differences and racial tensions between the two groups who differ in nationality but share a common heritage. Bourdain situates the othering of Latinos and Chicanos as a framework abated by the diversity of the American cultural fabric: "Los Angeles, like much of California, used to be part of Mexico. Now Mexico, or a whole lot of Mexicans, are a vital part of us" (*Parts Unknown*, 2017). His construction of minority identity in L.A. appears to reflect a local sentiment, if only from those he interviews, which becomes evident in the final words of his episode from a local Latino man: "You're never white enough for this country and you're never brown enough for Mexico … but I know that we are Californians … and I am Los Angeles" (*Parts Unknown*, 2017).

Conclusion

This study's qualitative textual analysis has examined the intercultural meaning-making of *Parts Unknown*, hosted by Anthony Bourdain to develop a nuanced understanding of travel journalism's role in cultural mediation. Through a textual and conversation analysis of two episodes, it has been revealed that Bourdain takes a very different approach to cultural mediation than traditional travel journalism. First, Bourdain represents the ordinariness of a featured location through an exploration of the interplay between political structures and the cultural practices of common citizens. The host investigates citizen behaviour in familial, communal and leisure activities as these experiences relate to national laws and freedoms. Second, Bourdain criticises his profession's unintended propagation of self-serving tourists to a featured location without condemning it, an amoral stance uncommon and therefore largely unstudied in the field of travel journalism (Hanusch, 2010, p. 76). Instead of catering to an imagined audience seeking exotic thrills, Bourdain frequently subverts his epicure arche-type by using traditionally entertaining scenes, such as a family-run restaurant or tourist hotspot, to discuss the benefits and burdens of foreign travel. Third, Bourdain constructs representations of otherness through conversations about everyday life with locals as contextualised with documentary style historical nar-ratives and accompanied with the host's self-reflective commentary. As a result,

Bourdain encourages Hall's definition of cultural competency through his search for local meaning and discussion of complex social issues.

Bourdain's embrace of unpredictable moments, informed search for the ordinary of a place and intermittent self-reflection in his role as cultural mediator does not fit the rigid scope of Hanusch's dimensions. Additionally, Bourdain's absence of strict behavioural rules for his audience complicates the placement of *Parts Unknown* along Hanusch's model of travel journalism. This study's initial look into *Parts Unknown* from a cultural perspective should encourage future models of travel journalism to accommodate reporters that find entertainment in the ordinary and information from the exotic. Bourdain investigates issues of culture, race, ethnicity and power relations in foreign places through a dialogue with local voices. Bourdain does not seek self-indulgent experiences that avoid inconveniences, nor does he exploit the strangeness of foreign travel for cheap entertainment or laughs. His graciousness reflects a humility in his fortune to travel that contrasts Hanusch's description of the "self-centred traveller" who marginalises a destination (2010, p. 73). Bourdain's journalistic integrity, devotion to hearing local perspectives and curiosity for the ordinary of a foreigner's daily life makes a television series that showcases unique cultural findings. In a media genre historically saturated with entertainment reliant on "making phenomena strange" (Carey, 1989, p. 7), Bourdain's 'ordinary' comes off as fresh and informative.

References

August, T. (2016) 'What's eating Asian American studies', *American Quarterly*, 68(1), pp. 193–203.

Bennett, M. J. (1998) 'Intercultural communication: a current perspective', in Bennett, M. J. (ed.) *Basic concepts of intercultural communication: selected readings*. Yarmouth, ME: Intercultural Press, pp. 1–20.

Buzinde, C. *et al.* (2014) 'Authorizing others: portrayals of Middle Eastern destinations in travel media', in Hanusch, F. and Fürsich, E. (eds) *Travel journalism: exploring production, impact and culture*. London: Palgrave MacMillan, pp. 193–210.

Carey, J. (1989) *Communication as culture*. New York and London: Routledge.

Corrigan, P. (1997) *The sociology of consumption: an introduction*. London: Sage.

Dow, B. J. (1996) *Prime-time feminism: television, media culture, and the women's movement since 1970*. Philadelphia: University of Pennsylvania Press.

Drive (2011) Directed by Nicolas Refn [Film]. United States: Bold Films.

Fürsich, E. (2002) 'Packaging culture: the potential and limitations of travel programs on global television, *Communication Quarterly*, 50(2), pp. 204–226.

Fürsich, E. (2009) 'In defence of textual analysis', *Journalism Studies*, 10(2), pp. 238–252.

Gerbner, G. *et al.* (2002) 'Growing up with television: cultivation processes', in Bryant, J. and Zillmann, D. (eds) *Media effects: advances in theory and research* (2nd ed.). Mahwah, NJ: Erlbaum, pp. 43–67.

Greene, D. (2017) 'At home, he's a tourist: the odyssey of Anthony Bourdain', *Film Criticism*, 41(3). doi: 10.3998/fc.13761232.0041.314.

Grgurinović, I. (2012) 'Anthropology and travel: practice and text', *Studia Ethnologica Croatica*, 22, pp. 317–337.

Hall, E. T. (1976) *Beyond culture.* New York: Anchor Books.

Hamilton, J. M. and Jenner, E. (2004) 'Redefining foreign correspondence', *Journalism,* 5(3), pp. 301–321.

Hanusch, F. (2010) 'The dimensions of travel journalism, exploring new fields for journalism research beyond the news', *Journalism Studies,* 11(1), pp. 68–82.

Hanusch, F. (2011) 'A profile of Australian travel journalists' professional views and ethical standards', *Journalism,* 13(5), pp. 668–686.

Hanusch, F. (2014) 'The geography of travel journalism: mapping the flow of travel stories about foreign countries', *The International Communication Gazette,* 76(1), pp. 47–66.

Hofstede, G. (1984) 'Cultural dimensions in management and planning', *Asia Pacific Journal of Management,* 1(2), pp. 81–99.

Hofstede, G. (2001) *Culture's consequences: comparing values, behaviours, institutions and organisations across nations* (2nd ed.). London: Sage.

Kassaye, A. *et al.* (2016) 'The relationship between media discourses and experiences of belonging: Dutch Somali perspectives', *Ethnicities,* 16(6), pp. 773–797.

Kristensen, N. and From, U. (2015) 'Cultural journalism and cultural critique in a changing media landscape', *Journalism Practice,* 9(6), pp. 760–722.

Ksiazek, T. B. and Webster, J. G. (2008) 'Cultural proximity and audience behaviour: the role of language in patterns of polarization and multicultural fluency, *Journal of Broadcasting & Electronic Media,* 52(3), pp. 485–503.

Lischke, J. (2006) *Reisejournalisten: Akteure im Spannungsfeld [Travel journalists: actors in a field of tension].* Unpublished M.A. thesis. University of Munich.

Lustig, M. and Koester, J. (2006) *Intercultural competence: intercultural communication across cultures* (5th ed.). New York: Harper Collins.

Martin, J. and Nakayama, T. (2012). *Intercultural communication in contexts* (6th ed.). New York: McGraw Hill.

Parts Unknown (2013) CNN Television, 14 April.

Parts Unknown (2017) CNN Television, 30 April.

Meyrowitz, J. (1989) 'Media and community,' *Critical Studies in Mass Communication,* 6(3), pp. 326–334.

Nicolau, J. and Mas, F. (2006) 'The influence of distance and prices on the choice of tourist destinations: the moderating role of motivations', *Tourism Management,* 27(5), pp. 982–996.

Richardson, L. (1990) *Writing strategies.* Newbury Park: Sage.

Rodríguez, I. (1998) 'News reporting and colonial discourse: the representation of Puerto Ricans in U.S. press coverage of the Spanish American war', *Howard Journal of Communications,* 9(4), pp. 283–301.

Santos, C. A. (2004) 'Perception and interpretation of leisure travel articles', *Leisure Sciences,* 26(4), pp. 393–410.

Santos, C. A. (2006) 'Cultural politics in contemporary travel writing', *Annals of Tourism Research,* 33(3), pp. 624–644.

Schiller, H. (1976) 'Communication and cultural domination', *International Journal of Politics,* 5(4), pp. 1–127.

Steves, R. (2009) *Travel as a political act.* New York: Nation Books.

Tompkins, K. W. (2005) 'Literary approaches to food studies: food, culture & society', *Journal of International Business and Cultural Studies,* 8(2), pp. 243–258.

Yoo, E. E. and Buzinde, C. (2012) 'Gazing upon the kingdom. An audience reception analysis of a televised travelogue', *Annals of Tourism Research,* 39(1), pp. 221–242.

6

THE IMPACT OF SOCIAL MEDIA IN LIFESTYLE JOURNALISM IN MEXICO

Serving citizens versus creating consumers

Sergio Rodríguez-Blanco and Dalia Cárdenas-Hernández

In the first quarterly report of 2015 from GlobalWebIndex on the latest trends in social networking (2015, p. 8), Mexico was globally ranked first in the use of social networks on a mobile—with a 65 per cent use by the population between 16 and 64 years old; it was also ranked the first country in the use of YouTube, second in the use of Facebook and sixth in the use of Twitter, in terms of hours spent on those platforms (GlobalWebIndex, 2015, p. 17). As a reference, the U.S. was 26th in the use of YouTube, the 22nd for Facebook and the 19th for Twitter, while the U.K. was 28th in the use of YouTube, the 24th for Facebook and the 18th for Twitter (GlobalWebIndex, 2015, p. 17).

As the popularity of social media in Mexico was growing a decade ago, the main Mexican newspapers started to open their own accounts on different social media platforms. *El Universal* launched its Twitter and Facebook accounts in 2008, while *Reforma* did it a year later, followed by *Excélsior* in 2010 (Twitter) and 2011 (Facebook). In the case of fashion-, travel- and gastronomy-specialised magazines attached to the most influential publishing houses in the country, Condé Nast and Expansión first opened their Twitter accounts in 2009 and 2010 respectively, and did the same on Facebook and other social media like Instagram and Pinterest about one year later.

All these transformations—not only in technology, but also in fields such as journalism, economy and cultural industries—are an effect of the so-called "digital convergence", a concept that Henry Jenkins uses to refer to "the flow of content across multiple media platforms, the cooperation between multiple media industries and the migratory behaviour of media audiences" (2008, p. 14). Bernardi (2011) emphasises that digital convergence impacts journalistic work, as it requires a permanent updating of technological skills, since journalists must plan their coverage to be disseminated through different platforms that have their own specific languages and conventions. This generates a versatility of the journalist (García Avilés, 2006), whose work is no longer confined solely to writing. In journalism, digital convergence has modified work routines and created a new professional culture, bringing about the idea of the "convergent journalist" (Meneses, 2011), who must work for various media platforms and do more hours on the job. This journalist requires technical skills that must be learnt quickly and must do the work that was once carried out by different people. But what are the specificities of digital convergence in social media used as platforms for lifestyle journalism?

The present investigation aims to analyse how work routines were modified in lifestyle journalism after the installation of digital social media in 2008, and identify some practices that characterise the treatment of information published through these platforms in the accounts of supplements and Mexican journals that specialise in soft news, where, it could be argued, the requirement of immediacy has modified the parameters of truthfulness and rigor. In this chapter we seek to determine how, in the so-called "convergent journalism" (Meneses, 2011), technical skills have contributed to the precariousness of the profession by demanding greater labour flexibility, multi-specialisation and technical skills in constant update under the premise that, in the digital age, journalists must, above other qualities, have the ability to adapt to change.

Journalism (of any type) ceases to be so if its primary function is not to provide citizens with the tools to understand the world and their position within it (Richardson, 2007, p.7). According to John Hartley (2000), Thomas Hanitzsch (2007), Elfriede Fürsich (2012) and Folker Hanusch (2012), the main characteristics of lifestyle journalism are the fact that it gives advice on goods and services, creates content that acts as an interpreter of reality in increasingly complex societies and presents an orientation towards the market, which favours and promotes consumption and places lifestyle journalism closer to the economic sphere than to politics (Hanusch, 2012). Our research poses the question, ultimately, of whether this adaptation to change has also implied, in Mexico, that digital social networks uncritically legitimised the agendas and discourses of the fashion, gastronomy and cultural industries (Rodríguez-Blanco, 2017, p. 114), establishing a hybrid discourse in which the journalistic contents merged with publicity. Although these two dimensions have been present since the origins of journalism, the connection has acquired a much wider, visible and evident presence as a result of the reach of digital social networks.

Method

In order to study the impact of social media on lifestyle journalism in Mexico, between 2017 and 2018 we conducted in-depth interviews with seven editors and reporters who experienced this change, who are specialists in soft news and also digital migrants. The respondents were all working as editors or reporters between 2008 and 2011, when digital social media was established as part of the information offer of national newspapers and magazines. We decided to exclude reporters and editors who began to work after that period and digital natives, in order to focus on the transformations of the working environment. The seven key informants were chosen for their experience working in the main outlets for national lifestyle media: Grupo Editorial Expansión (*InStyle, Elle, Singular, Life & Style, Aire, Accent, Travel and Leisure*, etc.), Grupo Editorial Televisa (*Esquire*), Editorial Condé Nast (*Vanity Fair, Vogue*, etc.), Iasa Comunicación, Grupo Imagen Multimedia, TV Azteca (*Central*), *Reforma* and *El Universal*. These last two were the first Mexican newspapers to include specific sections on gastronomy, fashion and travel, as well as being among the first national newspapers to incorporate social networks into their information offer.

Based on the method that corresponds to what Orozco and González (2012) call a "semi-structured interview", a research instrument was designed to include the following categories of analysis: process of appropriation of new technologies in digital migrants; transformation of journalistic routines in lifestyle journalism; increasing precariousness of the profession; new job profiles; multi-specialisation; reporting practices; professional values; treatment of information; and implementation of a journalistic discourse that fuses information and publicity.

The impact of digital convergence on Mexican lifestyle journalism

The seven key respondents interviewed for this research acknowledged the fact that the new platforms entirely transformed the way journalism is practised by becoming the main vehicle to attract readers, a task that was relatively easy for younger journalists:

> I started using social networks as part of my work. On a personal level, I didn't want to use them, I valued my privacy and I didn't see any justification in exposing my privacy all the time; but at work, if you wanted to have healthy results [in terms of impact and visibility], you had to be in social networks.
>
> *(Informant 4, editor-in-chief, 40 years old)*[1]

They also express the perception that older and more experienced journalists found it difficult to conform to the new demands of their job, either because they were not particularly interested in these new platforms or because they did not belong to the group of users of digital tools:

> There are editors ten years older than me who have not been on the digital boat because they have not been required to be, or because they feel they have not needed it. It is complicated because if they are not immersed in this digital environment, it is difficult for them to understand the scope and approaches of it.
>
> *(Informant 6, editor, 33 years old)*

The demand to keep readers informed at all times implied the need to generate content that ensures the positioning of the publication as the main reference source for their readers, forcing media professionals to adopt much higher response speed, as immediacy is one of the main values for information posted online (Romero-Martínez, 2012; Bastenier, 2009). It meant considering not only several products, but also different markets and languages, distinguishing the borderlines between different formats and their needs, a multi-specialisation that requires ongoing adaptation to change: "In social media you need to think differently, speak differently, spread your message in a different way" (Informant 6, editor, 33 years old).

The need to technically control social media in beats such as fashion, beauty, travel and gastronomy has led to the employment of younger reporters, co-editors and editors. This practice is increasingly more common on the grounds that, aside from being regular users of said platforms, they possess the ability to talk to the audience the publication is trying to attract or retain, leaving aspects such as experience and research ability in the background:

> It scares me that people think that anything can be published on social media. It is fine that they are young, but not that they make the decisions. Yes, it is fine to publish tweets or make videos or propose creative products, but I do not feel comfortable when they feel they are in charge. It is the logic that governs a newspaper or any company: you need some experience to be in charge, and it is the same in the digital media industry.
>
> *(Informant 7, editor, 41 years old)*

> We need to differentiate two things: a community manager obviously has to be young because he or she knows how to manage Facebook, Twitter, Instagram, but it is one thing to know how to manage a network and another thing to know how to communicate on social networks.
>
> *(Informant 2, editor and digital strategist, 38 years old)*

Aside from acquiring new skills, lifestyle reporters and editors acknowledge social media potential insofar as they are platforms that have allowed them to broaden the scope and impact of their jobs by providing them with the possibility to maintain a closer relationship with readers and offer content that challenges them to be increasingly creative. They also value the possibility of releasing content in a direct and simple manner, and with a wider scope. This is part of a process that has added to the democratisation of information by allowing virtually anyone with access to these platforms to generate and share their own content.

In addition to the approach and immediacy, having millions of points of view is one of the greatest things that social media has contributed to journalism. Now, each person can be in the place of events and be recording what happens;

this is one of the great contributions, the democratisation of information, the possibility to say: "I can also tell everyone what is happening" (Informant 4, editor-in-chief, 40 years old).

However, this scenario has also fostered the emergence of 'improvised' media, in which alleged opinion leaders set their stance on facts that have not been properly researched and contrasted, and that might be entirely based on rumours or come from unreliable information sources. Likewise, there is a perception that has become more difficult for people to distinguish a properly researched piece of news from alleged events that are mainly based on rumours and are spread by sites that are not actual communication media, thus contributing to misinformation.

> A negative aspect of social media has been the birth of these untrustworthy media sources, which disseminate information that people validate as true. They have also created a tremendous laziness, and this means that there is no longer the same interest. I don't want to generalise, but there are people who think "why should I buy this magazine or newspaper if I already read about it on social media?"
>
> *(Informant 5, digital editor, 42 years old)*

New profiles in lifestyle journalism

The new dynamics brought by social media have resulted in the development of a new professional profile: the community manager. Our research in Mexico suggests that this position is generally aimed at young communicators who, as users of social media, thoroughly understand how the different platforms work, but who, due to their age, do not yet have the skills required to handle the task with sufficient journalistic expertise. In parallel, bloggers and influencers emerged as figures who began to call themselves specialists, but with an academic and professional background different from that of the journalist and, therefore, with different objectives such as measuring their impact, scope or influence through the number of likes and subscribers to their accounts (Masip, 2016; Quintana, 2018). This is perceived as leaving the traditional objectives of journalism in a second place:

> In many platforms, it was understood that a specialised unit needed to take charge of social media; other media are still working with those people who managed to make this type of information. At the same time, figures like bloggers appeared, and although they had more enthusiasm than real expertise on the subject, the journalists and the specialists had to learn to compete with them in a certain way.
>
> *(Informant 1, lifestyle journalist, 38 years old)*

With regard to readers, new profiles have been set up as a consequence of the growth of lifestyle content in Mexico: for example, 'foodies', as gastronomy connoisseurs are called, or 'fashionistas', as people with a great interest in fashion are known, who use the digital platforms to show their looks. Different characters have emerged from the success of these social media accounts who, due to their high number of followers, have become a reference point in the industry, and who even seek to play a 'journalistic' yet nebulous role (Marchetti, 2005; Reich and Godler, 2017). This role has been legitimised, at least in Latin America, by public relations agencies, which have incorporated bloggers and influencers as part of the press who are invited to their events.

> Social media should be given relevance in the creation of content. Not all young people who have a good number of followers on their personal Twitter accounts or who know how to use Facebook can carry a brand. Before, this was done by publicists, people who studied the market; now, the only thing that counts is to have a good base of followers that supposedly gives you enough influence.
>
> *(Informant 6, editor, 33 years old)*

Information and advertising in lifestyle journalism on social media

The demand for immediacy and the competition to be first have also impacted the processing of information in aspects ranging from source verification to spelling errors. The way in which information is worded, the use of Anglicism and of informative spaces to express opinions or to openly advertise brands and products with which the publication has entered into commercial agreements is a common practice. This has favoured the development of a hybrid philosophy that benefits the commercial interests of the media and its advertisers, establishing a mixture of information and advertising that, although already present in lifestyle journalism prior to digitalisation, now finds in the new platforms a scenario in which soft news content achieves a wide exposure that seeks to exert a greater influence on the readers (Castelló-Martínez, 2010):

> The line between advertising and information is getting thinner, but this is something the media have allowed, and advertisers have also take advantage of it. At the same time, the advertisers were very astute in using figures such as bloggers, which are marketing tools that the same brands use to promote their products and that people consider as independent voices, when they really are a tool to position a new product, idea or trend.
>
> *(Informant 1, lifestyle journalist, 38 years old)*

The use of social media by newspapers and magazines for promoting brands and products is something that particularly concerns the interviewees, as something that, in the old regime, was considered a compromise with regards to media objectivity. Nevertheless, it is acknowledged that it is important to recognise how new platforms help to promote commercial relations between the media and their advertisers, as well as an alternative to attract more traffic by taking advantage of the audience that certain brands have obtained through their position as leaders in their field.

> A magazine like *InStyle* talks about the beauty products you can have, it gives you advice but it's still a magazine that talks about products. In the case of social media there is a game between media and advertisers, a dialogue in which if you tag Chanel you will have more people who read you than if you do not tag it. But you have to be very smart so that this is not perceived as something paid; the media have to defend their autonomy.
>
> *(Informant 4, editor-in-chief, 40 years old)*

It is important to remember that the crisis faced by newspapers and magazines in the last few years has led to incorporation of new formats that allow them to remain competitive and to maintain good profit margins by offering their advertisers different approaches to make their products available to the readers, typically through editorialising these commercial proposals. Even though these editors acknowledge that editorial independence is one of journalism's fundamental values, they also accept that the industry must become closer to advertisers to remain profitable.

> The challenge is to find the balance between the content you want to publish and the presence of the advertisers, so we do not do publicity, but editorial work with advertisers. We have to be clever enough to separate the commercial terrain from the publishing field to continue having our independence.
>
> *(Informant 6, editor, 33 years old)*

In spite of this, it is interesting to note that, given the lack of experience and the absence of a formal style to manage new digital media, different outlets adopted social media in the same way that Mexican lifestyle journalists managed their personal accounts (Hohmann, 2011; Diezhandino *et al.*, 2012), even if this meant using the media's social networks to voice opinions that may compromise the credibility of the publication or its interests, commercial or editorial. By performing a similar role to that of a columnist in the printed or digital version, these authors adopt the position of an expert in a relevant source or topic.

> I like to have my favourite critics in the media. As a critic, you have to be professional and have strong opinions to speak on behalf of a medium. If you are being given that space it is because you are a specialist and because you are going to contribute, if not, just use your personal social media where you are not speaking on behalf of anyone.
>
> *(Informant 4, editor-in-chief, 40 years old)*

The processing of soft news information in the digital era

Adding social media to the information offer of Mexican lifestyle journalism considerably multiplied the editorial spaces devoted to information about new products, the launching of collections of big fashion houses or the venues the public must visit. The interviewees speak of the apparent triviality of the topics addressed, yet, although they admit that often the treatment given to some content is inadequate, it is certainly the publication itself and the journalist that set up the parameters for the way they cover the information, and the way in which said information is presented to the readers. Therefore, even though the topics covered lack the sense of urgency of the topics traditionally attached to hard news, that does not mean the public cannot be presented with thorough and well-conducted research that offers valuable, useful and interesting information.

> The strength of lifestyle journalism is that it does not deal with information that is a matter of life and death. What the editor of a travel magazine can tell us is not the same as what financial, economic or political journalists will tell us. Lifestyle journalism could be seen as journalism without rigour, but the depth that you want to give your information depends on each media source and on each journalist.
>
> *(Informant 6, editor, 33 years old)*

The need to attract increasingly more traffic therefore requires journalists to think creatively and look for topics and angles that stand out. In the specific case of social media, we must consider that updating takes place 24/7, which forces editors and reporters to provide information that, although it may be of interest to their readers, does not necessarily place lifestyle content in the realm of news or exclusivity.

According to the interviewed editors, the lack of rigor in language—spelling and punctuation mistakes, poor writing and excessive use of neologisms—is precisely one of the negative aspects of the content shared, a situation that responds to the need to update these platforms at a high rate. On social media, aspects such as spelling and choice of words are not considered very important: "It is a mistake to think that digital media requires less solemnity in the use of language because it is aimed at a younger audience. You can be as playful as you want by writing well" (Informant 1, lifestyle journalist, 33 years old); "Printed journalism is richer and more complex than online journalism. Many rules have been broken on the web because no matter what you say or how you say it, it is simply 'say it'" (Informant 3, web editor, 40 years old).

Given the speed with which news must be shared through these platforms, fact verification has often taken a backseat. Unlike the printed version and even the web version, in digital social media, practices such as verification of sources, contrast of information and other rules of traditional journalism are often omitted, giving priority to other aspects like the speed with which information is updated on Facebook and Twitter. The permanent demand for content that generates increasing traffic has led to the need to publish information that is becoming a trend, but which lacks the rigor that used to be imposed as a standard for all sources, including lifestyle journalism. For writer and journalist Humberto Musacchio (in Lara Klahr, 2005), the lack of general knowledge is one of the problems affecting quality of content, especially among younger generations, who perfectly know how to use new digital media but lack the experience necessary to assume the responsibility involved. This view resonates with that of our interviewees:

> You think a lot about young people because they live on social media, but it is a very senior level of responsibility because we are in a moment where everyone is involved in Facebook, reading the news and watching videos. The person in charge of that is the community manager or the social media editor. I think the high level of responsibility of this job does not correspond with the low profile of many community managers and social media editors.
>
> *(Informant 5, digital editor, 42 years old)*

Despite the fact that social media serve as platforms to share fake news, rumours or information that has not been confirmed, it is, at the same time, difficult for journalists not to use them as information sources and as a tool to remain updated with what happens in the world. Even journalists who do not place social media as among their main sources of information recognise the value of new digital platforms in monitoring news that may emerge. These media have become the fastest way to know which topics people are talking about, and to determine where the informative trends are headed.

> When I get the newspaper in the morning, I feel like I am missing something. I know that information was written by people like me the night before and in those twelve hours that passed, that information may have changed completely. Reviewing the old media is only a routine, but if what you really want is to see the latest updates, you do have to access the electronic and digital media.
>
> *(Informant 4, editor-in-chief, 40 years old)*

In view of the proliferation of accounts attempting to join the news spectrum without formal establishment as mass media, it is the editorial groups themselves that must find, within their information processing and journalist professionalism, the vehicles to guarantee their survival in an environment where digital tools have provided the public with the possibility to become transmitters of messages, along with the inherent risks this implies. The key point lies in the fact that whoever possesses information is bound to account for the way they use it. To the extent that it is used responsibly, the impact of social media can be highly favourable; otherwise, we are facing the risk of misinformation, which represents a great danger for a society like that of Mexico, where many people obtain information through Facebook and other social media.

Conclusion

Little more than a decade after Mexican news outlets started to manage their own social media accounts, the challenges lifestyle journalists face now are not only focused on generating contents for these platforms, but also on the creativity and skills necessary to address coverage in order to ensure their feasibility. At least in Mexico, the most innovative proposals have emerged not from the traditional media, but from alternative media that were born in the virtual environment itself, and which stand out for their close relationship outside and beyond the journalistic realm, such as marketing and advertising. Our research suggests that this context presents opportunities to traditional outlets—such as increasing the reach and audience of lifestyle content, and generating revenues for the news outlets—but is perceived as a hybrid between information and advertising by practitioners who oversaw the transition from analogue to digital journalism. It would be of great importance to do further research about the content being produced, as Mexico tops the list of the ten nations with the highest use of social media (GlobalWebIndex, 2015), which has become one of the main information and leisure sources for the population that uses the Internet.

Added to this scenario is the configuration of new professional profiles, such as bloggers and influencers who, due to the reach of their social networks, have managed to build an identity that positions them as opinion leaders. These new influencers base their expertise on the number of followers and likes their posts obtain, in which the content is usually linked to themselves or to the advertisers that pay them to obtain coverage. For established journalists, this is a crucial diversion from the primary function of journalism as a service to citizens, historically backed by the credibility that the media itself have built among their readers by providing them with the information to understand reality in all its complexity.

Note

1 All interviews were originally conducted in Spanish and have been translated by the authors.

References

Bastenier, M. (2009) *¿Cómo se escribe un periódico? El chip colonial y los diarios en América Latina*. Mexico: Fondo de Cultura Económica, Fundación Nuevo Periodismo Iberoamericano.

Bernardi, M. T. (2011). 'Las rutinas periodísticas en los sitios de noticias regionales', in Bianchi, M. P. and Sandoval, L. R. (eds.) *Jornadas Patagónicas de estudios sociales sobre Internet y tecnologías de la comunicación*. Comodoro Rivadavia: Universidad Nacional de la

Patagonia San Juan Bosco. Available at: http://tecnologiaycultura.com.ar/actas2011/doc/m9bernardi.pdf (Accessed: 17 December 2018).

Castelló-Martínez, A. (2010) 'Una nueva figura profesional: el community manager', *Revista de la Red Académica Iberoamericana de Comunicación*, 1, pp. 74–97.

ComScore (2018) 'Global digital future in focus. 2018 international edition'. Available at: http://adepa.org.ar/wp-content/uploads/2018/03/Global-Digital-Future-in-Focus-2018.pdf (Accessed: 17 December 2018).

Diezhandino, M. P. *et al.* (2012) *El periodista en la encrucijada*. Barcelona: Fundación Telefónica.

Fürsich, E. (2012) 'Lifestyle journalism as popular journalism', *Journalism Practice*, 6(1), pp. 12-25. doi: 10.1080/17512786.2011.622894.

García Avilés, J. A. (2006) *El periodismo audiovisual ante la convergencia digital*. Elche, Alicante: Universidad Miguel Hernández.

GlobalWebIndex (2015) 'GlobalWebIndex's quarterly report on the latest trends in social networking'. Available at: http://www.thewebmate.com/wp-content/uploads/2015/05/GWI-Social-Report-Q1-2015.pdf (Accessed: 17 December 2018).

Hanitzsch, T. (2007) 'Deconstructing journalism culture: toward a universal theory', *Communication Theory*, 17, pp. 367–385.

Hanusch, F. (2012) 'Broadening the focus', *Journalism Practice*, 6(1), pp. 2–11. doi: 10.1080/17512786.2011.622895.

Hartley, J. (2000) 'Communicative democracy in a redactional society: the future of journalism studies', *Journalism Studies*, 1(1), pp. 39–48.

Hohmann, J. (2011) *Las 10 mejores prácticas para medios sociales. Guías útiles para las organizaciones periodísticas*. Austin, Texas: ASNE, American Society of News Editors.

Instituto Nacional de Estadística y Geografía (2018) 'En México 71.3 millones de usuarios de internet y 17.4 millones de hogares con conexión a este servicio: ENDUTIH 2017', 20 February. Available at: http://www.beta.inegi.org.mx/contenidos/saladeprensa/boletines/2018/OtrTemEcon/ENDUTIH2018_02.pdf (Accessed: 17 December 2018).

Instituto Nacional de Estadística y Geografía (2018) 'Disminuye la población lectora en México: Módulo de Lectura (MOLEC) 2018', 27 April. Available at: http://www.beta.inegi.org.mx/contenidos/saladeprensa/boletines/2018/EstSociodemo/MOLEC2018_04.pdf (Accessed: 17 December 2018).

Jenkins, H. (2008) *Convergence culture. la cultura de la convergencia de los medios de comunicación*. Barcelona: Paidós.

Lara Klahr, M. (2005) *Diarismo: cultura e industria del periodismo impreso en México y el mundo*. Mexico: Editorial E.

Lutz, B. (2017) 'Alimentación y clases sociales en la Ciudad de México', *Estudios Sociales*, 27(49), pp. 295–305.

Marchetti, D. (2005) 'Subfields of specialized journalism', in Benson, R. and Neveu, E. (eds) *Bourdieu and the journalistic field*. Cambridge: Polity Press, pp. 64–84.

Masip, P. (2016) 'Investigar el periodismo desde la perspectiva de las audiencias', *El profesional de la información (EPI)*, 25(3), pp. 323–330.

Meneses, M. E. (2011) *Periodismo convergente: tecnologías, medios y periodistas en el siglo XXI*. Mexico: Porrúa.

Orozco, G. and González, R. (2012) *Una coartada metodológica*. Mexico: Tintable.

Quintana, A. R. H. (2018) 'Resilencia de la organización de la información en la era de la posverdad', *Revista Cubana de Información y Comunicación*, 6(14), pp. 47–59.

Reich, Z. and Godler, Y. (2017) 'The disruption of journalistic expertise, in Peters, C. and Broersma, M. (2017) *Rethinking journalism again: societal role and public relevance in a digital age*. London: Routledge, pp. 64–80.

Richardson, J. E. (2007) *Analysing newspapers: an approach from critical discourse analysis.* New York: Palgrave MacMillan.

Rodríguez-Blanco, S. (2017) 'El periodismo cultural y la cómoda jaula de la cultura institucionalizada. Por un periodismo crítico ante la narrativa hegemónica de la cultura en Iberoamérica', in Ángel, J. (ed.) *Cultura y comunicación. Acercamientos críticos, narrativos y analíticos.* Mexico: Intersecciones, pp. 111–140.

Romero-Martínez, P. (2012) 'Los problemas de la inmediatez: "Hemos matado a Steve Jobs"', *Cuadernos de Comunicación Evoca,* 8, pp. 11–15.

Watlington, L. (2013) 'Periodismo digital', in *International Centre for Journalists. Guía de periodismo en la era digital,* pp. 7–16.

We Are Social (2018) *Digital Report 2018.* Available at: https://www.smartinsights.com/social-media-marketing/social-media-strategy/new-global-social-media-research and https://wearesocial.com/uk/blog/2018/01/global-digital-report-2018 (Accessed: 17 December 2018).

PART III

New players and lifestyle actors

7

COMMUNICATIVE VALUE CHAINS

Fashion bloggers and branding agencies as cultural intermediaries

Arturo Arriagada and Francisco Ibáñez

In 2016, during the Milan Fashion Week, four editors of the U.S. version of *Vogue* magazine—a well-known, printed fashion magazine founded in 1892—criticised bloggers for wearing sponsored outfits and blamed street-style photographers and clothing brands for contributing to fashion week chaos. Bloggers responded that *Vogue*'s article exemplified fashion journalists' resentment vis-à-vis their success, especially with younger audiences (Topping, 2016). Bloggers have emerged as new actors within the field of fashion, sometimes replacing the work of mainstream journalists as consumers' sources of information (Rocamora, 2011). Fashion blogs and printed magazines "feed into each other" by reproducing similar content and exchanging roles between writers to produce content about fashion (Rocamora, 2011: 104). A blogger can contribute content to a printed magazine, while a fashion journalist can be a blogger.

Vogue's example demonstrates the extent to which bloggers and journalists are increasingly in competition with each other for visibility and attention from audiences and sponsors in the constantly changing field of fashion media (Vos *et al.*, 2011). More broadly, they compete over the power to validate different forms of taste, to consecrate in front of their audiences the work of designers, models and brands (Entwistle and Rocamora, 2006). However, as Julie Bradford (2015) suggests, if bloggers and journalists share similar interests and practices in the field of fashion media, there are also important differences. Print and digital, for instance, can have different expectations and results. Fashion journalism, as a professional practice, demands that news and stories must be reported "as a mirror" (Zelizer, 2004, p. 31), without bias, to give audiences a true account of the events. However, in working with brands, fashion blogging shares some of the consumer oriented elements of lifestyle journalism, defined as a "distinct journalistic field that primarily addresses its audiences as consumers, providing them with factual information and advice, often in entertaining ways, about goods and services they can use in their daily lives" (Hanusch, 2012, p. 1).

The story of how these actors—bloggers and journalists—emerge as "taste-makers" participating in the global flow of fashion consumption, invokes Pierre Bourdieu's concept of "cultural intermediaries" (1984). Bourdieu developed the concept of cultural intermediaries to refer to those professionals who have a key role in the reproduction of consumer economies (1984, p. 326). For Bourdieu, cultural intermediaries were observed in professions and trades such as advertising, journalism and even included executives in the tourism industry. As market actors, cultural intermediaries construct value "by mediating how goods (or services, practices, people) are perceived and engaged with by others (end consumers and other market actors including other cultural intermediaries)" (Smith Maguire and Matthews, 2014, p. 2).

One of the key aspects of fashion blogging is how bloggers display a set of strategies to promote themselves as brands and with brands (Duffy and Hund, 2015). For instance, by commenting on fashion trends and reviewing products, among other activities, fashion bloggers are promoting an 'authentic' and 'personal' lifestyle based on the consumption of goods (Duffy, 2017;Marwick, 2015;Duffy and Hund, 2015). Similarly, bloggers are promoters of consumption by associating brands and goods with special moments of everyday life (Duffy, 2017). In this sense, bloggers as cultural intermediaries can mediate the perception consumers have of brands and goods, but also shape consumers' taste and consumption choices (Smith Maguire and Matthews, 2014). However, they do not do this by themselves; they are part of a network of economic and social relations linking different actors, e.g. branding agencies, audiences and platforms.

Drawing from a series of semi-structured interviews with a group of Chilean fashion bloggers (N = 35), we will discuss how fashion bloggers become cultural intermediaries by working with other intermediaries, specifically branding agencies, in order to create content and experiences around brands and products on digital platforms. We will explore how fashion bloggers and branding executives—themselves cultural intermediaries—establish social and economic relations to promote brands and consumption, and the knowledge they display to validate their practices as 'experts' in addressing their audiences as consumers. Social media operates as a space through which bloggers accumulate audiences that are attractive to branding agencies in order to incorporate their work—as both promoters of consumption and 'ideal consumers'— into the brands' communicative value chains. Through these relations, different tensions emerge around bloggers' practices, particularly when they are understood as forms of digital labour. How do these different types of cultural intermediaries work together? How do they put into practice their knowledge and expertise in a specific field of cultural production, and what, if anything, do they share with lifestyle journalism? What kinds of tensions emerge in order to validate different forms of expertise across digital and non-digital audiences?

Method

Data for this project comes from two different sources: the first is a sample of in-depth, semi-structured interviews with 35 social media influencers (mostly fashion and beauty bloggers) based in Santiago de Chile in 2017. Our sample was mostly women (N = 26) and a few men (N = 9), all college educated. Interviews were conducted in person and recorded with participants' consent. Interview topics included participants' backgrounds and expertise; processes of content creation, distribution and promotion; self-presentation strategies; and their relationships with brands and branding agencies. During interviews, we also revised and discussed some Instagram pictures with participants to have more information about their examples and content creation practices. Interview transcripts were coded and analysed using a grounded theory approach, analysing the data as it was collected and contrasting each interview's topic with the other (Glaser and Strauss, 1969).

A second source of data was ethnographic fieldwork in a branding agency, specifically observation of campaign meetings with branding executives and a group of fashion bloggers. These observations gave us an overview of how branding campaigns are organised and executed by the branding agency and a group of influencers, and gave us insight into the criteria for branded content.

Results and discussion

Connecting actors in a communicative value chain

Branding started as a strategy for companies to provide a narrative, a myth through which consumers could integrate themselves or with which they could empathise; in today's media landscape, brands are capable of reaching out to consumers and becoming part of their everyday lives. In the last decade, branding consultants have been pursuing this goal, not only by incorporating social media into to their campaigns, but, most importantly, by inviting a specific type of consumer to be part of those campaigns. These consumers are active in the promotion of products online, writing reviews and evaluating their experiences with brands (Baym and Burnett, 2009), which, at face value, is not entirely different to what lifestyle journalists do, particularly when they are producing branded content. The work of fashion bloggers, as active social media users who create digital content about brands and products, catches the attention of branding consultants (Rocamora, 2018), and as a result products are presented and inserted as part of bloggers' daily activities, such as eating, drinking coffee, going for a walk, or, more spectacularly, travelling and attending private events (e.g. parties or marketing events). As a well-known fashion model-turned-blogger explains: "We sell branding spaces, but what interest brands most is content creation. They give you the products, you try them, and then you tell your audiences about your experience as a user" (Female blogger, 34 years old).[1]

Some bloggers have a spontaneous approach to these encounters, with little or no experience and few expectations in their dealings with brands or agencies. Others are making explicit efforts to reach these agencies and start building work alliances with them.

> Everything started by mail, you start getting mails from agency X telling you that they're working with this brand, and they're interested in working together in this thing, and having a meeting or knowing if I'm interested, so you start answering. So, it begins, it depends, there are two ways, because as I didn't know anyone; I don't know, they came to me, out of nowhere ... but there were people who started and were very active, meeting other people, sharing databases and promoting themselves by sending mails to agencies. That is not my case—everything that has come to me was because it came to me, because they reached me. The first big campaign I was involved with, the agency contacted me, telling me they liked a lot my site's graphic design.
>
> *(Male fashion blogger, 22 years old)*

The first thing that catches agencies' attention is the number of followers bloggers have across different platforms (e.g. blogs, Instagram, YouTube). Agencies aim to harness bloggers' existing reach on social media to display their own products and services, and in turn measure the potential impact and exposure they might get if they work with bloggers. As an experienced female blogger describes:

> I was considered a Twitter influencer, I have lots of followers on Twitter; I was one of the first to create an account, so they sent me stuff, and I work as an influencer for a brand, like food-related stuff ... then, beauty products started to arrive as a result of my blog ... agencies started asking for my address to send me new products.
>
> *(Female fashion blogger, 32 years old)*

Branding agencies' commercial endeavours might begin tentatively, putting bloggers on a sort of trial collaboration, of narrow scope, with few risks for the agencies. Bloggers use this opportunity to wear clothes, present products and produce content (e.g. photos and videos) to showcase them in a specific context. From there, they may prove their value and thus gain access to new opportunities or even convert their relationship with agencies into something more stable, e.g. a lengthier campaign or an official endorsement as a brand ambassador, which in turn brings better economic rewards. A blogger involved in this process describes it thus:

> It's not that the agency calls me to do an advertising campaign with me. What we've done was a kind of campaign, not official, it's not that Arrow (the brand) grabs my photos and spreads them all around Santiago. What

they did is that they lent me their facilities, their store, and told me to pick whatever I wanted, to do whatever I wanted, based on me choosing looks, giving them a context and carrying out that collaboration with pictures and videos, sharing on social media. They were very happy and they're analysing the possibility of giving me more stable work.

(Male fashion blogger, 32 years old)

What binds bloggers and agencies together is not only economic relationships, but the alliances forged on a daily basis, founded on the mutually beneficial exchange of information. These alliances are not the result of previous friendships or close personal relationships. On the contrary, they arise out of a sense of professional engagement with each other, which grows stronger over time. No longer restricted to regular working schedules, these relations can encompass daily life as a whole, including meals, night events and travel. As a blogger describes:

In the end it's not that you become friends with people (from the agencies), but I don't know, when they invite you to events, when they send you information, when I've needed information and I've asked … you start developing a relationship with them. So, later they tell you 'hey, it's part of job in the end'. (People from agencies) tell you 'hey we have this release event … can you help me with the promotion online? Do you want to come to the event?' Then you'll have content for your readers or you'll use the product.

(Female fashion blogger, 34 years old)

Producing branded content online for consumers niches

From a communicational standpoint, the importance of having an online presence is already clear to brands, to varying degrees. This depends on the type of product—for example, a luxury brand—which can lead them to make great efforts to consolidate their brand image. However, the next step for bloggers is to translate online communications into sales. As a blogger who recommends outfits and clothes describes it:

[For brands] branding was the first stage, and now the ones that have lots of followers online … they are interested in conversion. Basically, like generating a coupon that consumers bring to the store and at the end you measure how many people from social media came to the store.

(Female fashion blogger, 32 years old)

From the bloggers' perspective, there is little-to-no systematised know-how with respect to the specific ways through which online presence and content creation can be monetised. This leads to some clumsy attempts from agencies to do this in a formal way, for instance, proposing content to influencers that displays their products in a very unsubtle way, which looks much closer to advertising than fashion and lifestyle material. Such content is defined by bloggers as 'inorganic', and undesirable for both brands and bloggers. That is the case for 'publi-post', a form of branded content created by bloggers and paid by agencies to promote specific brands. An experienced blogger who works with branding agencies describes this:

> There are people and there are agencies that have no idea how to carry out these collaborations. Then, they offer you a toothpaste so you make a post and publish it on your social media, and suddenly you realise … well, let's see, this is a 'publi-post', its advertising, it's not worth a toothpaste, and this is much more valuable. For instance, considering how many people it's reaching, and you have to start checking how much your site is worth, how much a post is worth, how much a tweet, and then you have to start learning these things, and at the beginning there are many mistakes in this regard.
>
> *(Female fashion blogger, 38 years old)*

In this context, bloggers have had to find out where and how to position themselves, by learning when to say no to deals that might be unfair to them or are inconsistent with their own brand and values, or by defining how to charge branding agencies for different kinds of services and recognising who is who when they are offered to them. The way in which products are presented also requires several decisions to be made, not only by choosing the best format for doing it (e.g. as a review, through a contest, a photo or video); how to do it (through a specific technique, text or aesthetic); but also when not to do so. Defective product experiences have been ignored by reviewers, or given to someone who can test their effects in a trial and error manner, especially in the case of beauty products. In the case of an extremely bad performance or management by agencies, bloggers might upload an unfavourable review, jeopardising their possibilities of working again with that brand. As a blogger explains:

> It happens because of the exchange for reviews. The agency gives me stuff so my audience participate in a contest, and [the brand] reaches a broader audience. Sometimes, agencies send me stuff and I don't like it … once, I got a [beauty] mask that gave me an allergy, and I told them it gave me an allergy, that I almost went to the hospital, and the guy from the agency told me to not upload it. But there are times when products really have been so bad, or the attention has been so bad that I published anyway and it's like sorry, or they get mad and don't hook up with me anymore. I'm not going to die because one brand gives me the cold shoulder or gets mad at me because I reviewed them poorly.
>
> *(Female fashion blogger, 26 years old)*

Generally speaking, brands are always looking for people who can give them the most exposure. Thus, they tend to look for already established celebrities. But brands have also started looking for credible voices in social media who will present their products seamlessly as part of their everyday lives. Some of these bloggers serve as average users, while others might vary from actual experts with credentials to "amateur experts" (Baym and Burnett, 2009). As a male fashion blogger describes it, what they can offer in terms of 'expertise' is to communicate honesty and knowledge across platforms:

> Now, what we bring to the table is a more realistic point of view, and I've talked about it personally with the agencies. Brands hire advertising agencies, and advertising agencies reach out to us so we generate advertising, clearly the brands look for TV personalities, other types, because they generate much more visibility, but brands also look for [YouTubers, Instagrammers], people who have a blog, because it's a much more realistic everyday outlook, it's like more honest. Based on what I've talked about with people from the agencies, they look for that, and that's what we can offer.
>
> *(Male fashion blogger, 32 years old)*

Despite their relationship of collaboration and mutual exchange, bloggers may perceive agencies as a threat to the validity of their work creating content. Some of the high-profile bloggers (those with bigger volumes of followers, likes, online activity and perhaps commercial deals) consider agencies as enablers of commercial relationships, but also as competitors in the field. Agencies, as intermediaries, are perceived by bloggers as agents that add little value in the process of content creation, while nevertheless taxing part of the income that bloggers could receive without intermediation. A blogger who occasionally works directly with brands explains how bloggers compete with agencies as intermediaries:

> They'll never want bloggers do (the work) better than them. They think like this … if I bring you to Adidas, I'm going to want to win too. It's common sense, this is business. Instead, if I go straight to Adidas, it's convenient for Adidas and for me, because Adidas doesn't lose money (paying an agency) and you earn more.
>
> *(Female fashion blogger, 27 years old)*

Tensions between bloggers and agencies

Problems do not arise only from competition between actors in the same field of cultural production. Bloggers also struggle with agencies to define the value of their labour, with the latter not recognising their effort in the way the former expect. In part, this is because of the nature of the work involved, which agencies perceive as a part-time activity or a hobby. Bloggers, however, see their labour as demanding work, which involves producing and uploading content, and developing and maintaining communities around it. It is worth the money and they expect to earn some from promoting the consumption of clothes, food or accessories on their online spaces. They also point at the hypocrisy in agencies treating this form of exposure as 'amateurish', when they should be dealing with it as they do with any other kind of publicity in other media. This leads to situations where the exchange between both actors—agencies and bloggers—isn't perceived as a fair deal for bloggers:

> [Brands and agencies], in the end they use your platform. If they want to use my platform and my curatorship in the content I give them … that's valuable work. Finally, keeping up a community is tons of work, and work that no one pays for. You do it because you like it, as a hobby, it's one of your interests, but if a brand wants to tell you like 'hey, may I use your platform?' I'm not going to accept them giving me a gift card of 50 thousand Chilean pesos in Dijon [a cheap local retail franchise]. Pay me what I'm worth and what my community is worth. It's the same you would pay for an ad on the radio.
>
> *(Female fashion blogger, 31 years old)*

Brands can be reluctant to give some of their creative control over their campaigns to bloggers, which results in attempts to try to reproduce a traditional marketing approach in an online environment. This is contested by bloggers, who see their own work diminished, and even their image damaged, because they would have to upload low-quality content, something that might clash with their own personal branding efforts.

As some interviewees describe it, an important part of their appeal as bloggers is precisely their distance from the companies, that they are not seen as direct representatives of the companies' goals and values. This semblance of autonomy is crucial to bloggers' practices of content creation and similar to journalists who share an orientation towards objectivity and independency as key values in reporting news and creating media content (Schudson, 2001).

However, for bloggers, it is important not be controlled by agencies, as they need creative freedom to communicate brands' values and identities. This process of negotiation between brands and agencies is described by a blogger:

> It's super important that agencies give you space to express what you are as a blogger, and not force me to fit into their things, interfering in my way of doing things. Instead, they should give me space for being myself with the brand. That's very different. In order for the blogger to have the power they have, the brand has to let bloggers be themselves, if not they lose their whole appeal.
>
> *(Female fashion blogger, 17 years old)*

Some agencies might even go as far as to present their relationship with fashion bloggers as a favour done to them, reversing their interchange, stating that bloggers are the ones benefitting by getting exposure from brands. There's no way to tell if this way of thinking is sincere or just a cost reducing strategy, but this approach, which can come off as condescending, only elicits a negative reaction from content creators. When bloggers perceive that agencies see them as the last part of a brand's value chain, they establish boundaries in terms of their involvement in campaigns. As one of them explains:

> I'm the kind of blogger that rejects lots of stuff because it seems to me absurd, like 'hey, post this', not even 'what do you think about doing this?' Lots of emails are like 'we are a company that doesn't have money' and, dude, you're McDonald's, don't tell me you've got no money and I'm obliged to post about your 'Hamburger Day'. That's the shamelessness in that you should be grateful a brand is calling you. As I told you, I rejected various things for content that has nothing to do with me, or maybe the way agencies try to do things.
>
> *(Female fashion blogger, 31 years old)*

Conclusion

This chapter has analysed how a group of fashion bloggers work together as cultural intermediaries as part of communicative value chains. In today's digital landscape, fashion bloggers and branding agencies are cultural intermediaries that mediate how brands and goods are perceived by bloggers' audiences and final consumers (Smith Maguire and Matthews, 2014; Moor, 2008; Moor, 2014). Bloggers and agencies are interesting case studies of some elements of lifestyle journalism, particularly in relation to the creation of 'branded content' as part of a contemporary media landscape. By focusing on three key moments in the establishment of their relationship, we described how different forms of knowledge and expertise merged together to create experiences around brands and products on digital platforms. They do so, first, through the connections forged between bloggers and branding agencies in order to produce and promote branded content across digital platforms. Through distinctions around the number of followers online, the ability to promote content as part of bloggers' everyday activities and the potential to incorporate, in a formal way, their work as content creators, agencies incorporate bloggers into a communicative value chain, comprised of actors (e.g. bloggers, branding consultants), technological devices (e.g. social media) and their practices.

Second, as part of communicative value chains, bloggers display their technical knowledge and thereby validate their practices as a form of labour that is subject to valuation by branding agencies. At this stage, bloggers and agencies start competing with each other. On the one hand, agencies want to control bloggers' practices of content creation; on the other hand, bloggers would prefer to work directly with brands. Thus, as a result of this competition with agencies, where bloggers—especially the more established ones—realise that their work is being treated as a form of paid advertising, they reclaim their social position as experts who work with brands to promote their qualities in a more honest way. They produce content that is related to different dimensions of their daily lives, from the mundane to the luxurious, from 'amateurish' to expert, all coexisting next to each other (Duffy and Hund, 2015). Part of their expertise relies on developing a cohesive narrative, using their lives as the raw material. This is done in a trial and error fashion, accumulating the necessary knowledge to understand the tools of each platform, the best ways to produce adequate content, understanding the desires and responses of both the brands they represent and their own audiences.

Through the content they produce, fashion bloggers present products and brands, and they use these as ways of presenting themselves. A skilled blogger is one who is able to build a strong relationship between himself and his brands in an organic way: non-forced, 'natural'. Otherwise, it might be regarded as blatant advertising, a failure to differentiate themselves enough from the brands and exert their own individuality, or in other words, to make the boundaries between the agencies, brands and everyday life disappear.

Finally, in the context of Chile's fashion media field, where fashion journalists move between celebrity journalism and a handful of work in the field of fashion, bloggers have occupied the vacant space of fashion journalism. Specifically, by presenting themselves as 'experts', promoting fashion trends to new audiences, especially younger ones, and also by functioning as intermediaries for the interests of brands and branding agencies through the type of content they create, based on authenticity and affect as its core values (Duffy, 2017). However, bloggers are also aware that, because Chilean fashion is not an industry unto itself, and everything from fashion trends to garments is 'imported', it is difficult to get remunerated for their activities.

Funding

This research has been funded by Chile's National Fund for Scientific and Technological Development (Project 11150095).

Note

1 All interviews were originally conducted in Spanish and have been translated by the authors.

References

Baym, N. K. and Burnett, R. (2009) 'Amateur experts: international fan labour in Swedish independent music', *International Journal of Cultural Studies*, 12(5), pp. 1–17.
Bourdieu, P. (1984) *Distinction: a social critique of the judgement of taste*. Boston, MA: Harvard University Press.
Bradford, J. (2015) *Fashion journalism*. London: Routledge.

Duffy, B. E. and Hund, E. (2015) '"Having it all" on social media: entrepreneurial femininity and self-branding among fashion bloggers', *Social Media + Society*, 1(2), pp. 1–11.

Duffy, B. E. (2017) *(Not) getting paid to do what you love*. New Haven: Yale University Press.

Entwistle, J. and Rocamora, A. (2006) 'The field of fashion materialized: a study of London Fashion Week', *Sociology*, 40(4), pp. 735–751.

Glaser, B. G. and Strauss, A. L. (1969) *The discovery of grounded theory: strategies for qualitative research*. New Jersey: Transaction Publishers.

Hanusch, F. (2012) 'Broadening the focus: the case for lifestyle journalism as a field of scholarly inquiry', *Journalism Practice*, 6(1), pp. 2–11. doi: 10.1080/17512786.2011.622895.

Marwick, A. (2015) 'Instafame: luxury selfies in the attention economy', *Public Culture*, 27(1(75)), pp. 137–160.

Moor, L. (2008) 'Branding consultants as cultural intermediaries', *The Sociological Review*, 56, pp. 408–428.

Moor, L. (2014) 'Branding', in Maguire J. S. and J. Matthews J. (eds) *The cultural intermediaries reader*. London: Sage, pp.77–88.

Rocamora, A. (2011) 'Personal fashion blogs: screens and mirrors in digital self portraits *Fashion Theory*, 15(4), pp. 407–424.

Rocamora, A. (2018) 'The labour of fashion blogging', in Armstrong, L. and McDowell, F. (eds) *Fashioning professionals: identity and representation at work in the creative industries*. London: Bloomsbury, pp. 65–81.

Schudson, M. (2001) 'The objectivity norm in American journalism', *Journalism* 2(2), pp. 149–170.

Smith-Maguire, J. S. and Matthews, J. (eds.) (2014) *The cultural intermediaries reader*. London: Sage.

Topping, A. (2016) 'Vogue editors accused of hypocrisy after declaring war on fashion bloggers', *The Guardian*, 29 September. Available at: https://www.theguardian.com/media/2016/sep/29/vogue-editors-declare-war-fashion-bloggers (Accessed: 10 December 2018).

Vos, T. *et al.* (2011), 'New media, old criticism: bloggers' press criticism and the journalistic field', *Journalism*, 13(7), pp. 850–868.

Zelizer, B. (2004) *Taking journalism seriously: news and the academy*. California: Sage.

8

ARE FOOD BLOGGERS A NEW KIND OF INFLUENCER?

Sidonie Naulin

Understanding contemporary lifestyle journalism involves exploring its margins and borders. Since the 2000s, food blogs have precisely occupied the margins of food journalism and have challenged its borders. Food blogs appeared at the beginning of the twenty-first century; they are personal websites on which food bloggers publish posts in reverse chronological order and can interact with their audience. Most of the posts are about recipes but they might also deal with food products, utensils, cookbooks, food events or restaurants. As Andrew Cox and Megan Blake (2011) put it: "Food blogging typically represents a complex interweaving of 'foodie' or gourmet interest in cooking, blog writing (and so Internet use) and photography" (2011, p. 4). In the 2000s, the technological context of the development of the Internet as a medium of expression, the growing popularity of food in the media and the effects of the recession with a promotion of 'do it yourself' culture with the potential to receive freebies, have contributed to the success of food blogs. The status of 'foodies' then changed from being mere recipients of the food discourse to becoming actual news producers. And even though food bloggers consider themselves as different from journalists, some of their peers, readers and food companies consider them as information providers and influencers. As such, food blogging shares similarities with lifestyle journalism, "a distinct journalistic field that primarily addresses its audiences as consumers, providing them with factual information and advice, often in entertaining ways, about goods and services they can use in their daily lives" (Hanusch, 2012, p. 2). This questions both the specificity of the journalistic work and the professional identity of journalists as a whole: who is legitimated to give advice concerning food and cooking?

Method

Many studies about food bloggers rely on content analysis or interviews with a small sample of highly visible bloggers. This chapter is based on an online survey of 621

French food bloggers and on 15 interviews. Ethnographic observations have also been conducted during two food-blogging events. Both the interviews and ethnographic observations were conducted in 2010. In March 2011, the questionnaire was distributed to 1,387 active French bloggers registered by the owners of the website *750grammes*. Their list of active food blogs was fairly exhaustive for France at this time. The objective of the survey is threefold: first, it seeks to map the French food blogosphere; second, it looks to uncover the digital and social practices of food bloggers; finally, it attempts to identify and quantify 'professionalisation'. The activity of food bloggers is compared with that of 41 French food journalists interviewed at the same time. During this period, food blogging was booming and online social networks (Facebook, Twitter, Instagram) were not extensively used by food lovers to share their passion yet. Media were starting to question the challenges that the online expression of lay people represented for professional journalism. These questions are still accurate and the results of this study about food blogging can be used to understand the current phenomena of online lifestyle news production by unqualified persons, be it on social networks or on a blog and other media platforms.

Results

A social profile close to that of food journalists

Bloggers share many characteristics with food journalists dealing with recipes and products. Similar to journalists, the vast majority of bloggers are female. While women account for 84 per cent of the contributors of *Cuisine et Vins de France*, a major French food magazine, between 2000 and 2010 they account for 94 per cent of the food blogger sample. This gender imbalance suggests that food blogs, like most food magazines, are closer to domestic cooking than to professional cooking. Studies illustrate that in France, 74 per cent of women cook daily, as opposed to 37 per cent of men (INSEE) and 63 per cent of 'foodies' are women (Dynegal, 2013); on the contrary, among professional cooks, only 25 per cent are women (FAFIH OPCA, 2011). The domestic orientation of food blogs is confirmed by the words used to depict blogs: the most frequent is 'day-to-day cooking'. Food blogs can thus be seen as promoters of a "new domesticity" (Matchar, 2013) or a "post-feminist domesticity" (Salvio, 2012) that rebrand the traditional female role into something chosen and desirable.

Like food journalists, food bloggers have attained a higher level of education than the general female population. This is surprising since there is apparently no barrier of entry for food blogging and, like lifestyle journalism, it should be considered as an activity "requiring no particular expertise" (Swick, 1997). Since cooking is not an academic discipline, this higher level of qualification may be explained by the computing and writing skills necessary to feed a blog. Food journalists often have degrees in literary disciplines because, according to them, their most important skill is writing (Naulin, 2017). Another common feature of food bloggers and food journalists is the importance of 'learning by doing'. Both claim they have significantly improved their skills in cooking and writing—and photography, for food bloggers—since the beginning of their activity in the field.

Concerning their other social characteristics, food bloggers are mainly middle-aged working women: half of them are between 30 and 44 years old and 70 per cent are in employment, even if the blog was often started during time-off: expatriation, unemployment, sabbatical, maternity leave. Their profession, social class, income and geographic location are fairly similar to that of the general female population. The latter characteristic is a noticeable difference with food journalists who are over-whelmingly located in the Paris area, where most of the newspapers' offices are situ-ated. Bloggers have features in common with culinary journalists—notably, feminisation and a relatively high-level of education—but they are also different. They blog in addition to their main professional activity and they have varied socio-demographic profiles; from teenager to retiree, from farmer to dentist, from rural to urban. The hobbyist's world does appear, then, to be less socially discriminating than the journalist's.

Food bloggers as passionate hobbyists

The research established that 78 per cent of bloggers created their blog to "share their passion". The centrality of the interactive dimension of blogging often leads scholars to analyse blogs as a means of expression that participates in the construc-tion of identities (Allard and Vandenberghe, 2003; Cardon and Delaunay-Téterel, 2006). When asked about why they blog, bloggers first state personal satisfaction (75 per cent of bloggers), then recognition from their relatives (29 per cent) and finally recognition from other bloggers (27 per cent). At first, it is often blogs' prac-tical or even utilitarian functions that are the pull factor, rather than the opportunity they offer to reach out to people and create new links. For instance, 54 per cent of bloggers say they started blogging to "keep their recipes". This is the case for a 24-year-old laboratory technician who created her blog two years ago:

> It was the desire to share my recipes, that the family could have them without giving them all the time, it was easier. And even for me, when I search for old recipes, it's easier to have them on the blog. So, I share my recipes with everyone.
>
> *(Female blogger, 24 years old)*[1]

Food blogs can thus be considered as practical personal archiving instruments, the dematerialised equivalent of the traditional family recipe book. Also, it is the very practice of blogging that leads to a gradual inclusion of amateur cooks in a community of previously unknown peers.

According to Patrice Flichy (2010),

> what distinguishes amateurs from professionals is less their lower skill than another form of engagement in social practices. Their activities do not

depend on the constraint of a job or an institution, but on their choice. They are guided by curiosity, emotion, passion, attachment to practices often shared with others.

(2010, p. 12)

Food bloggers are amateurs in the sense that they are passionate about cooking. Perhaps, surprisingly, this is not automatically the case for food journalists, according to my study of the careers of 25 food critics. Passion for cooking is far from being a prerequisite for their engagement in this activity: some of them became food journalists because they were asked to by editors or because they could not find a job in the journalistic specialty they like (Naulin, 2017). Moreover, those who define themselves as "journalists" rather than "food journalists" argue good journalism is an attitude—define by values and practices such as curiosity, investigation, fact checking—rather than a passion for a topic. This is different for food bloggers, as several elements illustrate their passion: first, food bloggers often cook extremely intensively, spending on average 2h53 on weekdays and 3h19 on weekends. These figures are significantly higher than those of the general French cooking population, which spends 1h03 on weekdays and 1h08 on weekends (INSEE). Second, they spend significant time blogging, which includes taking pictures, writing texts, answering comments and reading to get inspired. Third, they also spend significant money to feed their passion: for example, they are compulsive cookbook collectors. Half of the bloggers own more than 30 cookbooks and 13 per cent own more than 100 cookbooks; many bloggers also collect food magazines, and 83 per cent of them had read at least one culinary magazine in the two months before the survey. These figures highlight that there is a clear complementarity between digital and analogue magazines and books. Cookbooks are the most frequently cited source of inspiration for bloggers (75 per cent), while recipe websites are the fifth most frequent. Money is also spent on buying food products, kitchen, computing and photographic equipment. Having a blog encourages bloggers to test novelties and develop creativity, as a 24-year-old food blogger says:

> Yes, I cook more [since I started the blog], and different products, for example, new products that I see in other blogs. I think that it can be nice. There are plenty of products that I was not used to cooking and that I do now after I have seen them in other recipes. Basically: squash or stuff like that, [...] agar-agar, or that kind of thing.
>
> *(Female food blogger, 24 years old)*

Blogging thus seems to be a "serious leisure" activity (Stebbins, 1992) that is rewarding but time consuming and potentially costly. This hobby seems to contrast with food journalism.

A leisure activity distinct from food journalism

Food journalists are paid by organisations to produce and disseminate information about food. Unlike them, bloggers' primary concern is to share their passion with other hobbyists. On average, they receive 324 unique visitors per day and each post gets eight comments. Interactions are often the driving force behind the continuation of their activity, and there is an implicit norm that high frequency publication is required to maintain one's readership. The most frequent periodicity of publication is two to six times a week, and roughly two-thirds of the sampled food bloggers (64 per cent) publish at least once a week. Frequent posters want to maintain their high frequency and those bloggers who publish little content want to increase their publication rate. Very few bloggers (8 per cent) wish to slow their publication rate.

Bloggers themselves are a significant part of the readership. Whereas non-blogger readers are often perceived through statistics as an anonymous mass, richer interactions are established with other bloggers. Many comments come from other bloggers and cohesion is reinforced by rules of reciprocity like answering comments, visiting commentators' blogs and exchanging blog links. Food bloggers are both the principal intended readership and the main inspiration, and 69 per cent of food bloggers find recipe ideas in other blogs. It seems that the blogosphere produces both emulation like 'covers' of recipes from one blogger to another, incentives to try new products and techniques, and inducements to overcome one's personal limits in terms of creativity and technicality. These forms of exchange do not only obey Internet sociability norms, they also allow actors' work to become more visible (Dupuy-Salle, 2014). Two out of three bloggers leave comments on blogs in order to promote theirs, which is why they tend to target high traffic blogs. Dense interactions between amateurs reveal a universe that is fairly closed on itself and where this "virtual community" (Rheingold, 1993) materialises in "real life" during meetings like the Salon du Blog Culinaire in France or the International Food Blogger Conference in the U.S. Almost half of French bloggers have already met some of their peers in real life.

As they form a community of amateurs, food bloggers evolve in a separate world from that of culinary journalism. Unlike restaurant review bloggers, whose key figures are professional food critics, bloggers who publish recipes are rarely professional culinary journalists. Only 22 out of the 621 food bloggers surveyed have already worked as a food journalist, and it is the main profession of only three of them. In contrast, very few culinary journalists indicate that they have a blog. Food bloggers feel that their activity is quite distinct from that of food journalists. When asked about potentially turning it into a career, they suggest other activities—cooking teacher, food product seller, cookbook writer, private chef, brand consultant, food photographer—rather than journalism. They position themselves as media consumers rather than media producers competing with traditional media. This is the case for a 33-year-old, stay-at-home mum who was a sales director in a web services company and who created her food blog one year ago:

It remains amateur, we remain amateurs, and everyone stays in his place here. I feel very small. Well, when I see professionals, I put myself in my place. I am an amateur. We mustn't mix everything up. I am pretty much self-taught. […] I'm not trying to get anything from it: some fun, that's all. For me, it remains a hobby, a source of pleasure, and maybe in six months I will stop, I don't know. I do not want to end up chained to it.

(Female food blogger, 33 years old)

Economic returns—money, freebies or professional opportunities—are regularly presented in the media as a reason for becoming a blogger. However, it seems that the economic returns are far less of a pull factor for bloggers than the symbolic ones. Asked about the satisfaction their blog brought them, only 2 per cent of bloggers mention money, and it is the least frequently cited benefit. This low figure should not be attributed to underreporting, as only 3.5 per cent refuse to say how much money they make from their blog, and 35 per cent say that their blog offers them either money or freebies. Other economic returns are also among the least mentioned ones, where 11 per cent of bloggers indicate that the blog leads to professional opportunities and 28 per cent say that it allows them to test new products for free.

Indeed, two-thirds of bloggers do not earn either money or freebies through their blog and, among the ones who do, three quarters (73 per cent) get less than 50 euros a month. The idea of making a living out of one's blog seems to be more of a dream than a tangible reality. In France, the number of food bloggers who earn the equivalent of the minimum wage from their blog is very low. But blogs can be a trigger for income generating activities since they reveal a passion for cooking, offer contacts with professionals or act as a business card that showcases professional skills. In other words, money does not result directly from the blog but from the opportunities the blog creates. Only 9 per cent of food bloggers already work in the food sector and 83 per cent wish to remain amateurs. They consider living off their passion as a non-desirable utopia since it would turn pleasure into a constraint. A food blogger, whose blog is one year old and gathers 50 to 80 visitors a day, expresses the reasons why she prefers to remain amateur: "I think that after a while being in the kitchen every day, with professional constraints, I won't enjoy it so much. And I want it to remain a pleasure".

If food bloggers are mere hobbyists who feel very different from food journalists, why is a comparison between the two groups relevant?

Similarities to food journalists in terms of influence

From the outside, food bloggers seem to be the same kind of information producer as food journalists (Gillmor, 2006). Just like them, they write recipes, product or restaurant reviews and articles about news and events in the food industry for a wide audience. Doing so, they promote certain lifestyles and give consumers advice. This leads them to build relationships with PR professionals just like food journalists who have a "high market orientation" (Hanitzsch, 2007) and get significant volumes of information through press releases and press lunches (Naulin, 2017). Usually, two criteria are used to differentiate amateurs from professionals: the skill criterion and the remuneration criterion (Weber and Lamy, 1999). Neither of them fully differentiates food bloggers from food journalists.

Since in France the profession of journalist is 'open' and does not require a specific qualification, most food journalists do not have formal training in journalism or cooking, for that matter. Their knowledge has been learned through practice and experience. It is the same for bloggers, who, like journalists, have a high level of education and can benefit from the growing accessibility of knowledge on the Internet (Flichy, 2010). This convergence of professional and amateur skills is summarised by the neologism "pro-am" (Leadbeater and Miller, 2004). This might partly explain the proximity of the content produced: even though not all food blogs can compete with what is produced by journalists, some blogs offer relatively similar content in terms of writing quality, angle, aesthetics and reliability. It creates a competition with food journalists. All the bloggers who became food journalists or who have participated in events with food journalists express the suspicion and contempt they raised. For example, a 37-year-old food blogger who became a food journalist says:

> Bloggers who became journalists stress out food journalists because they do not consider bloggers as 'pro'. It is probably stupid, because there are people who write well. You don't need to have been to a school of journalism to be a journalist.
>
> *(Female food blogger, 37 years old)*

Historically, in France, the income criterion has been chosen to delineate the "professional jurisdiction" (Abbott, 1988) of journalists: to be recognised as a "professional journalist", a person must earn more than 50 per cent of his/her income as a journalist (CCIJP, no date). This criterion allows us to distinguish food journalists from the mass of amateur bloggers who earn nothing from their activity and do it as a hobby. Nevertheless, the existence of some bloggers seeking to earn a living from blogging means the two categories overlap somewhat, especially since most food journalists do not actually live exclusively off their journalism. That some bloggers now have business cards presenting their blog and the emergence of blogging agencies (Mäkinen, 2018) indicate that some bloggers are committed to self-promotion and making a profit.

Same relationships with the food industry

For PR professionals, food bloggers can influence readers' consumer decisions. This is why they send them information, products and money, just like they do with food journalists. However, not all bloggers are comparable to food journalists in terms of influence. Bloggers' influence is often measured by audience (Agarwal *et al.*, 2008). As in other online worlds, food bloggers' audience distribution follows a power law: 20 per cent of bloggers—those who have more than 350 unique visitors a day— attract 75 per cent of the readership (see Figure 8.1).

A multiple correspondence analysis and an ascending hierarchical classification performed on 529 French food bloggers show different profiles of food bloggers (Naulin, 2014). Only those most invested in the blogging activity and those who encounter audience and commercial success can be considered as influencers. 'Local influencers' are bloggers with high blogging intensity but limited commercial success: they seem to be well integrated within the bloggers' community but not known outside it. On the contrary, a minority (12 per cent) of 'elite bloggers' combine high blogging intensity and commercial success (more than ten hours per week spent blogging; more than two posts published per week; more than 1,000 daily visitors; more than three products tested a month; earning more than 50 euros a month, etc.). Their influence goes beyond the food blogosphere as shown by the frequent mentions of their blogs in the media. Men, highly educated people, executives, people living in big cities and those earning more than 4,000 euros per month are overrepresented in this category, which is the most likely to compete with food journalists.

More precisely, relationships with brands take different forms according to the capacity of influence given to bloggers. The most visible and widespread form of relationships between bloggers and the food industry is advertising. More than two-thirds of food blogs include ads, often (77 per cent) run by the blog-hosting platforms. Advertising is weakly correlated with the characteristics of blogs and has little impact on bloggers' activity. It generates earnings that vary according to the number of readers (e.g. 5 euros for 815 visitors per day). More direct blogger-brand

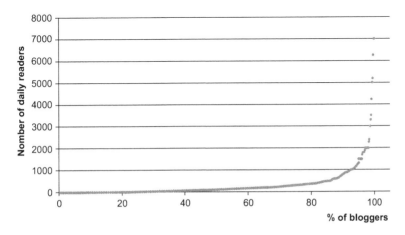

FIGURE 8.1   Audience distribution among bloggers
Source: Author

collaborations are called 'partnership'. These are highly positively correlated with readership, measured by the number of unique daily visitors. They are also positively correlated with the bloggers' investment in promoting their blog on the Internet, like having a Facebook page or publishing a newsletter. In the case of partnerships, what is visible on the blog is a message whose content is co-created, to varying degrees, by the blogger and the brand, in exchange for material or monetary reward. There are, in order of increasing earnings and blogger subordination: product-exchanges when bloggers receive freebies that they are free to review; sponsored posts when bloggers receive money for writing articles; paid service provision for long-term collaboration, participation in cooking shows, hosting events, etc. Not all bloggers are involved in this kind of brand relationship: one in two (55 per cent) has already received products to test, but only 8 per cent have already published sponsored posts. These figures indicate that brands do not only focus on the most influential bloggers, but that when their involvement goes beyond just sending freebies, they are far more selective.

Bloggers who are enthusiastic about the monetary rewards provided by their influence justify it in different ways: it allows them to test new products that they may not have turned to spontaneously or that they could not afford; external constraints or parameters stimulate their creativity; freebies improve their daily lives; and, for those who actually receive financial compensation, it covers the costs of running the blog, such as the fee they pay to the hosting platform or their purchases of filming and editing equipment. Some bloggers refuse payment, and 14 per cent systematically decline brand proposals, while 40 per cent have already refused advertising propositions. Only 15 per cent of refusals are based on moral principles; the main reasons why bloggers reject partnership proposals are the lack of interest in the product, disagreement on the conditions imposed by the brand and the fear of being perceived by readers as corrupted. A female food blogger explains that her perception of what her blog should look like leads her to refuse partnerships:

> I had proposals like: 'We will send you a 50 euros voucher to spend on our website if you put our name on your blog'... 'Okay, I'll put it on my partner page' ... 'No, we need to be on the homepage' ... 'No, I do not want it there' ... So in the end, I prefer not to have the voucher and not to put you on the homepage. It's not the image I want to give.
>
> *(Female food blogger, 34 years old)*

Consequently, food bloggers appear not to be willing to monetise their influence at all costs. For them, it is more a side product of their activity than its mere purpose.

Discussion

Partnerships are the extension, in the blogosphere, of very common practices in traditional lifestyle media. Brands can send information or freebies to journalists and they can also pay for an article to be written about their products.

'Sponsored articles' are thus a less regulated form of 'advertorials'. The existence of similar relationships between brands and food journalists, on the one hand, and brands and food bloggers, on the other, tends to prove that both food journalists and bloggers are influencers.

However, their influence is not based on the same foundations. The influence of food bloggers derives from the qualities of bloggers and blogs. Precisely because bloggers are amateurs, contrary to food journalists, they are supposed to be disinterested, free to judge and quasi neophyte. They are, therefore, perceived as independent, sincere and trustworthy by readers. Unlike the more expert trust in food journalists, trust in food bloggers is "personal" (Karpik, 2010). The characteristics of food blogs as media also explain the influence of bloggers. Interactivity and real-time reactions allow quick information flows that lead to the buzz phenomena sought by viral marketing (Mellet, 2009). A civil servant in her thirties who has had a quite successful food blog for more than three years explains that phenomenon:

> Brands contact us a lot because when bloggers talk about something, sales take off. I am the first 'victim' of it: when a blogger has spoken about something two or three times, I run to buy it. In blogs, there is a feeling, and therefore an impression that the reader is closer to the blogger than to a magazine.
>
> *(Female food blogger)*

If food bloggers have a more 'personal' influence than the 'expert' one of food journalists, there is a question about the introduction of relationships with brands that would place bloggers in a similar position to professional journalists. Not only does the possibility of financial reward pave the way for a potential professionalisation of bloggers, it also raises new questions for them. Deontology, as a form of ethics, is regularly debated in the blogosphere: what is the line between information and promotion? How to manage relationships with brands? How to express one's real opinion without upsetting PR officers? Copyright is also an issue: do you have the right to publish and earn money from a recipe that is not yours? What if a commercial website uses your photographs without your consent? Despite the existence of regulatory instruments like the Consumer Code or the French law on confidence in the digital economy, those regulations are relatively unknown and have grey areas. Unlike debates among food journalists, these ones are carried out public. In the end bloggers, like journalists, must often rely on their personal ethics, for example to accept or reject partnerships, to disclaim or not relationships with brands, etcetera, and the strategies they adopt in order to maintain relationships with the industry in the long run are very similar to those of professional journalists.

Conclusion

Though it tends to consider itself as just a community of amateurs, the food blogosphere appears to be seen as part of the regular media by food brands and readers, and sometimes even by the traditional media (Lofgren, 2013). Indeed, it broadcasts news about food-related products, events and people to a large audience. However, the properties of the media—interactivity—and the status of its speakers—amateurs—create a brand new form of influence. Web 2.0 allows the formation of a personal relationship between consumers and bloggers and it gives birth to a new form of influence situated between that of personal networks ('word of mouth') and that of experts. For food brands, the more autonomous and 'amateurish' the blogosphere is, the greater its influence, compared to that of journalists. But brand involvement in the blogosphere reduces both its economic independence and its amateurism, and challenges the sustainability of this model. The existence of a minority of around 12 per cent of food bloggers who monetise their blogs extensively and develop relationships with PR companies, similar to those of food journalists, blurs the boundaries between food blogging and food journalism. The monetisation of influence leads bloggers to face new questions about their role, responsibility and activity.

Note

1 All interviews were originally conducted in French and have been translated by the author.

References

Abbott, A. (1988) *The system of professions: an essay on the division of expert labour.* Chicago: University of Chicago Press.

Agarwal, M. *et al.* (2008) 'Identifying the influential bloggers in a community', *WSDM '08 proceedings of the 2008 international conference on web search and data mining*, Palo Alto, 11–12 February, pp. 207–218.

Allard, L. and Vandenberghe, F. (2003) 'Express yourself! Les pages perso entre légitimation technopolitique de l'individualisme expressif et authenticité réflexive peer to peer', *Réseaux*, 117, pp. 191–219.

Cardon, D. and Delaunay-Téterel, H. (2006) 'La production de soi comme technique relationnelle. Un essai de typologie des blogs par leurs publics', *Réseaux*, 138, pp. 5–71.

CCIJP (Commission de la Carte d'Identitédes Journalistes Professionnels) (no date) *Conditions d'attribution de la carte professionnelle.* Available at: http://www.ccijp.net/article-10-conditions-d-attribution-de-la-carte-professionnelle.html (Accessed: 2 January 2019).

Cox, A. and Blake, M. (2011) 'Information and food blogging as serious leisure', *Aslib Proceedings*, 63(2)(3), pp. 204–220.

Dupuy-Salle, M. (2014) 'Les cinéphiles-blogueurs amateurs face aux stratégies de capitation professionnelles: entre dépendance et indépendance', *Réseaux*, 183, pp. 65–91.

Dynegal (2013) *Dispositif d'enquête.* Available at: http://www.dynegal.org/dispositif-d-enquete (Accessed: January 31, 2019).

FAFIH OPCA (2011) *Portrait sectoriel. Hôtellerie, restauration & activités de loisirs.* Available at: https://www.foodplanet.fr/app/download/5805929813/Fafih-portrait-national-hotellerie-restauration-2011.pdf (Accessed: 31 January 2019).

Flichy, P. (2010) *Le Sacre de l'amateur. Sociologie des passions ordinaires à l'ère numérique.* Paris: Seuil.

Gillmor, D. (2006) *We the media: grassroots journalism by the people, for the people.* Sebastopol: O'Reilly.

Hanitzsch, T. (2007) 'Deconstructing journalism culture: toward a universal theory', *Communication Theory,* 17, pp. 367–385.

Hanusch, F. (2012) 'Broadening the focus: the case for lifestyle journalism as a field of scholarly inquiry', *Journalism Practice,* 6(1), pp. 2–11.

INSEE (Institut National de la Statistique et des Etudes Economiques) (no date) *Enquête Emploi du temps 2009–2010.* Available at: https://www.insee.fr (Accessed: 31 January 2019).

Karpik, L. (2010) *Valuing the unique: the economics of singularities.* Princeton: Princeton University Press.

Leadbeater, C. and Miller, P. (2004) *The pro-am revolution: how enthusiasts are changing our economy and society.* London: Demos.

Lofgren, J. (2013) 'Food blogging and food-related media convergence', *Media/Culture Journal,* 16(3). Available at: http://journal.media-culture.org.au/index.php/mcjournal/article/view/638 (Accessed: 2 January 2019).

Mäkinen, K. (2018) 'Negotiating the intimate and the professional in mom blogging', in Taylor, S. and Luckman, S. (eds.) *The new normal of working lives.* London: Palgrave Macmillan, pp. 129–146.

Matchar, E. (2013), *Homeward bound: why women are embracing the new domesticity.* New York: Simon & Schuster.

Mellet, K. (2009) 'Aux sources du marketing viral', *Réseaux,* 157–158, pp. 267–292.

Naulin, S. (2014) 'La blogosphère culinaire. Cartographie d'un espace d'évaluation amateur', *Réseaux,* 183, pp. 31–62.

Naulin, S. (2017) *Des mots à la bouche. Le journalisme gastronomique en France.* Rennes: Presses Universitaires de Rennes.

Rheingold, H. (1993). *The virtual community in cyberspace.* Reading: Addison-Wesley Publishing.

Salvio, P. (2012) 'Dishing it out. Food blogs and post-feminist domesticity', *Gastronomica: The Journal of Food and Culture,* 12(3), pp. 31–39.

Stebbins, R. (1992), *Amateurs, professionals and serious leisure.* London: McGill-Queen's University Press.

Swick, T. (1997) 'On the road without a Pulitzer', *The American Scholar,* 66(3), pp. 423–429.

Weber, F. and Lamy, Y. (1999) 'Amateurs et professionnels', *Genèses,* 36, pp. 2–5.

9

AGENTS OF CHANGE

The parallel roles of trend forecasters and lifestyle journalists as mediators and tastemakers of consumer culture

Sabrina Faramarzi

In the Introduction to *The cultural intermediaries reader*, Julian Matthews and Jennifer Smith Maguire portray intermediaries as taste makers "defining what counts as good taste and cool culture in today's marketplace", and performing "critical operations in the production and promotion of consumption, constructing legitimacy and adding value through the qualification of goods" (2014, p. 1). The authors use Bourdieu's (1984) discussion of new occupations that emerged in the 1960s, including figures such as the arts promoter, the PR practitioner and the journalist, among others, as the starting point of a lineage of critical discussions that propose the interconnection between the realms of production and consumption, and aim to establish the role of intermediaries in the production of meaning (Matthews and Smith Maguire, 2014, p. 1). This chapter follows some of the concerns of Bourdieu's seminal text in terms of defining new occupations and talking about 'taste making', while also sharing Matthews' and Smith Maguire's understanding of cultural intermediaries as market actors defined by a certain claim to expertise. That claim to expertise would be unpacked through an analysis of two contemporary occupations: the lifestyle journalist and the trend forecaster. While the former is a relatively new occupation in the history of journalism, or at least one that has become more prevalent in recent times, the latter remains a figure that is less visible than other intermediaries, as it talks to agencies and other creative actors but not directly to the public at large.

The chapter draws parallels between the two roles and discusses how they both play key functions in the mediation of taste in society and the consumption of goods. It does this by placing the trend forecaster in relation to the lifestyle journalist and to lifestyle media more broadly, while also exploring the redefinitions of each role in contemporary digital culture; this transformation also exposes the new dynamics that define the role of intermediaries, perhaps not envisioned by Bourdieu's work. Because there is little academic research into trend forecasting or lifestyle journalism, it is useful to observe this through the lens of service journalism in order to understand the dynamics of 'service' in which both actors engage. Service journalism addresses its audience as "a hybrid social subject—part citizen, part consumer, part client" (Eide and Knight, 1999, p. 525), offering both help and advice; therefore, it comes close to the roles in which both trend forecasters and lifestyle journalists engage. Also, service journalism has its origins in the "expansion and aestheticization of the commodity economy" (Eide and Knight, 1999, p. 534), the same environment from which trend forecasting stems and to which it speaks.

One key aspect of Matthews' and Smith Maguire's definition of the "cultural intermediary" is to note how they construct value by "mediating how goods (or services, practices, people) are perceived and engaged with by others (end consumers, and other market actors including other cultural intermediaries)" (2014, p. 2). They produce "discrete and concrete" engagements between goods and individuals, and also influence the production and reproduction of discourses to different stakeholders, either "downstream"—client or consumer perceptions— or "upstream", to those in elite positions (2014, p. 10). As such, the authors argue, intermediaries are involved in the production of value and desire and they are useful for thinking about the present and future intersections between production and consumption, economy and value.

Trend forecasting has, to some extent, a stake in that formulation of the future, as it gathers contemporary trends in order to present a view of the patterns and changes occurring in cultural production. However, it articulates a different link between production and consumption. Unlike lifestyle journalists, trend forecasters talk to other stakeholders instead of consumers directly, thus both playing a key part but working in parallel to one another.

As part of the primary research, I have collected trend reports from three different trend agencies and cross-analysed those with pieces of lifestyle journalism, more specifically service journalism, to show how both agents approach trend content to serve each of their audiences. By working through the case studies, I began to find key patterns and elements used by each agent to explain social and/or cultural trends in their content; in the last section of this chapter, I have included three reports and articles as examples. The selection of case studies was based on three criteria: first, that both the trend report and article were published by a reputable trend agency and publication; second, that they were authored by different writers and come from different publications and agencies, in order to reinforce that the parallels roles of lifestyle journalism and trend forecasting are based on the services they provide, not on a particular style or format; third, that they have all been published in the last five years, to emphasise the convergent timeframes found in both areas. By working through the case studies, it is possible to establish that both parties work on similar themes (although on a slightly different timeline) and look to each other for validation but, given that they have different stakeholders and talk to different audiences, are never in direct competition.

These findings are also aided by my experiences working both as a trend fore-caster and a journalist, sometimes stepping into the role of both actors simultan-eously; for instance, I have featured simultaneously as an 'expert' (trend forecaster) and writer (journalist) even for the same publication.

Cultivating knowledge: the birth of the 'coolhunter'

Given that trend forecasting is not a widely known form of content creation, it is important to understand how this activity emerged and how it has been writ-ten about. The 'coolhunter' can be regarded as a pre-Internet cultural intermedi-ary, and exists in popular literature as an equivalent of today's trend forecaster (Gladwell, 1997). It was the first documented role of a job that tracks trends, unearths 'cool' and uncovers the 'next big thing' (Higham, 2009). Although writings about the 'coolhunter' started to appear much later, it is understood that this figure was born during the 1960s and emerged when fashion changed from trends trickling down from the top (couture houses) to trends trickling up from the bottom (Gladwell, 1997).

In his article 'The coolhunt', published in 1997 by *The New Yorker* magazine, journalist Malcolm Gladwell outlines the role of the 'coolhunter' as someone who has an ability to 'see', whose perception of society is more finely attuned than that of most people. "Coolhunting is not about the articulation of a coherent philosophy of cool. It's just a collection of spontaneous observations and predictions that differ from one 'coolhunter' to the next and from one moment to the next" (Gladwell, 1997).

The 'coolhunter' can be described as a professional people-watcher who tracks new behaviours on a mass scale, and then reports those behaviours to their clients so that they can produce cultural goods that supply that demand. In a pre-digital age, it would be possible to understand the 'coolhunter' to be the analogue version of the trend forecaster.

> What they have is what everybody seems to want these days, which is a window on the world of the street. Once, when fashion trends were set by the big couture houses—when cool was trickle-down—that wasn't import-ant. But sometime in the past few decades things got turned over, and fashion became trickle-up. It's now about chase and flight-designers and retailers and the mass consumer giving chase to the elusive prey of street cool—and the rise of coolhunting as a profession shows how serious the chase has become.
>
> *(Gladwell, 1997)*

The 'coolhunter' then became firmly positioned as a cultural mediator. However, after the introduction and mass adoption of the Internet, this role started to be per-ceived differently: whereas before trends could be spotted in a more informal and analogue way, dependent on this supposed observational research and gut intuition of the 'coolhunter', that reading became more complex and difficult.

[The] consequences of the Internet's immediacy for trend forecasting have been manifold. The most notable outcome being that instead of just a few trends emerging at one time, there are now multiple trends surfacing simultaneously and permeating within each other.

(Illingworth, 2016)

However, this alleged 'elusiveness' of trends was not absent from Gladwell's account, even though he was speaking about a pre-Internet past, as illustrated by this passage: "The paradox, of course, is that the better coolhunters become at bringing the mainstream close to the cutting edge, the more elusive the cutting edge becomes" (Gladwell, 1997). The author finishes with his well-known quote: "This is the first rule of the cool: the quicker the chase, the quicker the flight" (Gladwell, 1997).

Both this 'elusiveness' and the transformations brought by the Internet might offer an explanation as to why 'coolhunting' had to develop into a more formalised role, given that the rate of change became too overwhelming to track. Taking a more critical stance, it is possible to say that the role of the 'coolhunter' has been romanticised as that of a person who was able to discover 'cool' in an era when, particularly in fashion, "trends were dictated by a small upper echelon of designers, hence why even a cursory glance at fashion history will reveal how one look tended to dominate almost an entire era of dressing" (Illingworth, 2016). It can be argued that the 'coolhunter' made the business of trends and the business of cultural production more democratic, one that responded to the real needs of people with an attitude of supplying demand rather than creating it, to help both businesses and audiences.

Trend forecasting: finding the cultural anomalies

The emergence of trend forecasting as a more formalised role and a business-to-business service industry was an attempt to standardise an already existing collective language and interpretation of trends. Even though different methods have been developed by specific trend research agencies with formalised techniques, one of the first approaches to trend forecasting came from American forecaster Faith Popcorn in 1980; she is the author who coined the term "cultural brailing" (Popcorn, 1991), making a reference to Braille, the tactile writing system used by visually impaired people. "Cultural brailing" has been described as a way to "feel the bumps in culture" (Raymond, 2010, p. 36), a tactile reference that alludes to the trend forecaster's ability to read what others are not able. Martin Raymond explains this as the capacity to be "hyper-observant and alert to newness" (2010, p. 36); the activities of trend forecasters are imagined as "all-consuming and something you must do wherever you are or whoever you are with" (Raymond, 2010, p. 36). The fact that this is conceptualised as an activity that never ceases and therefore lacks very distinctive features might explain why the trend forecaster has limited visibility as a cultural mediator. Like a covert anthropologist, the trend forecaster's ability to hide in plain sight allows for a constant alertness to signals of cultural change.

"Cultural brailing" therefore becomes a metaphor that explains the 'soft' skills of the trend forecaster—not being able to 'see' the change, but to 'feel' the bumps of the change in culture. Popcorn describes it as an ability to "touch" as much of the cultural environment as possible to be able to make sense of its "whole" (1991, p. 21–22). She goes on to explain that cultural brailing is "compensating for tunnel vision by developing a different sensitivity" (Popcorn, 1991, p. 22) but fails to describe the makeup of that sensitivity. This is an issue that has brought both scepticism and confusion to the field of trend forecasting, and that has been described as "something that gurus revealed in expensive and closely guarded reports and presentations" (Mason *et al.*, 2015, p. 10).

In their paper 'How we became curators of cool', Pernille Kok-Jensen and Els Dragt explain trend research as "the art of looking sideways" (2015), which provides another interpretation of the "sensitivity" that Popcorn discusses. But these are not the only soft skills that live under the hybrid umbrella of trend forecasting. Raymond outlines two others: "intuitive forecasting" and "network forecasting" (2010, p. 92). The first one is based on the idea that trend forecasters match linear, rational and logical thinking with lateral, non-linear and creative thinking, and also alludes to the precarious position in which trend forecasters find themselves as mediators: they are supposedly expected to be able to live in the shoes of the coolest consumers, but also to understand the commercial needs of their clients. The second one, "network forecasting", explores the way in which forecasters can use social networks to gain information, similar to what social anthropologists, and indeed journalists, do to collect information about different groups of people. It could be argued that this is an attempt to portray the field as a pseudo science, another example of the formalisation process of trend forecasting in order to cement its position and authority in a digital landscape where information is freely found.

As networks "synthesise the knowledge of the many into a single view of the future" (Raymond, 2010, p. 94), the understanding of them constitutes a highly important dimension of trend forecasting. This is commonly known as the 'Law of the Few', a concept also discussed by Malcolm Gladwell in *The tipping point* (2000). There he outlines three types of people who create trends: mavens (information specialists, those who know about an idea), connectors (those who spread that idea) and salesmen (those who sell it in a persuasive manner); through this process trends reach mainstream audiences. The author states that "the success of any kind of social epidemic is heavily dependent on the involvement of people with a particular and rare set of social gifts" (Gladwell, 2000, p. 33), because "ideas and products and messages and behaviours spread like viruses do" (Gladwell, 2000, p. 7). The 'Law of the Few' deals with those agents who supposedly spread the virus, or trends, and is the way in which Gladwell himself, a journalist, alludes to the importance of social networks to spread information.

Even a percentage has been estimated to allude to the people who take a trend from its inception to its tipping point, before it spills out into the mainstream: they make up 20 per cent of the population yet influence the other 80 per cent. This is commonly known as the 80/20 Pareto Principle, named after Italian economist and sociologist Vilfredo Pareto: "the Pareto Principle states that for many phenomena 80% of the output or consequences are produced by 20% of the input or causes" (Dunford *et al.*, 2014, p. 141). It is this 20 per cent that trend forecasters seek in networks.

This 'Law of the Few' can be further contextualised within trend maps. There are many iterations of this, including WGSN's 'wave' (WGSN, 2017) or Henrik Vejlgaard's diamond shaped trend model (Juselius, 2012). Given the previously informal role of the 'coolhunter' explained above, these trend forecasting methodologies are formalised by agencies rather than scholarly thought. However, one academic framework that could be used—and is indeed used by trend forecasters—to understand how the 'Law of the Few' is key to the development of trends is the 'Diffusion of Innovations' developed by professor Everett Rogers (2003). The curve—similar to a soft hill that curves up and later slopes down—showcases how trends and innovations move through society, what key groups they hit and in which order. Rogers also calculates this through a percentage of society: each trend starts with "innovators" who make up 2.5 per cent of the population; "early adopters" who make up 13.5 per cent; "early majority" who constitute a 34 per cent; a "late majority" who make another 34 per cent; and "laggards" who make up 16 per cent (Rogers, 2003). Rogers explains that when the diffusion curve is leaving the "early adopters" and entering the "early majority" population, this is the moment when trends hit the mainstream, or what the author calls "Critical Mass" (Rogers, 2003), similar to the "tipping point". This timeline is key for discussion of the differences between the publishing of trend reports and the publishing of lifestyle journalism pieces below.

Consumption and advice in trend forecasting and journalism

These mediations between production and consumption and the dynamics of 'trends making' are further problematised if we look at the figure of the lifestyle journalist, first in itself and then in its relation to the trend forecaster. It would be possible to characterise the lifestyle journalist as someone who addresses his/her audience primarily as 'consumers' of a number of goods, fashions, cultural products or more recently 'experiences' (Hanusch, 2012). This is not to say that journalism has been evacuated from its more traditional roles of taking power into account, investigating social issues and others, yet at least one dimension of lifestyle journalism is closely linked to consumption, which explains its particular and potentially problematic position with regards to brands and advertising.

Indeed, it is possible to trace the rise of lifestyle journalism back as far as the 1950s and 1960s, with the emergence of consumer culture, when newspapers in many developed countries began to establish dedicated sections to areas that traditionally lay outside the main focus of the first few pages, and to include beats such as travel, food and health. This coincides with the transformation and expansion of lifestyle media more broadly, even though some authors have argued that lifestyle media belongs to a longer tradition, framing it in the context of industrialised, urban capitalism, and even before that (Bell and Hollows, 2005, 2006; Lewis, 2008, 2014). Yet, even considering this longer history, it could be argued that the contemporary version of lifestyle media has been shaped and aided by the development of lifestyle journalism, which now constitutes a large proportion of different news outlets' offer. As Luca Vercelloni (2016) has discussed, from the 1950s lifestyle-oriented media such as glossy magazines started to encourage readers to move away from a culture of 'making do' and come closer to one about buying commodities, mirroring the explosion of advertising. Consumer culture became the field to display a particular kind of individual sensibility:

> Increasingly a person's position in society could be defined in terms of his or her system of predilections: people were what they consumed, and they consumed what they desired, and desired whatever fascinated and bewitched them. Taste thus became the cornerstone of the process of aestheticization of social identities.
>
> *(Vercelloni, 2016, p. 103)*

The concept of 'a lifestyle' and, with it, the figure of the lifestyle journalist, became a central aspect of this landscape, and taste—as Bourdieu explored—became synonymous with 'good taste' and 'good culture', a supreme manifestation of discernment and the reconciliation of reason and sensibility (1984).

It could be argued that the formalisation of trend forecasting through designing evidence-based methodology from its more informal role of 'coolhunter', and the formalisation of lifestyle journalism through creating a permanent space for it in weekend magazines and supplements, is not only a direct response to a commercially challenged media landscape, but also an increased need for service and advice. In the academic literature about service journalism, this has been linked to self-knowledge and care, a form of "self-government" that Martin Eide and Graham Knight (1999, p. 541) have framed in Michel Foucault's conception of pastoral power as working through guidance and leadership: "If modernity brings everyday life into being, it does so by making the practice of living problematic and resolvable through the application of diverse and changing forms of knowledge, information and advice", the authors write (1999, p. 526). In their argument, the subject of service journalism is someone who receives the help and advice of others, while also having the agency to act and make choices for themselves (Eide and Knight, 1999, p. 541).

Like lifestyle journalism, trend forecasting also takes on the role of 'advice' to provide direct guidance to its readers; in this case, it advises its own stakeholders on how to capitalise on trends. Given that there are now more trends happening at the same time (Illingworth, 2016), some authors have argued that the function of both trend forecasting and lifestyle journalism has moved from merely 'tastemaking' to 'sensemaking' by reducing complexity and offering meaning to their audiences (Neuberger, 1996). Because of this, trend forecasting practices have shifted from a product focus—e.g. blue is the colour of the season—to a sociocultural practice where less emphasis is placed on the product and more on the format, delivery or message, effectively creating 'stories' about trends.

This change is also mirrored in some aspects of service journalism and popular journalism, in which the 'why' rather than the 'what' has become the focus, therefore offering, beyond consumer suggestions, advice that becomes "strategies for research that probe the social, cultural and economic context" (Fürsich, 2012, p. 12). Examples of this can be found through the burgeoning features supplements in UK newspapers such as *T2* from *The Times* and *G2* from *The Guardian*, that regularly address social and cultural shifts and give advice to their readers, as opposed to weekend supplements that focus more on things like recipes, interviews and product lists. Given that "the relentless complexity, novelty and reflexivity of modernity make everyday life difficult" (Eide and Knight, 1999, p. 526), these publications address consumers as individuals; 'sensemaking' (explaining) rather than 'tastemaking' (telling) offers readers the opportunity to make decisions for themselves as intelligent and autonomous consumers.

A portion of contemporary lifestyle journalism is very much based on 'trends reporting', with fashion being the most obvious example of the established editor's mantra of 'one is an example, two is a coincidence, three is a trend'. Yet more complex narratives of self-government can be found in it too, while also showing a life cycle that very much mirrors that of trends described earlier in this chapter. For instance, the 'rise and fall' of clean eating and its reporting—from an apparently healthy 'non-diet diet' to the demonisation of it, sometimes by the same news providers (Wilson, 2017)—follows the cycle that goes from innovators and early adopters to the 'critical mass', before slumping down and dying away. The role of digital influencers in this movement (Mahdawi, 2016) and in food trends more broadly (Severson, 2016), constitutes an example of Gladwell's 'connectors'.

Case study: same trends, different audiences

This last section illustrates this change from product to social storytelling with the analysis of three different trends against three different reports and pieces of journalism in the UK market. These pieces are from different agency outlets and publications to show that the trend forecaster and lifestyle journalist work as parallel partners across the media landscape.

'Healthy hedonism'—Future Lab and Evening Standard

The trend coined as 'healthy hedonism' is about people consuming alcohol in a guilt-free way in order to be aligned with a new 'wellness' philosophy. This is explored through a new micro-market of the beverage industry where drinks makers and cocktail bars are finding ways to satisfy their consumers who want to be social without consuming alcohol.

This trend is gathered in the report 'alco-health' by LS:N Global and authored by Jessica Smith and Hannah Stodell (2015), the editorial arm of the London-based forecasting agency The Future Laboratory. Their report is short, direct and formulated with a boxed-out bullet point section in the introduction that defines four key takeaway points. This is aimed primarily at a business audience, who may be short on time and who want to quickly distinguish whether this trend is meaningful to them and their business practice or not. As in journalism, the report also includes a quote taken from an original interview, showcasing journalistic formats and research methods.

The article 'Are you a healthy hedonist? Why we're swapping shots for superfood cocktails' (Service, 2016), published by the *Evening Standard*, is the journalistic take on the same trend. Taking the headline alone, the clear difference is that the article is speaking directly to the reader. Unlike the passive, more formal tone that is adopted by trend reports, the author has not just written in the first person, but she is also exploring the trend through her own experience of it. However, within the article, the journalist has interviewed a trend forecaster, one who is from The Future Laboratory. This is interesting because the journalist is using a quote from the trend forecaster to justify their exploration into 'healthy hedonism', so there is a role here for the forecaster to aid the journalist. We could assume that they are both spotting the same trends; however, the article is published nearly six months after the above trend report and is also using a trend forecaster to justify that positioning.

'Mysticore'—Stylus and Grazia

'Modern mysticism'—a trend report by London-based trends agency Stylus, explores the movement of modern spirituality through new ideas around witchcraft, rituals and magic (Stylus, 2017). Like the trend report from The Future Laboratory (and the format for most trend reports today), there are boxed-out areas of the report for those readers with limited time; it is organised by subtitles and fuelled mostly by examples. It also assumes a passive voice.

The report, published in August 2017, is posterior to the article from *Grazia* magazine: 'What is Mysticore and why has it cast such a spell on us?' (Crimmens, 2016), from late 2016. It could be argued, then, that the trend was initially spotted by the journalist, rather than the trend forecaster—and indeed the journalist coined the term 'Mysticore'—but the editorial piece also references a trend report by another trend agency to justify the journalist's observation and evidence of the development of this trend. Although working across different timelines, there is an argument that, within the cycle of trends, both the journalist and the trend forecaster inform and aid the work of one another. This harmony is able to exist because they speak to different audiences and as a consequence are never in competition.

'Millennial plants' – Canvas8 and The Independent

In the report 'Why Gen Y have become obsessed with plants' by London-based insight agency Canvas8 (2018), the author explores how young people are becoming increasingly fond of houseplants and indoor gardening. In this report, we find boxed areas again, which summarise key points of the content, but the text later constructs a story that resembles a journalistic article, with references to government policy, interviews and content from published sources to construct the argument that this trend is relevant. One of those published sources is *The Independent*'s piece 'Millennials are obsessed with houseplants because they can't afford kids' (Gander, 2017), which explores the trend by introducing it through a personal story and addressing the reader directly.

In all three examples, it is possible to identify the macro trend from which they stem: the practice and ideology of 'wellness'. By Illingworth's argument (2016), not only are different trends permeating one another, they are also rapidly creating new ideas and ecosystems around these new ideas.

Conclusion

This chapter has argued that some aspects of service journalism mirror the format and guidance that trend forecasters use and that both parties aid the work of each other. Although lifestyle journalism and trend forecasting have developed in parallel trajectories and offer similar forms of 'taste making', they are not in direct competition. Also, trend forecasting is a business and therefore closely linked to commercial gains, while journalism still presents values of public service and others, alongside the financial. However, through branded content, partnerships and affiliate links, news organisations are also generating income from lifestyle content through a combination of advice and service, and therefore it is plausible to think that they would work even closer together in the near future. This change from the heralding of products to exploring social and cultural change is, this chapter has argued, the reason why the two agents hold such power. By exploring a shift from 'tastemaking' to 'sensemaking', the trend forecaster and lifestyle journalist continue to offer guidance, albeit to different audiences and to differing degrees of depth.

Trend forecasters use reports to differentiate their consulting services. Trend reports serve as content to support the business of trend forecasting, which is primarily done through client consulting services. This role is now not dissimilar to the function of lifestyle journalism, in that it is not merely to satisfy the tastes of readers who want to consume more than just news: it holds a 'soft power' to shape the character of the publication in a landscape where differentiation is key, and to influence readers in their consumer choices.

Although both the trend forecaster and lifestyle journalist are relatively new roles, further research would be necessary to assess what value they bring to their hubs—the trend agencies and publications. How do trend-led pieces of service journalism in lifestyle supplements increase sales and deepen the readerships of publications? How do trend reports serve to help their agencies gain more clients in an increasingly competitive landscape?

References

Bell, D. and Hollows, J. (2005) *Ordinary lifestyles: popular media, consumption and taste.* Maidenhead: Open University Press.

Bell, D. and Hollows, J. (2006) *Historicizing lifestyle: mediating taste, consumption and identity from the 1900s to the 1970s.* Aldershot: Ashgate.

Bourdieu, P. (1984). *Distinction: a social critique of the judgement of taste.* Cambridge: Harvard University Press.

Canvas8 (2018) 'Why Gen Y have become obsessed with plants'. London: Canvas8.

Cohen, M., Brown, H. and Vergragt, P. (eds.) (2017). *Social change and the coming of post-consumer society: theoretical advances and political implications.* Abingdon and New York: Routledge.

Crimmens, T. (2016) 'What is "Mysticore" and why has it cast such a spell on us?', *Graziadaily*, 7 October. Available at: https://graziadaily.co.uk/life/real-life/mysticore/ (Accessed: 15 December 2018).

Dunford, R. *et al.* (2014) 'The Pareto Principle', *The Plymouth Student Scientist*, 7(1), pp. 140–148.

Eide, M. and Knight, G. (1999) 'Public/private service: service journalism and the problems of everyday life', *European Journal of Communication*, 14(4), pp. 525–547.

Fürsich, E. (2012) 'Lifestyle journalism as popular journalism', *Journalism Practice*, 6(1), pp. 12–25. doi: 10.1080/17512786.2011.622894.

Gander, K. (2017) 'Millennials are obsessed with houseplants because they can't afford kids', *The Independent*, 9 September. Available at: https://www.independent.co.uk/lifestyle/millennials-houseplants-children-kids-money-families-succulent-cactus-bonsai-how-to-dying-a7937021.html (Accessed: 15 December 2018).

Gladwell, M. (1997) 'The coolhunt', *The New Yorker*, 17 March. Available at: http://www.newyorker.com/magazine/1997/03/17/the-coolhunt (Accessed: 19 July 2017).

Gladwell, M. (2000) *The tipping point.* London: Abacus.

Hanusch, F. (2012) 'Broadening the focus: the case for lifestyle journalism as a field of scholarly inquiry', *Journalism Practice*, 6(1), pp. 2–11. doi: 10.1080/17512786.2011.622895.

Higham, W. (2009) *The next big thing.* London: Kogan Page Limited.

Illingworth, G. (2016) 'How valuable is trend forecasting in the post-Internet age?', *Notjustalabel*, 7 July. Available at: https://www.notjustalabel.com/editorial/how-valuable-is-trend-forecasting-in-the-post-internet-age (Accessed: 2 May 2017).

Jordan, A. (2016) 'Healthy tipples', *LS:N Global*, 26 January. Available at: https://www.lsnglobal.com/news/article/18888/healthy-tipples (Accessed: 15 December 2018).

Juselius, P. (2012) *Exploration to trends & product development: a framework to guide trend & consumer driven concept development.* M.A. Thesis. Aalto University. Available at: https://aaltodoc.aalto.fi/bitstream/handle/123456789/3932/optika_id_151_juselius_patrick_2012.pdf?sequence=1&isAllowed=y (Accessed: 15 December 2018).

Kok-Jensen, P. and Dragt, E. (2015) 'How we became curators of cool: what the Tumblr generation can teach us about doing research'. Paris: ESOMAR. Available at: https://www.warc.com/SubscriberContent/Article/How_we_became_curators_of_cool_What_the_Tumblr_generation_can_teach_us_about_doing_research/105924 (Accessed: 2 May 2017).

Lewis, T. (2008) *Smart living: lifestyle media and popular expertise.* New York: Peter Lang.

Lewis, T. (2014) 'Lifestyle media', in Matthews, J. and Smith Maguire, J. (eds). *The cultural intermediaries reader*. London: Sage, pp. 134–144.

Mahdawi, A. (2016) 'How clean eating devoured the diet', *The Guardian*, 3 August. Available at: https://www.theguardian.com/lifeandstyle/2016/aug/03/clean-eating-diets-chrissy-teigen-juice-soulcycle (Accessed: 19 January 2019)

Mason, H. *et al.* (2015) *Trend-driven innovation*. Hoboken, NJ: Wiley.

Matthews, J. and Smith Maguire, J. (2014) *The cultural intermediaries reader*. London: Sage.

Matthews, J. (2014). 'Journalism', in Matthews, J. and Smith Maguire, J. (eds). *The cultural intermediaries reader*. London: Sage, pp. 145–155.

Neuberger, Christoph (1996) *Journalismus als Problembearbeitung. Objektivität und Relevanz in der öffentlichen Kommunikation* (Journalism as problem solving: objectivity and relevance in public communication). Konstanz: UVK-Medien.

Popcorn, F. (1991), *The Popcorn report*. New York: Harper Collins.

Raymond, M. (2010) *The trend forecaster's handbook*. London: Laurence King.

Rogers, E. (2003) *Diffusion of innovations*. New York: Free Press.

Service, K. (2016) 'Are you a healthy hedonist?', *Evening Standard*, 25 February. Available at: https://www.standard.co.uk/lifestyle/esmagazine/are-you-a-healthy-hedonist-why-were-swapping-sambuca-shots-for-superfood-cocktails-a3188351.html (Accessed: 15 December 2018).

Severson, K. (2016) 'The dark (and often dubious) art of forecasting food trends', *The New York Times*, 27 December. Available at: https://www.nytimes.com/2016/12/27/dining/food-trend-predictions.html (Accessed: 19 January 2019).

Smith Maguire, J. (2014) 'Bourdieu on cultural intermediaries', in Matthews, J. and Smith Maguire, J. (eds.) *The cultural intermediaries reader*. London: Sage, pp. 15–24.

Smith, J. and Stodell, H. (2015) 'Alco-health', *LS:N Global*, 3 August. Available at: https://www.lsnglobal.com/micro-trends/article/17964/alco-health (Accessed: 10 December 2018).

Stylus (2017) *Modern mysticism*. London: Stylus.

Vercelloni, L. (2016) *The invention of taste: a cultural account of desire, delight and disgust in fashion, food and art*. London and New York: Bloomsbury.

Wilson, B. (2017) 'Why we fell for clean eating', *The Guardian*, 11 August. Available at: https://www.theguardian.com/lifeandstyle/2017/aug/11/why-we-fell-for-clean-eating (Accessed: 19 January 2019).

WGSN Insider (2017) 'Fidget spinners: the anatomy of a trend (aka how a trend is born)', July 12. Available at: https://www.wgsn.com/blogs/the-anatomy-of-a-trend-how-a-trend-is-born/(Accessed: 15 December 2018).

PART IV

Lifestyle, consumerism and branding

10

FOOD AND JOURNALISM

Storytelling about gastronomy in newspapers from the U.S. and Spain

Francesc Fusté-Forné and Pere Masip

Food and gastronomy are part of humans' basic needs, of community life, of culture and leisure. Nowadays, the rediscovery of food and gastronomy is presented as a pleasurable and valorised lifestyle practice (Jones and Taylor, 2013, p. 97) while, at the same time, food journalism has become a growing field in contemporary media (English and Fleischman, 2017; Hughes, 2010; Kristensen and From, 2012). In a broad sense, Kimberly Wilmot Voss (2012, p. 76) points out that writing about culinary topics touches the lives, traditions and memories of people. Also, current food journalism must be understood as a form of journalism that has established an indissoluble bond between two elements: forms of lifestyle and celebrities (Jones and Taylor, 2013). During recent decades, food and gastronomy have emerged as crucial topics of cultural reporting and they have reached unprecedented media coverage. This is due to several factors: on the one hand, tourism has led to more interest in food, a preoccupation fuelled both by locals and visitors (Hall, 2016), with an increasing and widespread use of food in promoting destinations (Du Rand, Heath and Alberts, 2003; Lee and Arcodia, 2011); on the other, thanks to the popularity of celebrity chefs and big-name restaurants, the media constantly strive to discover a new chef, a new producer or new culinary attractions before anyone else (Jones and Taylor, 2013; Naulin, 2015; Ray, 2007).

The goal of this chapter is to study how gastronomy is imagined in two mainstream newspapers, how it has been discursively framed and how it has evolved over the last decade. Following Folker Hanusch's suggestions (2012), a comparative approach across countries and media systems has been adopted, analysing food-based content published by *The New York Times* in the U.S. and *El País* in Spain. The study combines a quantitative content-analysis with a qualitative approach focused on the discourse produced by both newspapers about gastronomy and food. Findings suggest that star chefs play a central role in shaping the storytelling of contemporary interest on gastronomy. Additionally, results show how food journalism is introducing new crucial content such as products, food events and gastronomic tourist destinations, following the leading role carried out by celebrity chefs. While food preparation and eating are losing their purely utilitarian function, chefs have helped to popularise the 'pleasure of eating' and the 'pleasure of food'. They have contributed towards the engagement of people with the discovery of the culinary and gastronomic aspects of food.

Food, culture and lifestyle journalism

Lifestyle studies and lifestyle research are focused on a varied number of topics. Among them, food plays a significant role that signals its growing importance within the current media landscape. As Hanusch reports:

> recent decades have seen an apparently rapid rise in media content that falls outside what many have traditionally regarded as 'good' journalism. Increasingly, it seems, newspapers, magazines, radio, television and the Internet are preoccupied with what is generally referred to as 'soft news'.
>
> *(Hanusch, 2012, p. 2).*

Lifestyle journalism fits into this 'soft news' category (Hanusch, 2012; Kristensen and From, 2012; Lonsdale, 2015). Regarding this, John Hartley argues that lifestyle journalists who produce content for 'soft' genres have been able to "extend the reach of media, who teach audiences the pleasures of staying tuned, who popularise knowledge" (2000, p. 40). This helps us to understand lifestyle journalism as popular journalism of significant public value and as a crucial part of public life (Fürsich, 2012). The development of lifestyle journalism includes areas such as food and drink (Cole, 2005; Craig, 2016; Fürsich, 2012; Hanusch, 2012), which are commonly associated with the consumption of culture and leisure. In particular, "the rise of a consumer culture in the West, in line with increased amounts of individual leisure time, has obviously led to a demand for information about how to best spend the free time" (Hanusch, 2012, p. 7). In this sense, food journalism provides evidence on what is important to people with regards to gastronomy, and "food writers have considerable power to shape perceptions of food as high quality, fashionable, and worthy of attention from high status consumer" (Johnston and Baumann, 2007, p. 165). Here, gastronomy is understood as a landmark of different territories, both a cultural and natural symbol. Gastronomy and culinary heritages define who we are, our identity, our traditions and our lifestyles. Food, cuisine and gastronomy are a significant part of the heritage of societies (Bessière, 2013; Sims, 2009). This heritage is communicated through products, dishes, ways of consumption, events and tourism. All these aspects show the social dimension of gastronomy as part of a culture and as a form of cultural expression.

At the same time, gastronomy can be regarded as a tool for communication and cultural transmission. Gastronomy, as a heritage resource, has acquired a social dimension and a powerful capacity for the expression of identity (Duffy and Ashley,

2012; Sanjuán Ballano, 2007). In this sense, gastronomy is one of the foundational elements of any culture (Fischler, 1988) and draws very close links between cuisine, identity, territory, cultural traditions and lifestyles. Cultural landscapes in general and culinary landscapes in particular, represent intangible associations between a place and its gastronomy, history and heritage, as well as its structures, social relations and ways of life (Fusté-Forné and Berno, 2016). Nete Nørgaard Kristensen and Unni From put this as follows:

> today, the coverage of food includes good advice, recipes, reviews and expressions of taste and lifestyle, and the subject is therefore approached not only as guidance to cultural and/or gastronomic products or experiences (e.g. restaurant reviews) but also, like fashion, as a representation of ways of life and a symbolic marker of taste and lifestyle.
>
> *(Kristensen and From, 2012, p. 34)*

Consequently, media play a key role in the democratisation, socialisation and enhancement of gastronomy as part of cultural and lifestyle contexts. These contexts include "the ways that people live their everyday lives, their lifestyle choices and patterns" (Craig, 2016, p. 126). Within the framework of food journalism as a discipline of increasing academic interest (Fusté-Forné, 2017; Hughes, 2010; Jones and Taylor, 2013; Naulin, 2012), food has emerged as one of the key drivers to understand the simultaneity between communication and culture. Cooking, culinary heritages and gastronomy have progressively evolved to lifestyle fields that present multiple and diverse understandings.

Method

The objective of this research is to study how legacy media discursively shapes gastronomy. In particular, in order to better understand how print, mainstream newspapers narrate food and gastronomy, a qualitative content analysis was carried out. Specifically, content analysis was applied to the U.S. edition of *The New York Times* and *El País*, Spain, during the period 2005–2015. Both outlets are considered among the most influential in their countries, have a national circulation and have long-running food sections.

Given the size of the universe of analysis (N = 8.030), a sample was selected in order to carry out the research. First, odd years were chosen within the study period; second, a sub-sample was built using the technique of the composite week (Riffe, Aust and Lacy, 1993). Therefore, two days were selected for each week, meaning a total of 104 print issues per year, per newspaper (N = 624). Hard copies of both newspapers were manually reviewed and every article dealing with food and gastronomy topics was selected and added to an ad-hoc-created database. The selected articles were published in any section of the newspaper. For the whole period, a total of 708 articles from *El País* and 1,845 from *The New York Times* were analysed, meaning a total of 2,553 pieces.

Articles were manually coded following a codebook tested and used in previous research (Fusté-Forné and Masip, 2013). The codebook has two different sections: general features and thematic categories. The first section includes general data in order to identify each article: title, author, date, newspaper, genre, section and length. The second section refers to the thematic categories. These topics were divided into three groups (production, distribution and food and society), which in turn comprised 11 sub-categories. The final version of the codebook, including these categories, was the result of a pre-test analysis applied over a sample of food-based news published by two regional Spanish newspapers. Pre-test confirmed that all the contents fitted into these 11 topics, which served to classify the compiled articles. Furthermore, categories were described in detail, including quoted examples (Fusté-Forné and Masip, 2018) that illustrate the topics and justify what to include in each of them.

As a result of the process of definition of topics, thematic categories were divided into the three main aforementioned groups (namely production, distribution and food and society). These areas, in turn, comprised a variety of 11 themes or sub-categories, as follows: first, 'production', which includes the sub-categories of 'products', 'dishes' and 'chefs'; second, 'distribution', with 'restaurants', 'food selling points' and 'activities, awards and events'; and finally 'food and society', which includes 'gastronomy and arts', 'gastronomy as social fact', 'alimentation and nutrition', 'food and tourism' and 'gastronomy and media'. While the articles may develop different topics at the same time, it was crucial to identify the central theme. Logically, there were categories which, in a particular context, were bordering others, so some articles were classified into more than one sub-category. In addition to the quantitative analysis of the sample, a qualitative approach was carried out in order to identify the discourses drawn by both newspapers around food and gastronomy.

Storytelling about gastronomy in newspapers from the U.S. and Spain

While the current study takes a primarily qualitative approach, it is interesting to observe how, from a quantitative point of view, differences are also observed between the two studied newspapers. For example, *The New York Times* has double the number of food-based news during the period of analysis (1,845), compared to 708 pieces published by *El País*. Predominant categories are shared by both newspapers—'gastronomy as a social fact', 'restaurants' and 'products and dishes'—yet different ways of approaching them are identified. Additionally, the role of star chefs is particularly relevant, as described below.

Products: between popular and haute cuisine

While products are a very common issue in both newspapers, journalists approach them in a variety of ways. While *El País* pays special attention to local products and their preparation from a celebrity chef perspective, *The New York Times* predominantly focuses on products from different parts of the world.

Accordingly, there were a wide variety of products found within *The New York Times* for the period 2005–2015. Many pieces dealt with non-American products, such as India's national snacks, Belgian endive or Spanish Ibérico ham. Also, the discourse around products often relates to new foreign trends reaching American diners. Examples of this are texts such as 'Fans sour on sweeter version of Asia's smelliest fruit' (Fuller, 2007), about the durian fruit, or the piece about 'baijiu': 'The national drink of China heads West', whose challenging aroma was "described as resembling stinky cheese, anise, pineapples, musk and gasoline" (Risen, 2015). This provides evidence that international food and cuisine play a large role in American gastronomy, which is heavily influenced by other cultures and features Asian flavours quite significantly, as it is the case with the increasing use of wasabi. Other examples of products include pumpkin flavours or the new 'juicetails', a combination of cold-pressed vegetable and fruit juices, which was combined with tequila and vodka.

Journalists also report on the development of products with regards to their increasing popularity, and especially when celebrity chefs show interest in them. For example, an article explains the growing popularity of goat meat in restaurant menus, while another discusses products such as sorghum. In an article on granola, the journalist writes that "granola is no longer the lumpy woollen sweater of the food world; all over the country, small-batch entrepreneurs see granola as a booming growth sector, while chefs view it as an elegant and wide-open canvas for culinary experimentation" (Gordinier, 2013).

Products were also reported with regards to their seasonal availability or their relevance during special periods of the year—for example, Christmas. This is illustrated in an article showcasing a typical Spanish sweet made for Christmas, called *polvorones*. The journalist writes that "factories in Estepa, Spain, produce traditional sugary confections for the holidays, giving the local economy a much-needed lift" (Minder, 2013). Other examples of interfaces between food and traditions were found in an article about salt-curing olives in Middle-Eastern Jewish tradition or about *babka* as part of a Hanukkah meal.

In *El País* products were presented in a more homogeneous way. On the one hand, it was important to acknowledge the close relationship that products have with the territory where they are produced, but they were also discussed in relation to criteria such as innovation or quality. Unlike *The New York Times, El País* shows a stronger interest in quality products and their links with chefs who use them in '*haute cuisine*'. Thus, while *The New York Times* shows products from a daily-use perspective, the Spanish newspaper offers a more elitist vision of food, which not only contrasts with *The New York Times*, but also with other Spanish media (Fusté-Forné, 2017).

With regards to the quality of products, examples of articles are frequent. Some of them linked exclusivity to price, which is why products such as cherries (e.g. 'Cherries Glamour') or wine (e.g. 'La Ermita')—from Priorat, considered the most expensive in Catalonia—were highlighted. Other examples alluded to products with protected designation of origin (PDO), such as Sidra de Asturias. Also, journalists focused on the increasing use of certain products in haute cuisine by celebrity chefs. This is the case for nougat: for instance, one article states that

> although excellence has been in the hands of anonymous people for centuries, great chefs have been added to the curiosity for nougat. New shapes (elongated, curled, square, ovoid) and breaking textures and flavours appear in the trend of 'author' nougats.
>
> *(Rivas, 2013)*[1]

Articles also highlighted celebrity chefs like Ferran Adrià or Jordi Roca. This phenomenon was observed in other traditional products, such as olives, and in relation to innovative products such as yuzu fruit.

When chefs become celebrities

As discussed above, while star chefs play a crucial role in the popularisation of gastronomy through products in *El País*, this is often from an elitist perspective. In this sense, it is common to find articles that deal simultaneously with products and chefs. Here, Ferran Adrià, considered one of the best chefs in the world, occupies a central position. For example, stories describe how, in 2011, he toured China to get a better understanding of Asian cuisine, or, in 2013, he was willing to create a laboratory to internationalise Iberian ham.

Following the footsteps of Adrià, other Spanish chefs such as Carme Ruscadella, Angel León or David Muñoz stand out in the pages of *El País*. Thanks to all these chefs, who are owners of Michelin-starred restaurants, Spanish gastronomy and, extensively, the country's image, has been strengthened and commonly related to success, innovation and modernity. It could be argued that reporting on all these names allows the enhancement of national identity through food and gastronomy. However, international chefs are also present in *El País*, usually because of their gastronomic exoticism but also due to culinary novelty. These are the cases of Japanese chef Yoshihiro Narisawa, Mexican Enrique Olvera and several Nordic cooks. Furthermore, popular chefs such as the British media star Gordon Ramsay are also found in the publication.

Given this interest in star chefs, it is not surprising that the newspaper focused its attention on two of the events that regularly mark the annual gastronomy media calendar: the Michelin star awards and the publication of 'The World's 50 Best Restaurants', produced annually by William Reed Group. While coverage of these events can be considered of interest and newsworthy, only *El País* features these stories, particularly when Spanish restaurants were ranked among the top 50 or when they were awarded a new star; for instance, when, in 2007,

El Bulli by Ferran Adrià was named as the best restaurant in the world or when, in the same year, "Spain has placed four restaurants among the top 12, more than any other country" (Capel, 2007). In 2009, the results were similar, with Ferran Adrià ranked first for the fifth time and up to four Spanish chefs among the top 10. Similar news was found in 2011 and 2013, when El Celler de Can Roca restaurant won the distinction for the best restaurant in the world for the first time. In all the cases, the success of chefs is used to reinforce national identity.

Big-name chefs are also present in *The New York Times*, but the American paper focused its attention on signature restaurants' everyday activities and openings or closings, rather than reporting on awards and celebrities themselves. Interestingly, a piece regarding the closing of El Bulli was found; the article discussed the next step that chef Ferran Adrià was going to take in the culinary world, and also mentioned other influential Spanish and Catalan celebrity chefs. The article also highlighted one of the trends observed in *El País*, stating that "the Adrià monopoly on the international press may finally be broken" (Moskin, 2011).

Popularising food beyond restaurants and home-kitchens

Food-related events were widely covered by both newspapers, including festivals, fairs, contests and professional meetings. Gastronomy is shown as something more than eating in a restaurant; it has a ludic, leisure and lifestyle component that everyone can enjoy. Therefore, journalists frequently publish news about fairs and exhibitions focusing on a variety of products: wine, beer, chocolate, oysters, macaroons and seasonal products like *calçots*. National food from different countries and regions is also present through events such as Swedish Midsummer Festival, Lucky Rice, or fairs and festivals that take place in France, the Basque Country in Spain, Flanders in Belgium or the Scandinavian countries.

Awards, contests and competitions were also common topics in articles that dealt with The Vendy Awards to proclaim the best street-food vendor in New York City, the Manhattan Cocktail Classic or the Western Regional Barista competition.

It is also interesting to observe to what extent the relationship between gastronomy and society differed in both newspapers. The American newspaper frequently focused its attention on health awareness; indeed, health was one of the key drivers of the discourse around gastronomy as a social fact. For example, a piece by Marc Santora (2005) in *The New York Times* informs how the New York City health department urged all city restaurants to stop serving food containing trans fats, as the latest step in the "battle" against them; similarly, another piece describes how Philadelphia and New York City are offering financial incentives to supermarkets to make healthy food more widely available (Pristin, 2009). The topic of health also extended to celebrities: for example, an article in 2007 focused on Prince Charles as the owner of an organic farm in

Gloucestershire, England; another one, titled 'A new alliance in the fight against childhood obesity' (Severson, 2007) reported that Bill Clinton appeared on Rachel Ray's television and cooking show in order to promote programmes to fight childhood obesity. A similar connection between food, government and public policy is established in the article 'Michelle Obama's agenda includes healthful eating' (Swarns, 2009). Other news also focused on the White House, now concerning the appointments of chefs; again, a special interest on healthy and local food was seen as essential.

On the contrary, the relationship between food and society in *El País* is articulated through the links between food and tourism. Food and tourism appeared as a growing phenomenon for the enjoyment of gastronomy, related to products—such as wine, cheese or beer—and events and routes, which became important landmarks for different tourist destinations. Both at national and international levels, cities and regions were highlighted: examples of the former include the Ribera del Duero, one of the most relevant wine production areas in Spain, and Asturias for its production of cider; as sites of the latter, *El País* cites Brussels, Edinburgh, Washington and Boston as examples of culinary destinations.

Discussion and conclusion

Gastronomy-based journalism relies on understanding food as a source of knowledge and pleasure (Duffy and Ashley, 2012; Lonsdale, 2015). In particular, the interest on food journalism is founded on "both the sensory pleasures associated with the consumption of food and the pleasures associated with the knowledge of the production and preparation of that food" (Craig, 2016, p. 128). In this sense, Steve Jones and Ben Taylor (2013) affirm that gastronomy today is an issue of constant fascination for different media and, consequently, for their audiences. Gastronomy is a driving force capable of setting social trends and ways of life. Thus, media in general and newspapers in particular offer a pathway for the transfer of gastronomic knowledge to society, and fulfil a key role as agents of democratisation and popularisation of food through products, events, leisure and tourism. At the same time, gastronomy is a form of narration, whose study and understanding could be considered as an inheritance that reproduces the identity of a food culture (Counihan and Van Esterik, 1997; Duffy and Ashley, 2012; Jones and Taylor, 2001; Pujol, 2009; Song, 2016) in times of fast-changing contexts.

This chapter reflects contemporary trends in food writing and contributes to the understanding of the cultural and social role of food and gastronomy. Food has moved into a much broader social event that goes beyond family reunions and regular meals. Food and gastronomy are nowadays a fundamental part of people's leisure and lifestyles. It is important to acknowledge here that this socialisation of gastronomy did not slow down with the great economic crisis that has affected the world since 2008, which is reinforced by a journalistic message that continues to cover gastronomic issues. Here, it is also important to understand the crucial amplifying role played by television and social media. They are not in the centre of this chapter, but their role within the popularisation of gastronomy is a topic that might require further research and attention.

While the topics studied are presented in both newspapers in a similar way, the narratives that they construct present significant differences. Results reveal that *El País* often focuses on showing an elitist image of gastronomy, through high-end products or top-quality restaurants, which is an interesting fact given the context of the critical economic crisis mentioned above. Star chefs are included within the storytelling permanently, not only because of their signature restaurants: Spanish media also use them to narrate and promote a whole world of gastronomy. They are no longer recognised as chefs, but as artists, chemists, creators, designers and artisans; as brands that sell products, events, places and identity. In consequence, they allow audiences to incorporate food as an identity marker, as part of the culture and, importantly, as a lifestyle practice.

The elitist nature that often impregnates the gastronomic discourse of *El País* does not prevent it from being drawn to more popular food events, such as fairs and gastronomic festivals. People want to receive advice on what and how to experience gastronomic products, celebrations or tourist spots. Only within this context is it possible to understand the increasing motivation for food tourism, specialised and niche products, or phenomena such as slow food, among others. While linkages between food, heritage and tourism have been largely studied within the literature (see Bessière, 2013; Sims, 2009; Smith, 2015; Timothy, 2016), this chapter may lead to further investigations of them in relation to communication, media or lifestyle studies.

Food journalism practices in *El País* fit well within classic definitions of lifestyle journalism, with an evident market-driven strategy (Hanusch, 2017). In an interesting way, however, *El País* tends to avoid the review function attached to lifestyle journalism, favouring other roles such as giving advice or commercialisation. News on food and gastronomy were increasingly based on the description of products, places and restaurants, often elitists, owned by celebrity chefs. Thus, gastronomic contents have a clear aspirational component.

In *El País*, the use of gastronomy is also observed to offer a certain vision of national identity, through products, destinations or their protagonists. In this sense, chefs play a critical role, which is clearly linked to a sense of Spanish branding. The spread of Spanish national image through food-related media content is not new in Spain. For example, Àlvar Peris (2015) obtained similar results in his analysis of Master Chef reality show; at an international level, Andrew Duffy and Yang Yuhong Ashley (2012) also found a relationship between how food is represented in Singapore media and the promotion of national identity. Hence, food is used in certain contexts to create a sense of nation building. In this case, journalism promotes the identification with a collective identity based on food and gastronomy.

In the case of *The New York Times*, gastronomy is shown as a social event that includes a wide range of approaches and is explained from an international myriad. Narratives about eating, food and gastronomy in the paper are closer to Elfriede Fürsich's ideas about how "food journalism can also be examined for its discourse on global culture with an interrogation of concepts such as authentic, exotic or hybrid" (2012, pp. 16–17). In the American newspaper, there is a dialogue between novelty and tradition through restaurants, products or events. Consistently, narratives are found to be much more diverse and move beyond celebrity chefs themselves. While chefs form part of the newspaper's coverage, they are included within a broader perspective, which also responds to the diverse and global interests of the news provider's audience. Within the understanding of food as a critical communicative and media issue, journalistic practices in a lifestyle context show that narratives about food are not limited to a simple approach to products or dishes, or even events and tourism. Thus, they refer to a series of different topics that are strongly attached to the broader social and cultural context of a particular place.

Funding

This research was made possible thanks to the financial support of Aristos Campus Mundus 2015 (ACM 2015)—Campus of International Excellence, which allowed the first author to carry out a research stay at Fordham University, New York. It also forms part of the project funded by the Ministry of Economy and Competitiveness (Spain), reference: CSO2015-64955-C4-1-R (MINECO/FEDER).

Note

1   Quotations originally in Spanish have been translated by the authors.

References

Bessière, J. (2013) '"Heritagisation", a challenge for tourism promotion and regional development: An example of food heritage', *Journal of Heritage Tourism*, 8(2–3), pp. 1–18.

Capel, J. C. (2007) 'Estrellas en el firmamento culinario', *El País*, 28 April, p. 17.

Cole, P. (2005) 'The structure of the print industry', in Keeble R. (ed.) *Print journalism: a critical introduction*. Abingdon: Routledge, pp. 21–38.

Counihan, C. and Van Esterik, P. (1997) 'Introduction', in Counihan, C. and Van Esterik, P. (eds) *Food and culture: a reader*. New York: Routledge, pp. 1–8.

Craig, G. (2016) 'Political participation and pleasure in green lifestyle journalism', *Environmental Communication*, 10(1), pp. 122–141.

Du Rand, G. E., Heath, E. and Alberts, N. (2003) 'The role of local and regional food in destination marketing', *Journal of Travel and Tourism Marketing*, 14(3–4), pp. 97–112.

Duffy, A. and Ashley, Y. Y. (2012) 'Bread and circuses: food meets politics in the Singapore media', *Journalism Practice*, 6(1), pp. 59–74.

English, P. and Fleischman, D. (2017) 'Food for thought in restaurant reviews', *Journalism Practice*. doi: 10.1080/17512786.2017.1397530.

Fischler, C. (1988) 'Food, self and identity', *Social Science Information*, 27(2), pp. 275–292.

Fuller, T. (2007) 'Fans sour on sweeter version of Asia's smelliest fruit', *The New York Times*, 8 April, p. A3.

Fürsich, E. (2012) 'Lifestyle journalism as popular journalism', *Journalism Practice*, 6(1), pp. 12–25.

Fusté-Forné, F. (2017) *Food journalism: building the discourse on the popularisation of gastronomy in the twenty-first century*. Barcelona: Universitat Ramon Llull.

Fusté-Forné, F. and Berno, T. (2016) 'Food tourism in New Zealand: Canterbury's foodscapes', *Journal of Gastronomy and Tourism*, 2, pp. 71–86.

Fusté-Forné, F. and Masip, P. (2013) 'El periodisme especialitzat i futur del periodisme: anàlisi de la columna gastronómica', in Zilles, K., Cuenca J. and Rom, J. (eds) *Breaking the media value chain*. Barcelona: Universitat Ramon Llull, pp. 127–134.

Fusté-Forné, F. and Masip, P. (2018) 'Food in journalistic narratives: a methodological design for the study of food-based contents in daily newspapers', *International Journal of Gastronomy and Food Science*, 14, pp. 14–19.

Gordinier, J. (2013) 'Embracing the crunch (wild oats)', *The New York Times*, 20 February, p. D1.

Hall, C. M. (2016) 'Heirloom products in heritage places: farmers markets, local food, and food diversity', in Timothy D. (ed.) *Heritage cuisines: traditions, identities and tourism*. Abingdon: Routledge, pp. 88–103.

Hanusch, F. (2012) 'Broadening the focus', *Journalism Practice*, 6(1), pp. 2–11.

Hanusch, F. (2017) 'Journalistic roles and everyday life: an empirical account of lifestyle journalists' professional views', *Journalism Studies*, doi: 10.1080/1461670X.2017.1370977.

Hartley, J. (2000) 'Communicative democracy in a redactional society: the future of journalism studies', *Journalism*, 1(1), pp. 39–48.

Hughes, K. (2010) 'Food writing moves from kitchen to bookshelf', *Guardian Review*, 19 June, pp. 2–4.

Johnston, J. and Baumann, S. (2007) 'Democracy versus distinction: a study of omnivorousness in gourmet food writing', *American Journal of Sociology*, 113(1), pp. 165–204.

Jones, S. and Taylor, B. (2001) 'Food writing and food cultures: the case of Elizabeth David and Jane Grigson', *European Journal of Cultural Studies*, 4(2), pp. 171–188.

Jones, S. and Taylor, B. (2013) 'Food journalism', in Turner, B. and Orange, R. (eds.), *Specialist journalism*. New York: Routledge, pp. 96–106.

Kristensen, N. N. and From, U. (2012) 'Lifestyle journalism: blurring boundaries', *Journalism Practice*, 6(1), pp. 26–41.

Lee, I. and Arcodia, C. (2011) 'The role of regional food festivals for destination branding', *International Journal of Tourism Research*, 13, pp. 355–367.

Lonsdale, S. (2015) '"Roast seagull and other quaint Bird Dishes": the development of features and "lifestyle" journalism in British newspapers during the First World War', *Journalism Studies*, 16(6), pp. 800–815. doi: 10.1080/1461670X.2014.950474.

Minder, R. (2013) 'Sweets made only for Christmas are Spanish town's gift to itself', *The New York Times*, 24 December, p. E9.

Moskin, J. (2011) 'Spain's next wave in food (after El Bulli era, Spain looks forward)', *The New York Times*, 15 June, p. D1.

Naulin, S. (2012) *Le journalisme gastronomique. Sociologie d'un dispositif de médiation marchande*. Paris: Paris 4.

Naulin, S. (2015) 'Se faire un nom. Les ressorts de la singularisation des critiques gastronomiques', *Sociologie du Travail*, 57(3), pp. 322–343.

Peris, A. (2015) 'Els programes televisius de cuina i la identitat nacional. El cas de MasterChef', *Comunicació*, 32(2), pp. 29–46.

Pristin, T. (2009) 'Fresher food, with some help', *The New York Times*, 17 June, p. B6.

Pujol, A. (2009) 'Cosmopolitan taste: the morphing of the new Catalan cuisine, *Food, Culture and Society*, 12(4), pp. 437–455.

Ray, K. (2007) 'Domesticating cuisine: food and aesthetics on American television', *Gastronomica*, 7(1), pp. 50–63.

Riffe, D., Aust, C. F. and Lacy, S. R. (1993) 'The effectiveness of random, consecutive day and constructed week samplings in newspaper content analysis', *Journalism Quarterly*, 70, pp. 133–139.

Risen, C. (2015) 'The national drink of China heads West', *The New York Times*, 30 December, p. D4.

Rivas, R. (2013) 'El turrón de autor muerde mercado', *El País*, 3 December, p. 44.

Sanjuán Ballano, B. (2007) 'Información=Cultura. Mapas patrimoniales para ir de los medios a las mediaciones', *PH Cuadernos – Patrimonio Cultural y Medios de Comunicación*, 21, pp. 30–43.

Santora, M. (2005) 'Hold the trans fats, New York urges its restaurants', *The New York Times*, 11 August, p. A1.

Severson, K. (2007). 'A new alliance in the fight against childhood obesity', *The New York Times*, 25 April, p. F10.

Sims, R. (2009) 'Food, place and authenticity: local food and the sustainable tourism experience', *Journal of Sustainable Tourism*, 17(3), pp. 321–336.

Smith, S. (2015) 'A sense of place: place, culture and tourism', *Tourism Recreation Research*, 40(2), pp. 220–233.

Song, H. (2016) 'A Korean mother's cooking notes: maintaining South Korean cooking and ideals of housewives in global influences', *International Journal of Communication*, 10, pp. 1428–1445.

Swarns, R. L. (2009) 'Michelle Obama's agenda includes healthful eating', *The New York Times*, 11 March, p. D1.

Timothy, D. (2016) *Heritage cuisines: traditions, identities and tourism*. Abingdon: Routledge.

Voss, K. W. (2012) 'Food journalism or culinary anthropology? Re-evaluating soft news and the influence of Jeanne Voltz's food section in *The Los Angeles Times*', *American Journalism*, 29(2), pp. 66–91.

11

TRAVEL JOURNALISM AND THE SHARING ECONOMY

Airbnbmag and sourcing

Bryan Pirolli

Recent research on travel journalism focuses largely on new practices and social media (Duffy, 2017; Pirolli, 2018). This chapter pushes further to look at how the changing face of tourism—marked in part by the emerging sharing economy—offers new challenges and new opportunities for travel journalists, a category firmly implanted under the umbrella of lifestyle journalism. As house-sharing website Airbnb becomes a major player in the tourism industry, its segue into the media world with a printed magazine opens up new discussions about how travel journalists mediate travel between industry actors and consumers.

Before discussing Airbnb's magazine, it's necessary to summarise a conceptual framework for its evolution. Only recently, in the early twenty-first century, did the idea of a digital sharing economy develop, a concept based on individuals' ability to rent or sell unused items or services easily through online platforms (Guttentag, 2015). The term defines a type of exchange where there is not transfer of possessions, but instead a direct peer-to-peer exchange (Hamari, Sjöklint and Ukkonen, 2016; Taeihagh, 2017). Apartment sharing services, as alternatives to the traditional hotels, clearly illustrate this phenomenon. Online house-sharing platforms like Couchsurfing and, more importantly, Airbnb, have mainstreamed sharing economy practices in the tourism industry. By allowing homeowners to rent rooms or whole homes to travellers, the website has created a new commercial market, in direct competition with the established hotel industry. Research has attempted to study the impact of Airbnb on the hotel industry, showing that it can negatively affect segments of hotels, particularly lower-end properties (Zervas, Proserpio and Byers, 2017).

Some authors suggest that sharing economy models developed following the 2008 recession, as well as more environmental consciousness surrounding sustainability (Cohen and Kietzmann, 2014). Others point to a desire to humanise otherwise cold, faceless marketplaces (Schor and Fitzmaurice, 2015). Araz Taeihagh

(2017) summarises key features of the sharing economy, noting that it is disruptive; it involves the transactions of goods, services or resources; it relies on the Internet; it focuses on consumer markets through crowd-based online services and it engages with temporary ownership. The author creates links and distinctions between the sharing economy and the process of crowdsourcing, both of which function on a site like Airbnb, which includes reviews by users.

Airbnb, however, in 2017, disrupted even further, this time in the realm of travel journalism, as it segued into print media with *Airbnbmag*. The first two issues feature many sources, from Airbnb hosts and guests to other individuals not related directly to the company. It departs from branded travel publications like *easyJet Traveller* or other in-flight magazines because *Airbnbmag* is available to the general public, published by media company Hearst. Therefore, this magazine is a unique example of the sharing economy crossing over into mainstream journalism, bringing the virtual world to the printed press and further challenging professional travel journalism.

While *Airbnbmag* raises many questions about authority, independence and commercialisation of travel media, it also offers a chance to re-evaluate professional practice for travel journalists. This chapter takes a look specifically at the idea of sourcing in this publication. While it is expected that the magazine would be self-serving, promoting Airbnb's various endeavours, does the magazine offer anything beyond simple advertising? By understanding who the journalists interview and rely on for their stories, it becomes clearer how the sharing economy offers new opportunities for journalists that could be explored beyond branded publications. *Airbnbmag* takes user reviews from the virtual to print, allowing editors to curate them journalistically (Thorsen, 2013; Bakker, 2014). How does the idea of sourcing change in travel journalism as the sharing economy introduces new actors? To examine this niche, yet emerging field of study, this chapter addresses three research questions:

RQ1: Do all sources in *Airbnbmag* come from the Airbnb community?
RQ2: Do journalists indicate clearly when a source is connected to Airbnb?
RQ3: Does *Airbnbmag* provide content beyond its own brand interests?

Background/theory

Brand and consumer journalism

Before exploring how the sharing economy is intersecting with journalism, it is important to understand how *Airbnbmag* continues the tradition of brand journalism. Andy Bull (2013) detailed strategies for brand journalism, which he labels a hybrid of traditional journalism, marketing and public relations. Brand magazines are not novel; even the energy beverage Red Bull has a magazine, *The Red Bulletin*, focused on lifestyle issues important to its consumers. In the travel industry, airlines offer their own in-flight magazines, like *easyJet Traveller* and *N* by Norwegian airlines.

One rare study on in-flight magazines reveals how these publications reinforce certain stereotypes about consumption and power, appealing to elite travellers (Small, Harris and Wilson, 2008). The authors sum up the motivation of these magazines, writing, "Airline marketers strive to communicate their values through branding to secure customer loyalty to build market share, repeat business and profitability" (Small, Harris and Wilson, 2008, p. 20).

While studies on newer and successful branded publications remains elusive, the journalism behind it remains a topic of debate. Thomas Hanitzsch and Tim Vos (2018) suggest that individuals are flooded with options that they can choose from more easily than ever, especially with digital marketplaces. This complicates the task of creating identity as a consumer. For example, it's easier than ever to travel with online booking sites demystifying much of an industry that once required specialised knowledge. Today, however, the identity of a 'traveller' is not enough—people need to further distinguish themselves, and aligning with a certain brand or publication can assist. The researchers write: "This is where they need orientation for the management of self and everyday life, and for developing as sense of identification and belonging" (Hanitzsch and Vos, 2018, p. 158). *Airbnbmag* also illustrates elements of consumer journalism, like providing judgements of taste (Fürsich, 2012). Researchers point to seven ideal-typical roles of journalists in the domain of everyday life and some, including the 'marketer', the 'service provider', the 'connector' and the 'inspirator' all seem to correspond to travel journalists (Hanitzsch and Vos, 2018).

Something to note for this study, however, is the accessibility of branded magazines. Many branded travel magazines do not often make it to newsstands. Like in-flight magazines, *Airbnbmag* was designed for Airbnb hosts to display in their properties, but unlike its predecessors, it is also available for purchase to wider audiences—on sale through subscriptions, for example. Essentially, it is a marketing tool that goes beyond the limits of its website, reaching new customers through traditional means. At the same time, it opens up a new readership in order to attract advertisers to its pages.

Sharing economy: beyond reviews

Sharing economy marketplaces often rely on reviews by previous users to help future consumers make decisions, as discussed in one study on inherent bias in Airbnb reviews (Fradkin *et al.*, 2015). On Airbnb, for example, past guests are invited to leave reviews for a host, ensuring a closed reviewing system that is available for public consumption. These reviews, and the aggregate ratings that they provide, function much as a consumer journalist would. An individual will test a product and then write a supposedly honest review. While trust is always dubious in online communities, Airbnb reviews can only be written by someone who has actually booked. Such a system diverges from crowdsourcing sites such as TripAdvisor where anyone can review anything without actually experiencing it.

What *Airbnbmag* does that other consumer or branded publications have not yet done is to create and curate a unique type of content. Like Uber's *Momentum*, it is rooted in an online community, but *Airbnbmag* can also appeal to those beyond the community. Like *easyJet Traveller*, the magazine provides useful and engaging content for travellers, but again, breaks beyond the plane cabin and lands more globally—thanks, in part, to its partnership with Hearst.

Such crossover between websites and printed media are not commonplace. Rare examples exist, like the French website Doctissimo, which launched a magazine in 2017. Instead of travel advice and bookings, this magazine focuses on health issues. The original website functions as a forum for individuals to share symptoms and seek advice, in line with many of the lifestyle principles outlined by Folker Hanusch (2013). A major difference is that Doctissimo is not rooted in a sharing economy. *Airbnbmag*, therefore, is a fairly unique example of a magazine printed by a major publishing house in tandem with an online travel company.

What possible impacts could this have on the journalism produced within its pages—if we can call it journalism at all? Travel journalism's definition revolves around a few key points, according to Hanusch and Elfriede Fürsich (2014): it requires factual accounts, critical perspectives, an entertainment quality, treatment of audiences as consumers, ethical considerations and certain economic constraints in its production. A careful reading of *Airbnbmag* reveals all of these elements in some capacity. The two arguably most important elements in distinguishing travel journalism from other content are the ethics and economic constraints inherent to each story. While the economic constraints are arguably less worrisome when a lucrative company like Airbnb is commissioning the stories, the question of ethics remains omnipresent. How much are these stories simply gilding the lily of the company? Are they perhaps providing something more credible?

One way to assess the credibility of a news item—even in a lifestyle context—is through the sources used by journalists. The practice of contacting and quoting sources contributes to the idea objectively, a value made more complex due to emerging technologies (Deuze, 2005). Sourcing further leads to notions of credibility, central to journalists' ethical codes, and thus important to scrutinise even in a lifestyle or travel context (Franklin and Carlson, 2010, p 19).

Sources and journalism

While much of journalism seems to be in constant flux, some researchers suggest that certain features remain the same, such as a reliance on elite sources and enduring story structures (Carlson and Lewis, 2018). Academic research on journalism and sources tends to focus on the privileged relationships between the media and government officials, as discussed in prior studies (e.g. Berkowitz and Beach, 1993). Bob Franklin and Matt Carson write that "news sources not only provide details about a situation, but, more importantly, ascribe meaning to the events of the world" (2010, p. 9). More recently,

Daniel A. Berkowitz asks whether journalists or sources shape the news (2009, p 102). The relationship between both, he suggests, involves "the ability to shape ongoing meanings in a culture" (Berkowitz, 2009, p. 102). He lays out the framework for why sourcing from other individuals constitutes part of a journalist's ideology, concluding that both sides are taking a risk in depending on the other (Berkowitz, 2009, p 103). He also describes the 'routinisation' of sourcing: how getting information from regular sources can become difficult, while other organisational constraints may prevent the sharing of details needed for a story.

In a lifestyle context—particularly in travel—these frameworks don't apply quite as solidly. Hanitzsch and Vos suggest that journalism roles are too focused on Western democracy to account for wider interpretations, like those in non-Western contexts or those beyond political news (2018). Stepping back from these frameworks, then, allows us to re-evaluate specific contexts, to view them through a specific lens. As Hanusch and Fürsich explain, "most travel journalism considers audiences unashamedly as consumers, rather than citizens, even though that does mean some travel journalists do not also try to be critical in their reporting" (2014, p 10). Therefore, further research might focus on how travel journalism relies on sources, especially with the proliferation of online voices available to professionals.

In a travel context, at least historically, many of these routines that Berkowitz describes existed in one form or another. Offices of tourism, destination marketers, hotel owners and other PR factions have been sources for travel journalists, as well as providing them oftentimes with the experiences necessary to write their stories. Press trips and free hotel stays are standard examples of how travel journalists get their information as part of the privileged journalist-source relationship (Pirolli, 2018). The struggle, however, was less about power in shaping public opinion, as Berkowitz discussed, and more about independence in providing accurate, critical reviews without disrupting the source relationship. Travel journalists walk a fine line between advertising and editorial content, a main criticism that can be levied against the profession. On one end, they cannot always travel without the help of a tourism board or free restaurant experience; on the other end, they need to write critically and accurately without simply praising or recommending something at face value. Codes of ethics among journalists in the U.S. and Finland, according to one study, rarely deal directly with sponsored content, failing to separate editorial and commercial content clearly (Ikonen, Luoma-aho and Bowen, 2017). In a branded magazine like *Airbnbmag*, where all of the content is technically commercially oriented, research could further explore whether such divisions affect how the content impacts tourists.

Social media and sourcing

Social media has further disrupted these routines, whereby journalists can more easily source from a broader pool of individuals, such as customers who frequented a hotel or restaurant, someone who had a bad experience and is willing to discuss it or someone who may otherwise be off-the-radar of the journalist's usual networks. Researchers have explored how social media functions as a source, including Facebook and Twitter. One study on Belgian newspapers revealed that social media sources are commonplace, with journalists regularly monitoring various networks (Paulussen and Harder, 2014). Farida Vis examined the role of Twitter as a tool during the 2011 London riots (2013). She concluded that the tool was, indeed, a positive addition to journalists' routines and underscored the need to study these emerging, non-traditional practices.

Marcel Broersma and Todd Graham (2013) explore Twitter use's wide-ranging implications in British and Dutch publications. One result of their research suggests that Twitter is disrupting the once-privileged relationship between journalists and elite sources. They write:

> There is a loss of exclusivity because of the open nature of social media but reporters aggregate and select utterances that are still news to readers who do not follow Twitter. In other words, in a world where information is omnipresent, journalism has to redefine its relevance. Newspapers can make a difference in contextualizing tweets.
>
> *(Broersma and Graham, 2013, p. 461)*

While these studies, and others like them, discuss more hard news reporting—politics, breaking news, civic issues—there is no reason why the practices they are identifying cannot transpose to lifestyle media. Facebook and Twitter are two of the most prevalent networks studied, but social media exists well beyond these networks. In discussing Airbnb, the website is essentially one large social network, whereby users interact and leave commentary, both as clients of the service and hosts of homes or experiences. Travel journalists, therefore, can consider Airbnb a source just like any other social media outlet. Travel journalism is inherently linked to economic transactions on some level, so there is little argument to deny Airbnb hosts and clients as credible sources. *Airbnbmag*, essentially, is tapping into the vast pool of expertise and voices that Airbnb has cultivated. Yet, again, Airbnb is much more a marketplace than a true sharing economy at this point (Lessig, 2009). Still, looking at how the branded magazine uses sources reveals effective strategies that travel journalists more generally may be able to adopt, while also demonstrating how *Airbnbmag* walks a line between editorial and advertorial content.

Methods

To answer the research questions stated above, I used a simple content analysis of the sources quoted in the first three issues of *Airbnbmag* printed in 2017 and 2018. Because of the relatively small sample of content and the lack of any real comparison that could be made with another publication, this analysis was just a first step towards looking at this publication's model. Future study may consider comparing various branded magazines to understand what kinds of sources they use, but a lack of publications emanating from the sharing economy make more in-depth comparative studies difficult at present. For the moment, it is worthwhile to understand how commercially self-serving *Airbnbmag* is, or if there is some wider potential inherent in its model that journalists might discover.

It is also important to note that this magazine is as precarious as it is new—no set production-schedule seems to exist and little information is available to subscribers about how often editions will arrive. Subscription notices in the magazine advertise six issues available to clients, but with no mention of their frequency. There is a strong possibility that the magazine may not survive, similarly to the company's attempt at a lifestyle publication, *Pineapple*, which folded after one issue in 2014. Such concerns, however, should neither devalue current research nor discourage future endeavours. As Matt Carlson and Seth Lewis (2018) suggest, studying failures in journalism is arguably as important as studying successes, and *Airbnbmag* may fall into either of these categories by the time this chapter is published.

To this end, I went through the first three issues from 2017 and 2018 and noted the sources inherent in every feature story, spread or list who are identifiable by name. While initially interested in multiple categories, it became clear that there were really only two types of sources throughout the story: local experts not affiliated with Airbnb, and Airbnb employees or hosts of experiences and rentals. There were no voices from official tourism boards or other businesses, those whom we may consider elite sources. After categorising the sources, I was able to understand the breakdown of the two categories. A further content analysis into these sources reveals more specifically how the journalists used these two types of sources, revealing to what extent *Airbnbmag* provides both self-serving branded content and more traditional, non-branded stories.

Results

The results of this initial study revealed that the journalists and editors of *Airbnbmag* rely on sources from within the Airbnb community but also from outside it. In total, there were 195 attributed quotes or statements throughout the three issues. These included in-text quotations, interviews, and commentary. The breakdown of the two issues is as follows:

32 sources in the first issue were Airbnb-related
18 were not Airbnb-related
66 sources in the second issue were Airbnb-related
15 were not Airbnb-related

34 sources in the third issue were Airbnb-related
30 were not Airbnb-related

If we remove a two-page spread from the second edition that simply listed 33 tips from 33 Airbnb hosts—not really sources in a story as much as a simple list of ideas—the ratios of the first and second issues are relatively similar. The third issue illustrates a stronger leaning towards voices form outside the community. A closer look at how these attributions appear in the magazine, however, allow us to draw some conclusions about the credibility of these sources, and thus the journalists publishing in the magazine.

A few key examples help suggest that *Airbnbmag* has the potential for what we would consider ethically produced travel journalism, at least as far as attempts at objectivity are concerned. While Bill Kovach and Tom Rosenstiel (2014) affirm the impossibility for journalists to be truly objective, their method—including clear, transparent sourcing—can be. In the first edition, such attempts exist in a feature story on Los Angeles, entitled 'Los Angeles 4 ways'; in it, the writer interviews four different local experts to frame things to do for shoppers, adventurers, 'foodies' and families (Jaffe and Jones, 2017). The local experts, however, have no avowed connection with Airbnb. In the second edition, a similarly independent story entitled 'Rainbows over Beirut' discusses a burgeoning LGBT scene in the Lebanese city (Murphy, 2017). Again, local experts, including professors and activists, have no direct affiliation with Airbnb, but figure prominently as the main sources.

Other smaller stories, like an interview with a Brooklyn bookstore owner, a feature with an online influencer and short blurbs with various authors, highlight the fact that *Airbnbmag* is not entirely facing inwards towards its community. Its journalists have attempted to push beyond the brand to find other relevant sources for stories.

Alongside these—again, apparently—independent sources, unaffiliated with the brand, there are voices form within the Airbnb community. For example, in the article about Los Angeles, opposite the text, there are photos with a short blurb featuring recommendations from local hosts. In the LGBT Beirut article, similarly, there is a small sidebar where five local hosts share their tips for the city. In other features, there are voices from Airbnb hosts that stand on their own, like a multi-page spread presenting different unique rental homes, including interviews with the hosts. While this is not surprising, not every story follows this format. The third issue, for example, included a story about a photographer working with Indian women with no apparently link to a single destination or to Airbnb (Stein, 2018). The magazine opens up readers to trends, events and people beyond the community and beyond the company's interests.

Journalism or advertorial?

It is entirely expected that Airbnb would source from its hosts and users, preserving notions of community. Readers are likely using Airbnb anyway, so this sort of consumer travel journalism is useful. It is noteworthy, however, that the sources are not all framed commercially. One spread simply includes 33 tips from 33 hosts around the world, a clear example of how journalists can seek sources from the sharing economy without necessarily pushing a specific commodity. None of the voices in this spread link back to a specific listing on the site. Instead, the moniker of 'host' acts as a signal of authority, like 'professor' or 'researcher' might. Revisiting the initial research questions, these revelations become more apparent.

RQ1 Do all sources in *Airbnbmag* come from the Airbnb community?

No; roughly a third of each issue's voices come from sources from beyond the Airbnb community in the first two issues, while nearly half in the third issue are unaffiliated with Airbnb. Unsurprisingly, the majority of attributed sources come from within the Airbnb community, namely its hosts. It would seem that Airbnb has a built-in selection for sources, perhaps favouring people connected to the brand. A closer look, however, at the features and spreads in the magazine reveals that the longer, feature stories—arguably the more journalistic material on the pages—feature more non-commercial sources. A minority of sources have nothing to do with Airbnb, indicating that there is potential for a branded magazine to produce lifestyle journalism that is, technically, more independent from the brand. Such independence also reflects the outward-facing nature of the magazine as a supplement to its website, as something a non-Airbnb user may pick up and appreciate without actually having ever booked a service through the company.

To that end, we can ask whether the sourcing outside of the community helps frame the magazine as more than advertorial. The stories about Los Angeles and Beirut could arguably appear in almost any travel publication, suggesting that *Airbnbmag* is potentially fertile ground for travel journalism. As one marketing executive suggested, a platform like Airbnb isn't "just about the brands; they're about what the brands stand for" (Root, 2018). In the case of Airbnb, the brand promotes connecting with and living like locals when travelling, and so the magazine's content reflects these larger issues. While not the case for any branded content, for Airbnb, its values are applicable to audiences well beyond the online community of users. *Airbnbmag*, arguably, can interest any individual regardless of whether or not he or she travels using Airbnb, or is a simple armchair traveller who may not travel at all.

RQ2 Do journalists indicate clearly when a source is connected to Airbnb?

Yes, the editors and journalists identify all of their sources in detail, often providing links to their specific properties and experiences. The magazine is about giving a more personal voice to this form of travel journalism and *Airbnbmag* does just that by featuring its own community members. We cannot go so far, however, as to assume that every source that seems outside the community is, in fact, unlinked to the brand. It is possible that these seemingly independent sources and local voices—leaders, educators and business leaders, among others—are either hosts or customers, and as such part of the Airbnb community. It would be helpful, in future studies, to discuss how journalists for this magazine produce their stories, and if there is any regulation regarding transparency, which is often not the case (Ikonen, Luoma-aho and Bowen, 2017).

RQ3 Does *Airbnbmag* provide content beyond its own brand interests?

Yes—or at least presumably. The stories about Los Angeles and Beirut, for example, do not focus specifically on Airbnb properties, experiences or interests. Instead, they offer a look at current trends or issues more objectively, with a varied selection of sources. Brand interests appear only as ornaments for these stories, as sidebars or quotes on photo spreads, but not driving the stories. A possible argument is that the destinations themselves are important markets for Airbnb, and thus the stories are generating interest for these destinations without overtly advertising Airbnb experiences or rentals there. This is a constant consideration for travel journalism, and one that explains the multitude of travel articles about Paris or New York and very few about less commercially viable tourist destinations such as Ghana or Pakistan. The story in the third issue, however, dealing with a photographer focussing on Indian women being photographed, reveals that not every story needs a tie-in to Airbnb or a destination, opening the magazine up to sharing less commercially driven stories addressing more niche topics.

Conclusion

The sharing economy, as it infiltrates the media, challenges the way we think of journalistic independence and professional practice. Instead of travel journalists working for independent media brands dependent on advertisers, journalists at *Airbnbmag* work directly for the brand. There is less of a conflict of interest here, since readers clearly know who backs the publication, displaying a form of transparency that writers like John Greenman might espouse (2012). Where it becomes concerning for travel journalists is that the brand may filter out or limit the scope of sources in its stories due to financial interests. For example, it is fair to question why editors would bother commissioning stories about a destination with few Airbnb properties in the first place.

When discussing the nature of sharing economies, Lawrence Lessig suggests that true sharing economies eventually take on a more traditional marketplace role. He writes: "Thus, no distinction between 'sharing' and 'commercial' economies can be assumed to survive forever, or even for long" (Lessig, 2009, p. 150). Modern journalism, however, has always been marked by commercialisation, its own sort of marketplace, even more so as the Internet has increased competition (McManus, 2009). Travel journalism, furthermore, has traditionally embraced its consumer-oriented nature. All of this is to say that commercial issues have always been and will continue to be part of travel media—there is very little pure, benevolent exchange in travel media or in the tourism industry. Whether on Airbnb.com, in its magazine or in any travel publication for that matter, are there ever truly independent reviews? If branded magazines like *Airbnbmag* appear alongside more traditional publications, the lines continue to blur between the 'critical' aspect described by Hanusch and Fürsich and a more advertorial one. While this particular publication has managed to incorporate voices from beyond the online community, it is hard to remove the stories from some larger agenda. Does this agenda, however, undermine the journalistic integrity of the writing?

Looking at sources is just one way to examine the relationship between the sharing economy and travel journalism, but it is just the beginning. Further research will be needed to see how travel journalism more broadly, beyond *Airbnbmag*, deals with these new voices emanating from the sharing economy and social media more broadly. These new possibilities simultaneously present new challenges, but as the tourism industry changes, it is important to understand how travel journalism continues to adapt with it.

References

Bakker, P. (2014) 'Mr. Gates returns: curation, community management and other new roles for journalists', *Journalism Studies*, 15(5), pp. 596–606.

Berkowitz, D. A. (2009) 'Reporters and their sources', in Wahl-Jorgensen, K. and Hanitzsch, T. (eds) *The handbook of journalism studies*. New York and London: Routledge, pp. 102–115.

Berkowitz, D. A. and Beach, D. W. (1993) 'News sources and news context: the effect of routine news, conflict and proximity', *Journalism Quarterly*, 70(1), pp. 4–12.

Broersma, M. and Graham, T. (2013) 'Twitter as a news source: how Dutch and British newspapers used tweets in their news coverage, 2007–2011', *Journalism Practice*, 7(4), pp. 446–464.

Bull, A. (2013) *Brand journalism*. Oxon: Routledge.

Carlson, M. and Lewis, S. C. (2018) 'Temporal reflexivity in journalism studies: making sense of change in a more timely fashion', *Journalism*. doi: 1464884918760675.

Cocking, B. (2017) 'News values go on holiday', *Journalism Studies*. doi: 10.1080/1461670X.2016.1272066.

Cohen, B. and Kietzmann, J. (2014) 'Ride on! Mobility business models for the sharing economy', *Organization & Environment*, 27(3), pp. 279–296.

Deuze, M. (2005) 'What is journalism? Professional identity and ideology of journalists reconsidered', *Journalism*, 6(4), pp. 442–464.

Duffy, A. (2017) 'How social media offers opportunities for growth in the traditional media industry: the case of travel journalism', in Benson, V., Tuninga, R. and Saridakis, G. (eds) *Analysing the strategic role of social networking in firm growth and productivity*. Hershey, PA: IGI Global, pp. 172–187.

Fang, B., et al. (2015) 'Effect of sharing economy on tourism industry employment', *Annals of Tourism Research*. doi:10.1016/j.annals.2015.11.018.

Fradkin, A. et al. (2015) 'Bias and reciprocity in online reviews: evidence from field experiments on Airbnb', in *Proceedings of the sixteenth ACM conference on economics and computation*. ACM: Portland (Oregon), U.S., June 15–19, p. 641.

Franklin, B. and Carlson, M. (eds) (2010). *Journalists, sources, and credibility: new perspectives.* London: Routledge.

Fürsich, E. (2012) 'Lifestyle journalism as popular journalism: strategies for evaluating its public role', *Journalism Practice*, 6(1), pp. 12–25.

Greenman, J. (2012) *Introduction to travel journalism: on the road with serious intent.* New York: Peter Lang.

Guttentag, D. (2015) 'Airbnb: disruptive innovation and the rise of an informal tourism accommodation sector', *Current Issues in Tourism*, 18(12), pp. 1192–1217.

Hamari, J., Sjöklint, M. and Ukkonen, A. (2016) 'The sharing economy: why people participate in collaborative consumption', *Journal of the Association for Information Science and Technology*, 67(9), pp. 2047–2059.

Hanitzsch, T. and Vos, T. (2018) 'Journalism beyond democracy: a new look into journalistic roles in political and everyday life', *Journalism*, 19(2), pp. 146–164.

Hanusch, F. (ed.) (2013) *Lifestyle journalism.* London: Routledge.

Hanusch, F. and Fürsich, E. (eds) (2014). *Travel journalism: exploring production, impact and culture.* New York: Palgrave.

Harcup, T. and O'Neill, D. (2016) 'What is news? News values revisited (again)', *Journalism Studies*. doi:10.1080/1461670X.2016.1150193.

Heo, C. Y. (2016) 'Sharing economy and prospects in tourism research', *Annals of Tourism Research*. doi:10.1016/j.annals.2016.02.002.

Ikonen, P., Luoma-aho, V. and Bowen, S. A. (2017) 'Transparency for sponsored content: analysing codes of ethics in public relations, marketing, advertising and journalism, *International Journal of Strategic Communication*, 11(2), pp. 165–178

Jaffe, M. and Jones, R. (2017, Spring) 'Los Angeles 4 ways'. *Airbnbmag*, issue 1, pp. 83–91.

Kovach, B. and Rosenstiel, T. (2014). *The elements of journalism: what newspeople should know and the public should expect.* California: Three Rivers Press.

Lessig, L. (2009) *Remix: making art and commerce thrive in the hybrid economy.* New York: Penguin.

Malhotra, A. and Van Alstyne, M. (2014) 'The dark side of the sharing economy … and how to lighten it', *Communications of the ACM*, 57, pp. 24–27.

McManus, J. H. (2009) 'The commercialisation of news', *The handbook of journalism studies*, pp. 218–233.

Murphy, T. (2017, Fall/Winter) 'Rainbows Over Beirut', *Airbnbmag*, issue 2, pp. 98–105.

Paulussen, S. and Harder, R. A. (2014) 'Social media references in newspapers: Facebook, Twitter and YouTube as sources in newspaper journalism', *Journalism Practice*, 8(5), pp. 542–551.

Pirolli, B. (2018) *Travel journalism: informing tourists in the digital age.* London: Routledge.

Root, A. (2018) 'How branded content counters consumer scepticism. *Ragan's PR Daily'.* Available at: https://www.prdaily.com/marketing/Articles/24126.aspx (Accessed: 15 December 2018).

Schor, J. B. and Fitzmaurice, C. J. (2015) 'Collaborating and connecting: the emergence of the sharing economy', in Reisch, L. and Thøgersen, J. (eds) *Handbook of research on sustainable consumption.* Cheltenham and Northampton: Edward Elgar Publishing, pp. 410–425.

Small, J., Harris, C. and Wilson, E. (2008) 'A critical discourse analysis of in-flight magazine advertisements: the "social sorting" of airline travellers?', *Journal of Tourism and Cultural Change*, 6(1), pp. 17–38.

Stein, E. (2018, Spring) 'Written in the stars', *Airbnbmag*, issue 3, pp. 132–139.

Taeihagh, A. (2017) 'Crowdsourcing, sharing economies and development', *Journal of Developing Societies*, 33(2), pp. 191–222.

Thorsen, E. (2013) 'Live blogging and social media curation: challenges and opportunities for journalism' in Fowler-Watt, K. and Allan S. (eds) *Journalism: new challenges*. Bournemouth: Bournemouth University, pp. 123–145.

Vis, F. (2013) 'Twitter as a reporting tool for breaking news: journalists tweeting the 2011 UK riots', *Digital Journalism*, 1(1), pp. 27–47.

Zervas, G., Proserpio, D. and Byers, J. W. (2017) 'The rise of the sharing economy: estimating the impact of Airbnb on the hotel industry', *Journal of Marketing Research*, 54(5), pp. 687–705.

12

LIFESTYLE JOURNALISM AS BRAND PRACTICE

The cases of Uniqlo and Abercrombie & Fitch

Myles Ethan Lascity

Peddling different styles of clothing and different brand images, Uniqlo and Abercrombie & Fitch may not seem like they have much in common. Uniqlo, the Japanese retailer of basic garments and fashion diffusion lines, is known for its bright colours and extensive customer service. Meanwhile, Abercrombie & Fitch, during its peak, was known for its logo-laden clothing, risqué teen marketing materials and its exclusionary hiring practices. Further, Abercrombie & Fitch reached its peak influence in the late 1990s and early 2000s (Berfield and Rupp, 2015), while Uniqlo's global expansion came in 2007 and continues today (Ando, 2016; Wolf, 2017). Despite these differences, both used forms of content creation similar to lifestyle journalism to help build their respective brands. For Abercrombie & Fitch, this took the form of their magazine/catalogue hybrid, *A&F Quarterly*, while Uniqlo published its promotional materials as *The LifeWear Book*.

This chapter seeks to explore and compare how each brand used forms of lifestyle journalism in its efforts to build consumable images. In order to do so, this chapter will theoretically link lifestyle journalism and lifestyle branding before using each brand's marketing materials to perform an interpretative deconstruction in the vein of Consumer Culture Theory (Arnould and Thompson, 2005). From there, it will be possible to see these efforts within the same cultural genealogy (Mukerji, 2007) and draw some conclusions due to the historical contexts of each brand. Taken in tandem, this allows for both an exploration of how brands have embraced journalism-style writing for marketing ends and also suggests some ways the practice has changed and/or may be used to achieve different goals.

Giving life to lifestyle journalism

Folker Hanusch's (2012) call for broadening the focus of journalism studies toward lifestyle and other soft news is a useful starting point to expanding the field. He argues that the "softer side" of the news—from health and fitness to fashion and relationships—has not received as much attention from scholars, largely due to its close ties with consumer culture. Instead, professional journalists and journalism scholars have largely focused on and supported the work of the "watchdogs"—those who hold officials and businesses accountable to the wider public—(Hanusch, 2012, p. 3). Further, as Barbie Zelizer noted, journalists and journalism scholars have often worked to set the definitions of the field (2004), sometimes pushing aside certain types of journalism in the process (2011, p. 8). Meanwhile, Nete Nørgaard Kristensen and Unni From add that journalism categorisations are blurring and that lifestyle journalism, including coverage of fashion and food, are bleeding into cultural and consumer journalism categories, which traditionally included coverage of music and art, and cars and technology, respectively (2012, p. 26).

Lifestyle journalism has been seen as integral to consumer culture, including through the production of consumer guides and 'tastemaking'. Sharon Zukin ties this vein of reviews and articles from sources such as *Ladies' Home Journal* and *Good Housekeeping* to the development of 'lifestyle' through the cultural intermediaries she called "honest brokers"—the reviewers and critics who work to "personalise the objective qualities and objectify the subjective elements of what we like"—(2005, p. 172). It was in the 1960s that food reviews and other lifestyle topics were welcomed into the news fold, through a mix of technological factors (Hanusch, 2012, pp. 2–3) and career professionalisation (Zukin, 2005, p.181); honest brokers and others lifestyle writers came about in part to teach readers "how to live" (Zukin, 2005, p. 172). Seeking a more inclusive definition, Hanusch suggests that contemporary lifestyle journalists "see themselves as: cultural mediators, critics, entertainers, information providers and traveller" (2012, p. 5). By broadening the scope of lifestyle journalism, the field can be seen as "news which audiences can apply in their own lives" (Hanusch, 2012, p. 4), whether through travel suggestions or movie reviews.

Researchers have also turned their attention towards new forms of journalism: that of brand and branded journalism. Brand journalism is considered a hybrid form of advertising and public relations that allows organisations to communicate directly to the public (Bull, 2013, p. 1; Swenson, 2012, pp. 23–24). Comparatively, branded journalism is usually a journalistic endeavour that is sponsored by a particular company or organisation (Swenson, 2012, pp. 28–29). From both these examples and the increasing democratisation of journalism through the Internet and social media (Gilmor, 2004; Duffy, 2013, 2017), it is possible to consider journalism less as a process or specific profession and instead as a specific set of texts. Indeed, Zelizer noted some benefits to defining journalism as a text with "agreed upon features" (2004, p. 38); such a definition allows researchers to create finite, identifiable texts that can be read, analysed and referenced (Zelizer, 2004, p. 39). Moreover, since audiences do not necessarily know what goes on behind the scenes to produce journalism texts and—as recent work on native advertising has suggested—they may have a difficult time telling the difference between advertising and journalism

(Amazeen and Muddiman, 2017; Conill, 2016; Wojdynski and Evans, 2016), it makes sense to interrogate lifestyle journalism as the tangible text being presented. This means articles written in the style of journalism—full sentences and paragraphs, citing real sources—and offering consumers something they can use in their everyday lives.

Lifestyle branding has taken on a similar role of guiding tastes since Ralph Lauren's embrace of the concept in the 1970s and 1980s (Hancock, 2016, pp. 41–48). While largely accepted and promoted as a desirable business practice, the idea of lifestyle branding has also been subjected to definitional issues. Processes of cultural branding (Holt, 2004) and brand storytelling (Hancock, 2009) had been set out ahead of a fuller exploration of "lifestyle brands" (Saviolo and Marrazza, 2013). A lack of clear definitions of a 'lifestyle brand' largely emanate from competing of views of 'brand' (Allen, Fournier and Miller, 2008; Conejo and Wooliscroft, 2015) as well as the latter's dematerialisation and nebulousness (Manning, 2010).

Stephen Wigley, Karinna Nobbs and Ewa Larsen (2013) have suggested that intangible elements of a brand, including its associated lifestyle, are developed through tangible communications that are created about and often by the brand. These intangible elements can include concepts like brand image, personality, heritage and market position (Wigley, Nobbs and Larsen, 2013, pp. 249–255). Still, becoming a lifestyle brand—one that can influence other product categories beyond a brand's primary offering—is seen as a pinnacle achievement (Saviolo and Marazza, 2013, p. 48–49). In both lifestyle journalism and lifestyle branding, the goal remains to help shape consumers' tastes and purchases.

In the cases of *A&F Quarterly* and *The LifeWear Book*, both utilise lifestyle journalism articles while largely eschewing brand journalism proper. The articles, whether written by staffers of the publications or by contributing freelancers, rarely discussed the brands directly and did not provide information on the corporate organisation and its actions. Instead, both publications relied on other journalistic structures, such as profile pieces or pop culture reviews, in order to construct an intangible identity for its audience. Further, in the case of *A&F Quarterly*, some articles that were structured as a journalistic undertaking, such as an advice column and narrative features, were mixed with a heavy dose of fiction. Largely, the content in *A&F Quarterly* worked to create a lifestyle of activities and associated tastes while *The LifeWear Book* remained more closely related to the products sold. In both cases, however, much of the content could be used by readers and applied to consumers' everyday lives. The benefit for brands is that, while these articles may be interesting and useful to readers, they also support a lifestyle in which their products can be purchased and used.

Method

The following pages take a comparative case-study approach to better understand how lifestyle journalism can be used to cultivate specific brand images.

Accepting the premise that intangible brand elements are largely a creation of tangible communications (Wigley, Nobbs and Larsen, 2013), this analysis examines how lifestyle journalism texts are assembled into larger cultural constructions. This analysis will rely on an interpretative, qualitative analysis of brand texts to deconstruct the embedded meaning. Such methodologies are common within consumer research, when the goal is to understand how identities and lifestyle ideals are constructed for consumers (Arnould and Thompson, 2005, pp. 874–875; Stern, 1989).

The analysis focuses on the texts presented within the issues of Abercrombie & Fitch's *A&F Quarterly* from 2000 and Uniqlo's *The LifeWear Book* from 2015. Attention will be given to the types of articles presented within the publications, as well as the subjects of the pieces, in an attempt to deconstruct each brand's image. In doing so, the goal will be to set up two points in a cultural genealogy (Mukerji, 2007) and suggest that both brands are drawing from the same repertoire of knowledge and brand practices. From there, it becomes possible to draw comparisons between each brand's use of lifestyle journalism forms within their promotional efforts.

Results and discussion

Abercrombie & Fitch's A&F Quarterly

While the concept of a brand lifestyle predates Abercrombie & Fitch, the debut of its *A&F Quarterly*, a magazine/catalogue hybrid (sometimes called a 'magalog'), took place in 1997. Published to coincide with the school year—Spring Break, Summer, Back to School and Christmas—the publication contained risqué photography, which often featured nude or semi-nude models in sexually provocative positions as well as a variety of articles and profiles. The popular press noted that Abercrombie & Fitch sold a "Technicolor teen lifestyle" (Perman, 2000) that was as much a product of *A&F Quarterly* as its in-store branding. The marketing was powerful enough that the term 'Abercrombie' was adopted by teens as synonym for 'popular' (Goldstein, 1999). The brand's success was largely attributed to its CEO Mike Jeffries' tight control of its image (Berner, 2005), including heavy handed tactics which led to boycotts and discrimination suits (Denizet-Lewis, 2006). *A&F Quarterly* was a printed embodiment of the brand and was initially published until 2003, when a particularly sexual Christmas edition led the brand to stop further publication. Jeffries would later say it became boring to continue it (Berfield and Rupp, 2015), but the brand was already losing money and popularity when the publication was ended (Grinspan, 2014; WWD Staff, 2003).

A&F Quarterly was an archetype of the 'magalog' genre; not only did it include profile pieces, historical articles, reviews and celebrity profiles, but it also acted as a catalogue that sold the brand's clothing, complete with order forms. Meanwhile, *A&F Quarterly* blurred the lines of lifestyle journalism when some

elements, such as its 'Ask A&F' advice column, were written in the style of articles, but could be clearly identified as fiction. The advice column included
joking questions, answers and writers' names, while a narrative editor's note for
'A very Emerson Christmas' included fictional names and places (*A&F Quarterly*,
2000d, p. 2).

Beyond the blurred lines of reality, many of the articles included heavy sexual
innuendo and language that disparaged large swathes of the population. The
travel writing, which featured prominently in *A&F Quarterly* and was often written about far-flung, exotic locations, was no exception. In the opening editor's
note of the Spring Break issue, the 'travellers' write that they wanted to go
"where the wild things are" and that they realised it wouldn't be found "within
earshot of MTV" (*A&F Quarterly*, 2000a, p. 10). This included Costa Rica and
South Africa. Closer to home, the travellers visited Las Vegas and "got naked in
the woods" (*A&F Quarterly*, 2000a, p. 10). One piece declares: "Your Spring
Break will suck … unless you go to Costa Rica", and was accompanied by a list
of 50 reasons why everyone should visit the Latin American country; these
reasons included things like "beer is 50 cents a bottle", "no underage drinking
laws", "prostitution is legal" and "nude beaches" (Romando, 2000b, p. 173).
Other, more exclusionary and elitist tones were made with reasons like "no fat
people" and "no fast food" (Romando, 2000b, p. 173). A piece on South Africa
also played into the wealthy connotations of the brand, suggesting a trip where
round-trip tickets cost $1,500 and that longer-term travellers "often opt to buy
a cheap car for around $1,500" while in the country (Masterson, 2000, p. 207).
The travel pieces in the summer issue were more diverse in their destinations
and activities, but continued to highlight places that involved significant capital,
whether financial or otherwise, to access. In 'Forbidden snow', the writer trav-
elled to the Middle East on a snowboarding adventure in a search for the text
calls "untouched powder" (Blehm, 2000). Several other pieces also proved difficult to access, whether it was a location like Cuba (Levine, 2000), resources like
backpacking through Western Europe (Jeffries and Simmons, 2000) or travelling
like Jack Keroauc (Branch, 2000). Finally, the entire 'Back to School' issue was
focused on New York and combined elements of travel with more racy under-
takings. Pieces like 'Around the apple in 24 hours' (Johnson *et al.*, 2000) and
'Sex in the city' (*A&F Quarterly*, 2000c) both focused on things to do in the
city. While the first piece included a mix of restaurants, music venues and bars,
the second focused solely on sex-related activities including strip clubs, live sex
shows and massage parlours (*A&F Quarterly*, 2000c).

Beyond the travel pieces, there were several historical features that helped to
ingrain the brand's heritage, but also worked to place current activities within
a historic trajectory. In the New York issue, two features focused on formidable
thinkers of the city. 'The beat goes on' concentrated on the "hipsters who
started a youth revolution" including Jack Kerouac, William S. Burroughs and
Allen Ginsberg, noting that Kerouac "unwittingly helped pimp the Beats as
a faddish product"; Burroughs' *Naked Lunch* was called "psychopathological

filth" (and that he "shot his second wife dead" at a cocktail party); and "Ginsberg was tried on obscenity charges; his career as a social bandit and champion of free speech was set" (Van Parys, 2000, p. 164). Meanwhile, 'Harlem on my mind' featured biographies of black thinkers and artists, including descriptions of W. E. B. DuBois, Duke Ellington and Langston Hughes. These descriptions were written in a more proper tone, and contained less innuendo than those of beat writers. For example, the author noted that Angela Davis called DuBois the "most influential civil rights person of his day" and that Ellington "thought patterns blew people's minds". The most salacious detail in these brief biographies was a mention of Hughes being a "beneficiary of Charlotte Manson's largesse, up until the moment she cut him off in 1930" (*A&F Quarterly*, 2000b, p. 190).

Further, the interview pieces and the reviews worked to burnish the brand's credentials and raise its cultural capital. Interview and profile pieces ran the gamut from politicians like Rudy Giuliani (Carone, 2000) and Ed Koch (Romando, 2000a), to writers like Bret Easton Ellis (Sedaris, 2000a), comedians such as Jimmy Fallon (Sedaris, 2000b) and Amy Sedaris (Kon, 2000), and other noteworthy individuals including former Eagle Scout James Dale who sued the Boy Scouts for discriminating against homosexuals (Abadsidis, 2000). These profiles did little to connect the people to the brand or its products; simply the appearance within the 'magalog' and implication that these notables would be associated with Abercrombie & Fitch worked to promote the brand. Moreover, like in the other pieces above, they provided an identity and largely fictional lifestyle for consumers to buy into.

Uniqlo's The LifeWear Book

Years later, as part of their ongoing push into marketplaces around the globe, Japan-based Uniqlo began producing the biannual *The LifeWearBook*. The physical books were offered in-stores starting with the 2015 Spring/Summer and Fall/Winter collections and prominently featured clothing throughout. Uniqlo, which made a name for itself with its relatively cheap basics in multiple colours (Urstadt, 2010), wanted to be known for technological advances in fabric creation rather than a trendy clothier (Gaudoin, 2012). *The LifeWear Book* was named for a design philosophy the brand dubbed 'LifeWear' and explained that the encompassing clothing lines combine "respect for the traditions of [everyday essentials] while harnessing innovations to ensure that essentials keep meeting contemporary needs" (Uniqlo, 2017). 'LifeWear' included updates to denim and knits, as well as specialised fabrics and collaborative designs. While *The LifeWear Book* followed elements of lifestyle journalism, including personality pieces and travel-style articles, the pieces prominently featured the garments and fabrics in both story and image.

Each of the two issues started out with declarative statements about 'LifeWear', which worked to frame the rest of the material. The Spring/Summer 2015 issue began with a simple mission statement that read:

> What first began as everyday wear, Uniqlo has reinvented in Japan as Life-Wear. LifeWear isn't disposable clothing, but perfect components make with quality. We create LifeWear by evolving the ordinary, producing innovations big and small that benefit you every day.
>
> *(The LifeWear Book, 2015a, p. 1)*

The Fall/Winter issue was more extensive, but told readers that Uniqlo's apparel "comes from our Japanese values of simplicity, quality and longevity", and that the company continues to innovate "because your life never stops changing"; in sum, the pieces were: "Simple apparel with a not-so-simple purpose: to make your life better" (*The LifeWear Book*, 2015b, p. 1). These pieces work to set the brand apart from fast fashion retailers such as Zara and H&M, with which Uniqlo is often associated by consumers and industry professionals (see Lascity, 2018, pp. 83–86).

Both issues featured a combination of personality profiles and informational pieces that explained the technological developments of fabrics. The Spring/Summer issue included celebrities such as actresses Gennifer Goodwin (Borel, 2015a) and Nathalie Emmanuel (Borel, 2015b); magazine-editor-turned-entrepreneur David Zinczenko (Ryder, 2015a) and TV host Eden Grinshpan (Ryder, 2015b), as well as profiles of a florist (Crane, 2015), architect (Hayakawa, 2015a) and photographer (Hayakawa, 2015b). The Fall/Winter edition featured short pieces on celebrities such as tennis player Kei Nishikori, golfer Adam Scott (both of whom were sponsored by the brand), brand collaborator Ines de la Fressange (Pourhashemi, 2015) and sponsored wheelchair tennis player Shingo Kunieda (Matsuzawa, 2015). However, more space and in-depth profiles were written of a gallery owner (Ishida, 2015), a software engineer (Duncan, 2015), a professor (Newell-Hanson, 2015) and an explorer (Van Meter, 2015).

In these pieces, the individuals are discussing their everyday lives and interests, but connect back to Uniqlo's ideas of simplicity and change. For example, a profile of pottery artist Yuko Okazaki reads:

> As she has honed her craft, Okazaki has learned the best strategy for her to stay in a creative state of mind: 'It's living within the minimum. When you live in an environment with so much information and so many temptations, craftsmanship does not move forward …'
>
> *(Hayakawa, 2015c, p.11)*

Similarly, gallery owner Taka Ishii has much of the same emphasis, telling a journalist, "I like clothes that don't make the intentions of the designer too obvious. You still feel the presence of the person who made it. The same can be said with art" (Ishida, 2015, p. 56).

Each profile within both issues was accompanied by a photo of the subject wearing Uniqlo clothing—from a rayon blouse worn by Gennifer Goodwin to an 'Ultra Light Down Parka' and 'HEATTECH' cap worn by explorer and athlete Ben Saunders (Van Meter, 2015). Both the 'Ultra Light Down' and

'HEATTECH' lines are unique to Uniqlo and claim technological advancements that respectively allow for down-filled garments to be thinner and other garments to better-insulate wearers, while controlling odour and moisture. These photos were also given captions that promoted the garments shown. For example, one article states that Saunders' parka and other garments were "simple in appearance, powerful in performance" (Van Meter, 2015, p.72). A more in-depth description accompanied Goodwin's blouse:

> Spun from natural fibres that are thinner than cotton but soft like silk, rayon is the go-anywhere, do-anything fabric. Our Rayon Blouses feature wrinkle-resistant, easy-care functionality, so they're made to wash and go, which saves you time getting ready and looking great.
>
> *(Borel, 2015a, p.23)*

Beyond the profiles, each issue dedicated various articles to explaining the fabrics and design of particular garments. The Spring/Summer edition discussed the 'pocketable' parka (Pearson, 2015), mesh hoodie (Pesce, 2015a) and selvedge denim (Nomura, 2015), while the Fall/Winter edition went into event more background on the weaving of denim (Sakuma, 2015), the creation of the brand's 'HEATTECH' yarn (Lewis, 2015) and the differences of wool (Churchill, 2015). Some of these pieces involved a personal sales pitch, such as the 'pocketable' parka story, which reads:

> If you're taking off for Iceland, or your own private Iceland, go with one of these Pocketable Parkas. They look great … but they are much less likely to get lost since you can fold them up and stick them in your pocket or purse or wherever.
>
> *(Pearson, 2015, p.17)*

Other pieces focused much more on the construction and wear. A piece on 'DRY-EX', for instance, expresses how the "soft microfiber is enhanced with anti-odour properties, which limit the growth of odour-causing bacteria to suppress the unpleasant odour that result[s] from perspiration" (Pesce, 2015b, p. 39). Meanwhile, an entire feature was dedicated to 'How ['HEATTECH'] works', which explained that garments are "made up of four distinct fibres that are specifically engineers to work in tandem to provide the body with warmth and comfort" (Lewis, 2015, p. 44). Readers found out these fibres are rayon, polyester, polyurethane and a special micro-acrylic only available at Uniqlo. This piece also included in-depth illustrations showing how the fabric is assembled.

Conclusion

In both cases, elements of lifestyle journalism worked to help build the Abercrombie & Fitch and Uniqlo brands, although they did so in different ways.

The *A&F Quarterly* worked to create an immaterial lifestyle beyond what was inherent in the clothing. There is an unstated assumption that by purchasing the clothing, one could access the lifestyles described within the 'magalog'. Implications of class were apparent, as were other exclusionary issues, which have been covered elsewhere in the academic (McBride, 2005) and popular press (Denizet-Lewis, 2006).

Comparatively, Uniqlo's articles worked towards placing its clothing in everyday contexts. The professions of the individuals profiled—from professor to florist to software engineer—are more common and accessible than the subjects in *A&F Quarterly*. Still, these facts underline a subtler idea of class and status that infuse the *The LifeWear Book*. Uniqlo's advertising works to promote a forward-thinking and technological-heavy lifestyle that requires economic, cultural and even social capital of its participants. While the pieces of *The LifeWear Book* do not directly call out travel destinations or make direct judgements on lifestyle activities and tastes, they implied that people could travel like explorer Ben Saunders, should want the simplicity noted in various profiles and are interested in learning the fabrics' specifics. The market segmentations are less obvious, but nonetheless still there.

Largely, these approaches could be attributed to the differences in times and brands. Abercrombie & Fitch courted controversy in its attempt to appeal to teens; sex sells and so did Abercrombie & Fitch. In comparison, Uniqlo's aim is to appeal to entire families, including parents, grandparents and kids. As such, the same sexually suggestive and risqué advertising would work against its interests, but its more informative pieces still help to provide desired connotations to the brand. In this way, these articles are not only attempting to appeal to a specific subset of readers, but also to construct intangible elements of the brands and identities for consumers to buy into. A second reason for these differences goes back to the purpose and context of these materials. *A&F Quarterly* was part-catalogue that also aimed to literally sell the clothing, as order forms were included in each issue. Comparatively, *The LifeWear Book* did not include order forms and focused more on education than actually purchasing the garments. *A&F Quarterly* was published in the relatively early days of the web before Web 2.0 took hold and smartphones paved the way for quick purchases through apps. As such, Abercrombie & Fitch physically sold the 'magalog' in stores, but also shipped it across the country. Uniqlo, in contrast, gave away the promotional materials to those visiting a physical location. Practically speaking, Abercrombie & Fitch would need to be more engaging so readers would order the 'magalog' as well as order from it, since readers might not have physical access to stores. Comparatively, the Internet gives Uniqlo a wider reach already, so *The LifeWear Book* would target interested parties and those looking for more information on the products at hand, rather than promoting and selling the brand as the *A&F Quarterly* did.

That said, this returns to the most important point of these publications: to sell. While each publication did so in a different way, the promotional material is written in the style of lifestyle journalism. The producers of these publications were not following professional journalistic guidelines, nor were they under any obligations to produce content that did not fit their purposes. The most obvious problems can be seen in *A&F Quarterly*, where the overriding theme of its Christmas 2000 issue is a holiday gathering by a fictional family. This clearly blurs the lines of reality that a mainstream journalism organisation would certainly eschew. While *The LifeWear Book* did not contain obvious fictional accounts, several of the articles focused specifically on Uniqlo's developments of materials or what amounts to reviews of particular product lines. However, despite appearing as such, these are not objective reviews. As a hybrid publication mixing elements of journalism and marketing, this style of media production is open to questions of credibility.

Finally, it must be noted that while there are ongoing discussions over the blurring of advertising and journalism in the veins of branded journalism (Bull, 2013) and native advertising (Amazeen and Muddiman, 2017; Couldry and Turow, 2014; Conill, 2016; Wojdynski and Evans, 2016), this did not start nor are these issues confided to the Internet. As Rebecca Dean Swenson (2012) shows, firms have long-created publications through their efforts in marketing and public relations. The cases of both *A&F Quarterly* and *The LifeWear Book* show that these tactics are still in use and unlikely to go out of fashion anytime soon.

References

A&F Quarterly (2000a, Spring Break) 'Dear Class of 2000', *A&F Quarterly: wild & willing*, p. 10.

A&F Quarterly (2000b, Back to School) 'Harlem on my mind', *A&F Quarterly: New York*, p. 190.

A&F Quarterly (2000c, Back to School) 'Sex in the city', *A&F Quarterly: New York*, p. 112.

A&F Quarterly (2000d, Christmas) 'A very Emerson Christmas', *A&F Quarterly: a very Emerson Christmas*, p. 2.

Abadsidis, S. (2000, Christmas). 'Scout's honour', *A&F Quarterly: A very Emerson Christmas*, p. 150.

Allen, C. T., Fournier, S. and Miller, F. (2008) 'Brands and their meaning makers', in Haugtvedt C., Herr, P. and Kardes F. (eds) *Handbook of consumer psychology*. New York: Lawrence Erlbaum Associates, pp. 781–822.

Amazeen, M. A. and Muddiman, A. R. (2017). 'Saving media or trading on trust? The effects of native advertising on audience perceptions of legacy and online news publishers', *Digital Journalism*, 6(2),176–195. doi: 10.1080/21670811.2017.1293488.

Ando, R. (2016) 'Clothing giant Unqilo again the face of Japan's deflating economy', *Reuters*, 7 April. Available at: https://www.reuters.com/article/us-japan-economy-fastretailing/clothing-giant-uniqlo-again-the-face-of-japans-deflating-economy-idUSKCN0X507U (Accessed: 19 December 2018).

Arnould, E. J. and Thompson, C. J. (2005) 'Consumer Culture Theory (CCT): twenty years of research', *Journal of Consumer Research*, 31(4),868–882. doi: 10.1086/426626.

Berfield, S. and Rupp, L. (2015) 'The aging of Abercrombie & Fitch', *Bloomberg Businessweek*, 22 January. Available at: http://www.bloomberg.com/news/features/2015-01-22/the-aging-of-abercrombie-fitch-i58ltcqx (Accessed: 25 April 2018).

Berner, R. (2005) 'Flip-flops, torn jeans—and control', *Bloomberg Businessweek*, 29 May. Available at: http://www.bloomberg.com/bw/stories/2005-05-29/flip-flops-torn-jeans -and-control (Accessed: 26 April 2018).

Blehm, E. (2000, Summer) 'Forbidden snow', *A&F Quarterly: go play*, pp. 206–209.

Borel, K. (2015a, Spring/Summer) 'Actress Gennifer Goodwin shows how opposites attract', *The LifeWear Book*, p. 23.

Borel, K. (2015b, Spring/Summer) 'Actress Natalie Emmanuel gets a grip in *Game of Thrones*', *The LifeWear Book*, p. 3.

Branch, A. (2000, Summer) 'Make like Jack Kerouac', *A&F Quarterly: go play*, pp. 214–215.

Bull, A. (2013) *Brand journalism*. New York: Routledge.

Carone, P. (2000, Back to School). 'A Rudy awakening', *A&F Quarterly: New York*, p. 76.

Churchill, A. (2015, Spring/Summer) 'Heavenly bodies', *The LifeWear Book*, p. 18.

Conejo, F. and Wooliscroft, B. (2015) 'Brands defined as semiotic marketing systems', *Journal of Macromarketing*, 35(3), pp. 287–301. doi: 10.1177/0276146714531147.

Conill, R. F. (2016) 'Camouflaging church as state: an exploratory study of journalism's native advertising', *Journalism Studies*, 17(7), pp. 904–914. doi: 10.1080/ 1461670X.2016.1165138.

Couldry, N. and Turow, J. (2014) 'Advertising, big data, and the clearance of the public realm: marketers' new approaches to the content subsidy', *International Journal of Communication*, 8, pp. 1710–1726. doi: 1932-8036/20140005.

Crane, D. (2015, Spring/Summer). 'Florist Maurice Harris harnesses his flower power', *The LifeWear Book*, p. 12.

Denizet-Lewis, B. (2006) 'The man behind Abercrombie & Fitch', *Salon*, 24 January. Available at: http://www.salon.com/2006/01/24/jeffries/ (Accessed: 25 April 2018).

Duffy, B. E. (2013) *Remake, remodel: women's magazine in the digital age*. Chicago: University of Illinois Press.

Duffy, B. E. (2017) *(Not) getting paid to do what you love: gender, social media, and aspirational work*. New Haven, Connecticut: Yale University Press.

Duncan, F. (2015, Fall/Winter) 'Solving for X'. *The LifeWear Book*, pp. 58–61.

Fürsich, E. (2012) 'Lifestyle journalism as popular journalism: strategies for evaluating its public role', *Journalism Practice*, 6(1), pp. 12–25. doi: 10.1080/17512786.2011.622894.

Gaudoin, T. (2012) 'Uniqlo: cheap and very cheerful', *The Wall Street Journal*, 19 April. Available at: https://www.wsj.com/articles/SB1000142405270230444460457 7341394217275310 (Accessed: 26 April 2018).

Gilmor, D. (2004) *We the media: grassroots journalism by the people, for the people*. Sebastopol, California: O'Reilly Media.

Goldstein, L. (1999) 'The alpha teenager', *Fortune*, 20 December. Available at: http://arch ive.fortune.com/magazines/fortune/fortune_archive/1999/12/20/270530/index.htm (Accessed: 25 April 2018).

Grinspan, I. (2014) '*A&F Quarterly*: the story of Abercrombie's highbrow, controversial, sort of amazing magalog', *Racked*, 1 October. Available at: https://www.racked.com/2014/ 10/1/7574879/a-and-f-quarterly-abercrombie-magazine (Accessed: 26 April 2018).

Hancock, J. H. (2009) *Brand/story: Ralph, Vera, Johnny, Billy, and other adventures in fashion brand*. New York: Fairchild.

Hancock, J. H. (2016) *Brand/story: cases and explorations in fashion branding*. New York: Bloomsbury.

Hanusch, F. (2012) 'Broadening the focus: the case for lifestyle journalism as a field of scholarly inquiry', *Journalism Practice*, 6(1), pp. 2–11. doi: 10.1080/17512786.2011.622895.

Hayakawa, Y. (2015a, Spring/Summer) 'Architect Toshio Yada explores the unknown', *The LifeWear Book*, p. 34.

Hayakawa, Y. (2015b, Spring/Summer) 'Photographer ND Chow takes the eyes on a journey', *The LifeWear Book*, p. 21.

Hayakawa, Y. (2015c, Spring/Summer) 'Pottery artist Yuko Okazaki listens to the creative voice inside', *The LifeWear Book*, p. 11.

Holt, D. B. (2004) *How brands become icons: the principles of cultural branding.* Cambridge, Massachusetts: Harvard Business School Press.

Ishida, J. (2015, Fall/Winter) 'The art of dress', *The LifeWear Book*, pp. 52–57.

Jeffries, A. and Simmons, E. (2000, Summer). 'How I spent my summer vacation' *A&F Quarterly: go play*, p. 210.

Johnson, J. *et al.* (2000, Back to School) 'Around the apple in 24 hours', *A&F Quarterly: New York*, p. 111.

Kon, G. (2000, Spring Break) 'Stranger with candy', *A&F Quarterly: wild & willing*, pp. 276–277.

Kristensen, N.N. and From, U. (2012) 'Lifestyle journalism, *Journalism Practice*, 6(1), pp. 26–41. doi: 10.1080/17512786.2011.622898

Lascity, M. E. (2018) 'Brand tangents: semiotics and circulation in introduction', *Fashion Practice*, 10(1), pp. 78–98. doi: 10.1080/17569370.2017.1366687.

Levine, R. (2000, Summer) 'Cuba libre', *A&F Quarterly: go play*, p.213.

Lewis, J. (2015, Fall/Winter) 'Powers of warmth', *The LifeWear Book*, pp. 42–49.

McBride, D. A. (2005) *Why I hate Abercrombie & Fitch: essays on race and sexuality.* New York: New York University Press.

Manning, P. (2010) 'The semiotics of brand', *Annual Review of Anthropology*, Volume 39, pp. 33–349. doi: 10.1146/annurev.anthro.0128909.104939

Masterson, M. (2000, Spring Break) 'Ruling the coast', *A&F Quarterly: wild & willing*, p. 207.

Matsuzawa, K. (2015, Fall/Winter) 'Winner takes it all', *The LifeWear Book*, p. 9.

Mukerji, C. (2007) 'Cultural genealogy: method for a historical sociology of culture or cultural sociology of history', *Cultural Sociology*, 1(1), pp. 49–71. doi: 10.1177/1749975507073919.

Newell-Hanson, A. (2015, Fall/Winter) 'The iconoclast', *The LifeWear Book*, pp. 62–67.

Nomura, K. (2015, Spring/Summer) 'The next step for selvedge', *The LifeWear Book*, p. 28.

Perman, S. (2000, February 14) 'Abercrombie's beefcake brigade', *Time*, 14 February. Available at: http://content.time.com/time/magazine/article/0,9171,996083,00.html (Accessed: 25 April 2018).

Pesce, J. (2015a, Spring/Summer), 'Made for life in motion', *The LifeWear Book*, p. 9.

Pesce, J. (2015b, Spring/Summer) 'The DRY-EX effect', *The LifeWear Book*, p. 39.

Pearson, J. (2015, Spring/Summer) 'The parka by your side', *The LifeWear Book*, p. 17.

Pourhashemi, P. (2015, Fall/Winter) 'Growing up by Ines de la Fressange', *The LifeWear Book*, p. 8.

Romando, T. (2000a, Back to School) 'How am I doin'?' *A&F Quarterly: New York*, p. 280.

Romando, T. (2000b, Spring Break) 'Your spring break will suck …', *A&F Quarterly: wild & willing*, p. 173.

Ryder, C. (2015a, Spring/Summer) 'Entrepreneur David Zinczenko wants the good life for all', *The LifeWear Book*, p. 6.

Ryder, C. (2015b, Spring/Summer) 'TV host Eden Grinshpan speaks the global language of cuisine', *The LifeWear Book*, p. 14.

Sakuma, Y. (2015, Fall/Winter) 'A jean generation', *The LifeWear Book*, pp. 32–39.

Saviolo, S. and Marazza, A. (2013) *Lifestyle brands: a guide to aspirational marketing*. New York, NY: Palgrave Macmillan.

Sedaris, A. (2000a, Back to School) 'Bretorama', *A&F Quarterly: New York*, p. 214.

Sedaris, A. (2000b, Back to School) 'Those darned Fallon kids', *A&F Quarterly: New York*, p. 251.

Stern, B. B. (1989) 'Literary criticism and consumer research: overview and illustrative analysis', *Journal of Consumer Research* 16(3), pp. 322–334.

Swenson, R. D. (2012) *Brand journalism: a cultural history of consumers, citizens and community in Ford Times*. PhD thesis. University of Minnesota. Available at: https://conservancy. umn.edu/handle/11299/127279 (Accessed 19 December 2018).

The LifeWear Book (2015a) 'This is LifeWear', Spring/Summer, p. 1.

The LifeWear Book (2015b) 'This is LifeWear', Fall/ Winter, p. 1.

Van Parys, B. (2000, Back to School) 'The beat goes on', *A&F Quarterly: New York*, p. 164.

Van Meter, W. (2015, Fall/Winter) 'Outer limits', *The LifeWear Book*, pp. 68–73.

Uniqlo (2017) 'LifeWear NYC: Uniqlo celebrates everyday life Fall/Winter 2017', *Uniqlo News*. Available at: https://www.uniqlo.com/us/en/lifewear-fw17.html (Accessed: 26 April 2018).

Urstadt, B. (2010, May 9). 'Uniqlones'. *New York*, 9 May. Available at: http://nymag.com/ fashion/features/65898/ (Accessed: 26 April 2018).

Wigley, S. M., Nobbs, K. and Larsen, E. (2013) 'Making the marque: tangible branding in fashion product and retail design, *Fashion Practice*, 5(2), pp. 245–263. doi: 10.2752/ 175693813X13705243201577

Wojdynski, B. W. and Evans, N. J. (2016) 'Going native: effects of disclosure position and language on the recognition and evaluation of online native advertising', *Journal of Advertising*, 45(2), pp. 157–168. doi: 10.1080/00913367.2015.1115380.

Wolf, C. (2017) 'Uniqlo wants to be America's perfect fit, *Racked*, 11 April. Available at: https://www.racked.com/2017/4/11/14962056/uniqlo-wants-to-be-americas-perfect-fit (Accessed: 19 December 2018).

WWD Staff. (2003) 'Death of *A&F Quarterly*: Problem wasn't the sex but brand's loss of cool', *WWD*, 11 December. Available at: http://wwd.com/fashion-news/fashion-features/death-of-a-f-quarterly-problem-wasn-8217-t-the-sex-but-brand-8217-s -loss-of-cool-1315890/ (Accessed: 26 April 2018).

Zelizer, B. (2004) *Taking journalism seriously: news and the academy*. Thousand Oaks, California: Sage.

Zelizer, B. (2011) 'Journalism in the service of communication', *Journal of Communication*, 61(1), pp. 1–21. doi: 10.1111/j.1460-2466-2010.01524.x.

Zukin, S. (2005) *Point of purchase: how shopping changed American culture*. New York: Routledge.

INDEX

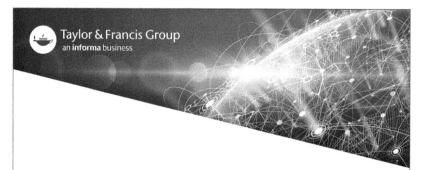